Samuel Augustus Tipple

Sunday morning at Norwood

prayers and sermons

Samuel Augustus Tipple

Sunday morning at Norwood
prayers and sermons

ISBN/EAN: 9783744745185

Printed in Europe, USA, Canada, Australia, Japan

Cover: Foto ©Lupo / pixelio.de

More available books at **www.hansebooks.com**

SUNDAY MORNINGS

AT NORWOOD

PRAYERS AND SERMONS

BY THE

REV. S. A. TIPPLE

SECOND EDITION: ENLARGED

LONDON: H. R. ALLENSON
30, PATERNOSTER ROW. 1895.

PREFATORY NOTE

QUITE tired of refusing what was persistently asked of me, I have reluctantly consented to this reissue of "Sunday Mornings at Norwood," with some slight addition, in the hope of forgiveness for my weak compliance, and not wholly despairing of some possible good to come out of it under that Divine order, in which our follies are often used for service.

And now, in reissuing the volume, I would dedicate it gratefully to the few left of those few who, with their sympathy and generous appreciation, unfailing through long years, have called forth from me whatever I may have ministered of any worth.

S. A. TIPPLE.

HILLCROFT, SOUTH NORWOOD HILL.

CONTENTS.

	PAGE

1. A GLORIOUS ASCENSION 5

    EPHESIANS iv. 8, 11.—"When He ascended up on high, He led captivity captive, and gave gifts unto men. . . . And He gave some, apostles; and some, prophets; and some, evangelists; and some, pastors and teachers."

2. A TIMELY DIVINE GIFT 22

    ROMANS viii. 3.—"What the law could not do, in that it was weak through the flesh, God sending His own Son in the likeness of sinful flesh, and for sin, condemned sin in the flesh."

3. THE PROPHET'S LAMENT 39

    JEREMIAH viii. 20.—"The harvest is past, the summer is ended, and we are not saved."

4. THE MEEK AND THEIR INHERITANCE ... 55

    MATTHEW v. 5.—"Blessed are the meek: for they shall inherit the earth."

5. SAMSON'S GIFT 72

    JUDGES xiii. 24, 25.—"And the woman bare a son, and called his name Samson: and the child grew, and the Lord blessed him. And the Spirit of the Lord began to move him at times in the camp of Dan."

	PAGE
6. THE ELECTION OF GOD	90

ROMANS ix. 11-13.—"For the children being not yet born, neither having done any good or evil, that the purpose of God according to election might stand, not of works, but of Him that calleth. It was said unto her, The elder shall serve the younger. As it is written, Jacob have I loved, but Esau have I hated."

7. UNCEASING PRAYER 109

1 THESSALONIANS v. 17.—"Pray without ceasing."

8. THE REJOICING OF CHARITY 126

1 CORINTHIANS xiii. 6.—"Rejoiceth not in iniquity, but rejoiceth in the truth."

9. CHRIST LEANING BACK ON GOD 143

JOHN xvi. 32.—"And yet I am not alone, because the Father is with Me."

10. THE JUDGMENT OF THE FATHER 161

1 PETER i. 17.—"And if ye call on the Father, who without respect of persons judgeth according to every man's work, pass the time of your sojourning in fear."

11. THE IMPORTANCE OF SELF-RESPECT ... 178

EZEKIEL ii. 1.—"And he said unto me, Son of man, stand upon thy feet, and I will speak unto thee."

12. TWO INCITEMENTS TO LOVE... 197

PHILIPPIANS ii. 1.—"If there be therefore any consolation in Christ, if any comfort of love, if any fellowship of the Spirit, if any bowels and mercies."

13. JOSHUA'S VISION. A Sermon for the New Year ... 215

    JOSHUA v. 13-15.—"And it came to pass, when Joshua was by Jericho, that he lifted up his eyes and looked, and, behold, there stood a man over against him with his sword drawn in his hand: and Joshua went unto him, and said unto him, Art thou for us, or for our adversaries? And he said, Nay; but as captain of the host of the Lord am I now come. And Joshua fell on his face to the earth, and did worship, and said unto him What saith my lord unto his servant? And the captain of the Lord's host said unto Joshua, Loose thy shoe from off thy foot; for the place whereon thou standest is holy."

14. GOODNESS AND MERCY BEHIND US 233

    PSALM xxiii. 6.—"Surely goodness and mercy shall follow me."
    ISAIAH lii. 12.—"The God of Israel will be your rearward."

15. EDIFICATION BY PLEASING 250

    ROMANS xv. 2.—"Let every one of us please his neighbour for his good to edification."

16. RESPECT OF PERSONS 267

    JAMES ii. 1.—"My brethren, have not the faith of our Lord Jesus Christ, the Lord of glory, with respect of persons."

17. CHRIST'S PROMISE TO HIS APOSTLES—PART I. 284

    JOHN xvi. 8-11.—"And when He is come, He will reprove the world of sin, and of righteousness, and of judgment: of sin, because they believe not on Me; of righteousness, because I go to My Father, and ye see Me no more; of judgment, because the prince of this world is judged."

18. CHRIST'S PROMISE TO HIS APOSTLES—PART II.   302

    JOHN xvi. 8–11.—"And when He is come, He will reprove the world of sin, and of righteousness, and of judgment: of sin, because they believe not on Me; of righteousness, because I go to My Father, and ye see Me no more; of judgment, because the prince of this world is judged."

19. THE VISION OF THE DYING CHRIST 320

    JOHN xvi. 8–11.—"And when He is come, He will reprove the world of sin, and of righteousness, and of judgment: of sin, because they believe not on Me; of righteousness, because I go to My Father, and ye see Me no more; of judgment, because the prince of this world is judged."

20. THE WHEAT AND THE TARES 339

    MATTHEW xiii. 25, 26.—"But while men slept, his enemy came and sowed tares among the wheat, and went his way. But when the blade was sprung up, and brought forth fruit, then appeared the tares also."

21. "WHOSOEVER HEARETH THESE SAYINGS OF MINE, AND DOETH THEM" 355
    (*A Reply to Count Tolstoï.*)

    MATTHEW vii. 24.—"Therefore whosoever heareth these sayings of Mine, and doeth them, I will liken him unto a wise man, which built his house upon a rock."

22. THE SILENCE OF CHRIST 380

    JOHN xiv. 30.—"Hereafter I will not talk much with you: for the prince of this world cometh, and hath nothing in Me."

SUNDAY MORNINGS
AT NORWOOD.

I.

PRAYER.

ALMIGHTY Father, whose glory is great in that perfect goodness of Thine which is far above ours as the heavens are above the earth; may that goodness shine upon our hearts, to excite within us the music of praise, to lift us into earnest worship, to set us longing afresh for the best things. May we receive the salvation of Thy goodness, for salvation there is in it when it is truly revealed to the soul. May it be effectual upon us to our redeeming—redeeming from all unwholesome glooms and melancholies; from all unworthy fears; from all impatience of ourselves and irreverence towards others; from all contented subjection to that in us which inclines to evil, and would listen to the voice of the Tempter. In the light of Thy goodness may we see our high calling, and with it be made strong to ascend.

Lord, here we are again in the church, talking of Thee, crying to Thee, stretching out our hands after Thee, and where art Thou—that Infinite Goodness which we have never beheld, which never meets us in the way? Art Thou in the summer air that comforts and brightens us?—in the solemn starlit skies that on still, lonely nights touch us with awe?—in the "moist flowers at even" that make us pensive and tender?—in the flame of the wondrous sunset that brings vague yearnings? In these Thou dost sometimes seem to us near; these do sometimes seem to speak of Thee. But it may only be fancy—there is no certainty; and other things to which we turn—on which we look—whisper often that it is but fancy. Where art Thou? Art Thou not most surely, most manifestly here in our own impulses toward, and aspirations after goodness; in the good that hides within us, and mixes with our evil, and rebels and fights against it; in the groans of prayer that break from us; in the higher desires that visit and disturb us; in the beautiful dispositions of a thousand human hearts; in the frequent grace of human lives; in the height of virtue and nobleness to which some men have risen; in the one surpassing radiance of the face of Jesus Christ? Yes; here is the very presence, here the sure sign and witness of a goodness which is above ours, which is more than all, which is the fountain and the source of all, of that Infinite Goodness unseen to which we pour out our souls. Man is weak and erring at his best, and stained with grievous stains, yet in man at his worst are motions and elements that bespeak the good God; and in the Man who is our head and crown, who is the amplest, richest flowering of our moral nature—in Him how does the good God declare Himself and shine?

Lord, out of whom we pray when we truly pray, receive our prayers, and in them come to us anew, and make Thine abode with us yet more largely, yet more intimately; may we have Thee not merely in our creed, nor yet merely in our thought and faith, but ever and increasingly in our ruling spirit, in the purity of our presiding affections, in the principles that actuate, in the sympathies that constrain us. Though we may not be remembering Thee or talking of Thee by the way; though at times we may be unable to feel Thee, and may lose that inward sense and conviction of Thy being which at other times we enjoy, may we always be possessing Thee and possessed with Thee in what we are, and are aiming and striving to be; *let our spirit*, with the expressions into which it runs, with the doings and endeavours which it prompts, be only full of God ; then shall we have risen to be with Him, then shall our prayers be ended. We seek Thee, without whom we are nothing ; give us of Thy love, that we may love with the love which is greater than knowledge and prophecies and tongues, greater even than faith and hope, and which faileth not, which rejoices not in iniquity, but rejoices in the truth, which believes all things and endures all things, than which there is no wiser teacher, no safer guide, no deeper well of life and blessedness. Give us of Thy love, that we may know how to give liberally, how to be most suitable, most beneficial in our relations and intercourse with men, how to work the very best work when we are wishing to work good. Keep us from marring and darkening the aspect of outward scenes, that would otherwise look fair enough, by indulgence in ill moods and ugly tempers ; from creating and diffusing disorder, by allowing within us a disorderly heart ; from begetting disease, by exhaling it ; from calling forth wrath, unkindness, or mean passion, by breathing and displaying them ; and, with utterances that are only lovely and right, may we make ever musical echoes, and understand what power we have in ourselves either to disfigure or transfigure those that we meet and the things which lie around us.

Teach us, we pray Thee, how much we have lost whenever we lose our way in wandering from Thy commandments ; how much is incurred of impoverishment and of mischief whenever we renounce fidelity to the light that is in us ; how much of beautiful strength is wasted whenever we yield to the temptation to indulge, in defiance of the whispers of conscience and the reluctance of the better mind ; how much is missed, alas ! when we miss being to another that something—that comfort or help—which we might have been.

Oh, God, let us not grow weary and sick when, with all our aims and efforts, we seem to accomplish so little and make so little way, or when our life seems taken up so much with inevitable trifles, with petty, vexing cares, and the great things that we would are made impossible for us. Instead of growing weary and sick, let us take rest in the thought that our times are in Thy hand; that our most broken aspirations cannot be in vain, because they are of Thee; and in the faith, that so long as we are faithful, we are doing and acquiring more than we know; that so long as we are faithful, a great education may be gained under the discipline of the narrowest occupations and the smallest cares, and will be gained, since Thou art giving us our lot.

Lord and Father of all, do teach us as we need, and teach through us our children, those who look up to us, and with whom we have influence. Teach the meek in judgment, and the transgressors the shame and evil of their ways; teach the tearful and stricken in their affliction, and the prosperous in their joy; teach such as fail for lack of a higher inspiration the inspiring faith of Thy Son, and such as are perplexed in their anxiety to deal prudently, the path of wisdom. Teach the complaining patience, the envious content, the cross-grained charity, the self-engrossed to look upon the things of others; and may the Christian Church be taught more, and more divinely than it has yet learned from Christ its Master, discerning more perfectly His principles and their application, and receiving more abundantly of His Spirit.

Father of Lights, lead Thou us on, even until, in the dispensation of the fulness of times, we come at last, if it may be, to the light without the shadow of a cloud; and in the meanwhile may the grace of our Lord Jesus, and the love of God, and the fellowship of the Holy Ghost be with us all, evermore.

SERMON.

A GLORIOUS ASCENSION.

" When He ascended up on high, He led captivity captive, and gave gifts unto men. . . . And He gave some, apostles ; and some, prophets ; and some, evangelists ; and some, pastors and teachers."—EPHESIANS iv. 8, 11.

WHEN I read in the New Testament Scriptures concerning Jesus Christ, how, after He had endured the cross, and seemed to His enemies utterly beaten and extinguished, He was carried up into heaven ; it is not of a miraculous rising through the air to higher and happier place that I am accustomed to think as constituting what is called His glorious ascension. That rising through the air, which the Apostles are described as beholding until a cloud received Him out of their sight, is to me but the figure of the true, the figure and sign of an ascension much more glorious, which can be shown to have followed His death, which did very manifestly, very strikingly, succeed it, and which He, we may be sure, would have considered much more glorious than any mere rapture of Himself, before the eyes of a few, from earth to paradise.

Were a number of persons asked to state severally what they should deem a grand ascent in their case—the proudest, the loftiest, that could happen to them—we should hear different replies given. Some would say one thing, some another, according to their several characters, and consequent tastes and aspirations. Each, probably, would have his own idea of beatific promotion—beatific exaltation. But what do you suppose would have been Christ's idea as He occupied His lot, and pursued His ministry in Palestine, as He sat among His disciples from day to day—the patient, anxious, yearning Teacher!—and from day to day went pouring out His soul in effort to quicken spiritually a slumbering people? Can you remember the constant labour of His life, the zeal that consumed Him, the discouragement and disappointment He was always suffering from the dulness, the prejudice, the stubborn resistance, or, at the best, the slow, halting progress of those whose culture He so earnestly sought? Can you remember this, and doubt that to ascend on high would have meant with Him, a large increase of His quickening influence, more power to act beneficially on human minds and hearts, to purify and energize, to inspire and elevate, as hitherto He had not been able? Yes; such, we must feel, would have been His conception of going up, of being advanced and aggrandized; to be made of richer Divine effect in men. That was His supreme ambition, the height for which He sighed; and was it not even thus that He went up gloriously at last from the cross and the grave, mounting from thence to be a greater saving and subliming force than He had ever been before, to beget repentance and remission of sins beyond what He had ever done?

Take, for example, the threefold statement of the text in which His ascension appears to me portrayed; His ascension, at least—for we must confine ourselves to this—as exemplified in what was wrought by Him posthumously among the *disciples* whom He left behind. First, He led captivity captive; in plain language, He captured the prisoners, making happy captives of those who were the victims of a miserable captivity, emancipating them from the bondage in which they were held, by bringing them into subjection to something better and worthier. Now here is one illustration. Do we not know that so long as Jesus lived in the flesh, His followers, notwithstanding all His endeavour to impress them differently, remained surrendered to false notions with regard to the Messianic kingdom and redemption? Though in daily communion with Him, they never rose above the current carnal imaginations about it; never ceased nursing fondly the dream of a temporal prince and political enfranchisement for Israel, and counting eagerly on its fulfilment as the choicest blessing in store. Such was the ideal with which they started, and which continued to possess and rule them, in spite of the Master's often contradictory behaviours and utterances, and the purely spiritual ardour He evinced, the purely spiritual aims on which He showed Himself intent. A royal deliverer for their nation, through whose mighty working, sooner or later, it was to tread down its oppressors, and acquire dominion over the heathen, and in whose court at Jerusalem they were to reign. Such was their vision of the brightest and the best that should flow from the Lord's anointed, of the great benediction to be waited for and reached after; nor could they be got to look and aspire higher. Not that His teaching and breathing had no correcting or refining effect on them; under it they were learning to be better men—sounder and healthier in soul than they had been—to see the beauty, to feel the claim of a righteousness transcending that of the Scribes and Pharisees; yet were they all the while in bondage to an idea of Christ, an idea of glory, to a hope, an ambition, that was earthy and low, and which, retaining its hold on them to the end, kept them to the end outside the understanding of much that fell from His lips, and that He would fain have had them enter into and share with Him.

It was thus with them, we know, until He died. Then gradually a great change took place in their views and sentiments.. Their horizon expanded, they began to think and desire more nobly. It was not merely that, as a matter of course, His death destroyed the expectations they had previously cherished, but that, from thenceforth, a nobler passion seized them. They saw and embraced, as they had not done, a Christ who had been given to bring good news of God, to reveal truth strengthening for duty, to communicate the secret of eternal life. They were captured by the vision of a spiritual redemption—a spiritual redemption, not for Jews only, but for peoples of all nations, for men everywhere. A new conception of Messianic power and Messianic blessedness awoke within them; a new enthusiasm was theirs, an enthusiasm for spreading light and righteousness. What fascinated them now, was the thought of imitating Christ, and endeavouring, with the exhibition of Him, to reconcile the world to God. They who had been captive to a low earthy ideal were brought into captivity to a higher. Great was the change, and wonderful in their central aspiration and aim; and a silent growth towards this change had been going on undoubtedly while the Master was yet with them. He had been laying in them the foundation for it, had been preparing in them the way to it; they had been learning, in association with Him, more than they knew, and more than He knew; had been secretly sown—beneath His tuition and influence—with germs of finer things, which it needed only the crucifixion and the resurrection to be the means of developing thus. In leaving them alone to mourn and wonder, to reflect on the cross, and look up from the grave, He drew forth upon them the ripe fruit of what they had blindly and little by little imbibed from Him. Oh, the richer blessing He became, the beautiful might to which He attained, in passing away! Then, at length, He rescued them from prison to be the bondsmen of a grander Lord; then, at length, He raised their ideal.

But what further says the Apostle? "He gave gifts unto men." Yes, indeed, as He gave often abundantly during the days of His flesh—new capacities, new possibilities, new means and resources—simply by liberating from the tyranny of some malady or affliction, some bodily defect or mental derangement. Loose him and let him go; and there was a man endowed at once with new wealth, with new powers of doing, enjoying, acquiring.

Admiring lately a cluster of fine fruit-trees literally robed in blossoms, the old gardener, standing by, remarked, with a shrewd, complacent air, "Well, sir, I might say that I gave them those;" and then, in answer to my questioning, he went on to tell me how for seasons the trees had borne scarcely anything, and how, at last, not content with pruning them above, he had pruned them also below, digging deep round them, and cutting in twain the long tap-root of each that struck down into coarse, sour soil, and drew from thence evil for the trees—so the old gardener represented it. "And that, sir," he said, "is how I gave them these beautiful blossoms—just, you see, by setting them free from the coarse, sour soil beneath, to which the tap-root bound them." Whether or no his notion was correct, it led me to consider what giving of gifts to men there may be, and often is, in just setting them free from something—from something unwholesome, mistaken, or wrong—to which they are in bondage. A little prejudice, for example;—in delivering from it, if you can,—what new vision you create, what new capabilities, perhaps, of appreciating and sympathizing, what new power of understanding or making progress! Emancipate a man, again, if you can, from the chain of an ever-haunting, ever-clinging self-consciousness; procure him escape from the thought of himself; assist him to lose it in some absorbing interest or worthy enthusiasm; and from thenceforth there may be developed in him a strength and a quality, sensibilities, braveries, which he had never previously displayed. How many a one in being released from a spirit of despondency that had long possessed him, from slavery, if you will—to a particular habit, or from hampering circumstances, mean contacts and associations—has been found presently blooming with energies and abilities, at the manifestation of which his friends were surprised; and they have said, "Who would have dreamed it? See how he has shot up and expanded; see how much more he has in him than we had suspected or could have imagined." A little redemption—the mere loosing of certain bonds with which they are entangled—is all, maybe, that some barren souls require to set them flowering beautifully; and nothing tends to bring forth in any, new and nobler things like their wakening from a lower to a higher love, or the flashing upon them of a higher ideal. What different creatures it made of the Apostles when once they were captured out of their captivity to coarse, carnal conceptions, and narrow and inferior aspirations, with regard to the kingdom of Christ, to be surrendered to the idea and inflamed with the ardour that came to be theirs after He had vanished from their sight! What enrichings and refinings it produced in them; what other and heavenlier gifts; how from that time they grew and were transfigured! Who has not been struck, for instance, with the remarkable alteration in Simon Peter; it is the same fervid, eager, impetuous nature as ever, but with such added solidity and dignity? We find in him, in connection with his old fire, quite a new self-possession and quiet persistence, a judgment, a power of patience, a meek receptiveness, a superiority to prejudice, in which he had been altogether wanting; and, while less dashing and adventurous, perhaps, was he not more heroically courageous? Under the influence of the greater sentiment and passion that had penetrated him greater things appeared in him.

The men who had been redeemed from their former sensuous dreams, to discern and follow the glory of the spiritual, began to blossom all over, became thereby more divinely endowed. Christ enriched them with a heritage of gifts, simply by detaching them from the meaner object on which their eyes were fixed, and binding them fast to a higher ideal. Gifts that are not ours do often lie hid and slumbering in us, waiting only for the application of the needed stimulus—healing or cleansing—to display themselves; and blessed is he who, with some disturbing, quickening touch, helps to elicit them.

But the text contains one other declaration with respect to the ascension of the Lord Jesus Christ in might. He gave some to be apostles, and some prophets, and some evangelists, and some pastors and teachers. You see it is not said that He left behind Him certain great institutions which He had built up and established, a whole machinery of offices and functions for carrying on His work and promulgating His religion. Nor did He. He had devised and prepared no system of things, arranging that there should be such and such departments of service—an apostolic department, a prophetical department, and so forth; appointing an order of evangelists and an order of pastors and teachers. He went away without making any arrangement of the kind. No hierarchy was founded or planned by Him. What He *did* leave behind Him, fashioned and shaped by His hand, was just that which the text intimates—*men* qualified and ready to labour in different capacities; *men*, out of whose several sanctified powers and faculties were gradually evolved the different offices and functions; *men*, some of whom had the gift of apostleship, some of whom took to prophesying and proved themselves prophets, some of whom became evangelists, some pastors and teachers. Here was the issue and fruit of Him. A number of living souls, whom He had been slowly training, on whom at last He had succeeded in impressing Himself; a number of living souls, at last in fellowship with His mind, understanding and sympathizing with His aims, inspired with His Spirit. It may not have seemed to be much; but what a grand achievement it was—how far-reaching and mighty in its results! Suppose that He had left as His issue and fruit, a code of fine rules and regulations, a complete Church constitution, an elaborate system of divinity, and withal, no such quickened, consecrated men as these; would He ever have been so wondrously diffused abroad? But these few men whom He had imbued and inflamed, do we not know what they accomplished for Him—what their love and zeal accomplished for Him, with no Church constitution, and no system of divinity to begin with, and with the world arrayed against them? Ah! how we think sometimes that much is going to be done by organizing committees, and appointing officials; or fondly hope to regenerate society with new franchises, new political arrangements, better legislation; when the real need is, that there should be some making and remaking of men, and the truest work would be to seek to promote the culture of individual minds and hearts. Nor let us doubt that *that* is always the divinest work—to get at a man, and be the means of ministering in some way to his healthier growth or finer inspiration; of helping him in some way to juster thought or loftier feeling. Get at a man, and send him from you into busy street and market-place, into the circle of which he is the centre, into the midst of his neighbours and friends with a greater spirit, with a breath of higher life in him, and who can tell what good you have not started and provided for in doing that?—who can predict whereunto that may not grow?—you have wrought, anyhow, for once in your life, an immortal work. The noblest sculptures and pictures will perish; the noblest utterances, the noblest poems may be forgotten; but any purifying or elevating effect which they have had upon a human soul,—that remains and dies not until the heavens be removed.

II.

PRAYER.

MAKER of all things, visible and invisible, and who hast made nothing in vain ; Thy creation is vaster and more wonderful than we know with all our knowledge and with all our admiration. Not yet have Thy works been sought out by the seekers who take pleasure therein ; discovery goes on ; but before and around us still, what an undiscovered country lies, to which, as yet, we have not come, of whose length and breadth and depth and height we dream not. "Lo, these are parts of Thy ways, but how little a portion is heard of Thee ! The thunder of Thy power, who can understand ?" And what is our knowledge often of that to which our eyes have been opened, which we have found and searched out, and can make report of ? Is not the light darkness after all ? What have we but a mystery named with a name ? Such strangers are we, at the best, upon the earth and in the Father's house, surrounded by locked chambers, seeing many things and perceiving not, taking illusion for reality, the shadow for the substance, knowing not, by reason of our ignorance, how modest and how lowly we should be ! Pity and forgive our excusable self-complacency, our pardonable conceit, even as we bear graciously with the like in our children, assured that they will be humbler when at length they are wiser.

How much we have yet to inherit ! What pleasure and joy of finding shall yet be ours ! For Thou who hast made us to thirst, and who hast been teaching us line upon line, little by little, Thou wilt lead us still toward greater things than these.

We thank Thee, the Father of lights, for all that has been

gradually learnt and comprehended by man in the course of the ages ; for all the treasures of knowledge and understanding that have been slowly accumulated and are now carried with us ; for all the clearer, deeper insights that have been gained, and the truer thought into which the world has struggled out of the chains of ancient error and mistake. We thank Thee for any delight of fresh beholding, and larger view, of resolving and ascertaining, which we ourselves have tasted ; for any sense of having gathered by the way what has permanently enriched the mind, and furnished and strengthened it for further gathering ; and especially for what we may have learnt that has led us to look around with more reverence, that has taught us to behave more wisely in life, has given us more sympathy with men, or made us more capable of communicating serviceably, and more generously enthusiastic.

We thank Thee for what man has been able to do with Thy works, with Nature, her beauties and effects, her secrets and forces, whether in the way of developing and applying, of utilizing for comfort and ministry, or in the way of representing and idealizing, to give delight, to the cultivation of the feelings. We thank Thee for the applications of Science, and for the creations of Art. Are not these also from the Lord, who is "wonderful in counsel and excellent in working," and shall we not praise Him for them?

Help, we pray Thee, the men whom Thou dost inspire and instruct, to recognize the sacredness of their gifts, and to labour with them in all pureness and sincerity ; and help *us* to do better for our *moral* culture, with the means and the material which Thou hast provided for that end, with the circumstances of our lot, with the encounters and adventures of the days, with the chances and changes of this mortal life. We would that with these there might be a finer making of us "to shape and use ;" that they might act upon us to more correcting and chastening effect. Thou dost send us sharp things sometimes, sharp troubles and distresses ; yet have we seen much sweetness wrought out under the pressure of such sharp things. We have known men in whom when they have passed, they have left an added grace manifest to all. Let not our sharp things, if we suffer them, be found to acidulate, but may they meet in us elements which shall determine them to sweetness. If we be exposed to the fire, let us be annealed by it, and not distempered or charred. Yet that, perhaps, for which we most need to pray is the sanctification to us of the small cares and vexations of life ; the petty frets and teasings which each day brings ; the dust and heat of the common round. For have we not failed ignominiously under these, at times, when a great trial had been nobly borne by us, when in a great fight of afflictions we had shown ourselves heroes? Have we not contended with the horseman and not fainted, and then in running with the footmen, they have wearied us? Pity, O God, our need of strength to bear gracefully, to our gracious discipline, little burdens—to behave grandly in little things.

We thank Thee for great examples, and chiefly for Christ, Thy great Son, the supreme Example of patient bearing and beautiful doing, and of a soul perfected through the strain and trial of life. May we consider such, and chiefly Him, and be braced and nerved by the contemplation. We thank Thee if we are more divinely anxious than we were in earlier days, while yet at the same time more divinely at peace within ; if we find ourselves caring more for some things than we did, even for truth and goodness ; for the progress of ideas ; for the triumph of just principles in society and government ; for the needs and miseries of others ; for the hastening of Thy kingdom ; while yet more able, in faith and hope, to cast our care on Thee, and to trust in an Almighty Father who rules. Let none of us be growing at all grosser in heart as we grow older ; less finely sensitive—less mindful of great things—less capable of noble passion, or less capable of committing the keeping of the world to Thee, in well-doing, as unto a faithful Creator.

Save, we beseech Thee, our nation from evil ; from irreverence and irreligiousness ; from moral decadence ; from indifference to righteousness. Guide us through our difficulties; teach and school us with our troubles. Out of confusion bring forth order; out of failure of faith—a faith purer and more vital. . Lead Thou the leaders : may our writers and thinkers be moved by the Holy Ghost. Let not poverty be a curse to the poor, and let none perish in the inner man of the heart through the multitude of their riches. Make our sons to be as plants grown up in their youth, our daughters as corner-stones polished after the similitude of a palace. And unto Him "who is of power to establish us according to the commandment of the Everlasting God, made known unto all nations for the obedience of faith—unto Him, the only wise, be glory, through Jesus Christ, for ever."

SERMON.

A TIMELY DIVINE GIFT.

"What the law could not do, in that it was weak through the flesh, God sending His own Son in the likeness of sinful flesh, and for sin, condemned sin in the flesh."—ROMANS viii. 3.

THE passage with which the previous chapter closes is one of the most interesting perhaps that St. Paul ever wrote, because, in describing there his own feelings and experiences, he has depicted so faithfully, so graphically, the feelings and experiences of all earnest souls. The passage narrates pathetic secrets of theirs, arrests them with a vivid pourtrayal of themselves. "What I would, that do I not; but what I hate, that do I. To will is present with me, but how to perform I find not, for the good that I would, I do not, and the evil that I would not, I do. I delight in the law of God after the inward man, but I see a different law in my members warring against the law of my mind, and bringing me into captivity to the law of sin that is in my members." What heart is there in which these words are not more or less echoed? Who among us does not exclaim to himself on reading them, "Even thus has it been with me"? If we have had any convictions of duty and any serious desire to follow them; if we have heard in silent hours the voice of commandments that spoke with authority, and at whose call we were constrained to rise and gird ourselves, anxious to go whither they pointed—have we not found always other motions within us, obstructing and opposing, making hard the way along which we sought to run fleetly, and often checking and turning us aside? Have we not known what it is, while perceiving and admiring the right, to be baffled by contrary impulses in our wish and purpose to practise it. We have seen its divine claim and majesty, and have meant, have craved and struggled to respond to it, yet could not, held down and overborne by the weight of something lower belonging to us.

> "As one whose footsteps halt,
>   Toiling in immeasurable sand,
>   And o'er a weary, sultry land,
>   Far beneath a blazing vault,
>   Sown in a wrinkle of the monstrous hill,
>   The city sparkles like a grain of salt."

The Apostle's experience had been, that he wanted power to do the good which he saw—the good which he saw and was persuaded of, and would fain have done; power to resist and vanquish the meaner self in him—"the flesh," as he terms it, which hindered; and have not men everywhere felt the same? If they could but have obeyed their heavenly vision, or plodded closely in the wake of their aspiration; if they could but have stepped to the divine music that fell upon their ears, and made them wistful and set them trying! It was not more ethical instruction that they needed, but more *strength*, for conformity to the commandment already delivered to them. Were we able only to realize the secret ideal of some extremely faulty, low-living neighbour, a beautiful life might be ours—the splendid creature, indeed, that might be constructed out of the occasional intentions and resolves, the occasional visions and aspirations of the least well behaved!

"Who shall emancipate me," cried St. Paul, "from the detaining, impeding element, and lift me above it? I discern what is good, and the solemn incumbency of performing it, but this clear perception and deep sense of obligation within me, is inadequate to produce the required obedience. The law, whose sacred imperative I hear, and to whose lofty fitness I entirely assent, is weak to shape me to itself, by reason of the flesh." Has not that been repeated continually in human experience? "I know well enough," many a one has said, "I know well enough that I ought to act thus and thus. I am alive to the law, to the beauty with which it shines, to the sanctions supporting and enforcing it. I believe in the peace, the blessedness which it promises: its penalties for transgression—have I not tasted some of their bitterness? and would that I could keep it. But I cannot. The flesh holds me down, and is not to be escaped from—is not to be surmounted. Here I lie, motionless, far off from a consciously better, worthier state, or feebly struggling, ever and anon, simply to fall back into bondage again. Here I lie, as it seems to me, for lack of a sufficiently strong impulse to loosen and carry me hence—an impulse stronger than mere knowledge gives. Knowledge! Have not men learnt times without number, through suffering, for example, the madness, the ugliness of their sins, yet only to return to them against their knowledge, and against the upward sighing and yearning, it had taught them; driven, dragged by the flesh. What they need, is help to *do* the nobler that they see and are drawn toward, in triumph over the sluggishness and averseness of the flesh. Help, help, for the divine law within them, weak through the flesh!"

But let us not doubt that help is never really needed for moral achievement, for moral victory, which is not near to us, and waiting to lend itself, if it be looked after; like the antidote which is said to grow always somewhere in the vicinity of the poison. Are we wavering and ready to yield before temptation?—there is always something that does but require to be remembered at the moment, and cogitated, in order to check and brace—the opening of the mind to which, to entertain and dwell upon it, would be for redeeming strength. There is always a saving or succouring thought at hand, if we could but lay hold of it, if we would but seek it. No man trembles and totters upon the brink of a fall, around whom ministering angels are not hovering, in the shape of considerations, to give admittance to which, would tend to steady and stay him. How often a memory, a reflection, has rushed upon one whose feet had well-nigh slipped, and made him strong to stand, and how often we might have conquered, instead of succumbing, had we but paused to consider! The very help you want, in your faintness, is never far from you. Only lift up your eyes and see it.

And what help toward acting above ourselves—above our meaner inclinations, we have sometimes derived from persons—from the touch of persons—not, perhaps, from any new life, any new ideas, they have communicated, but just from the influence of their personality! They flowed in upon us as we walked beside them, like a tide, on which we rose to higher things. There was that about them, and breathing from them, which drew us up to finer, firmer tone, stringing, inciting us : in intercourse with them we were polarized. For your assistance against what may be gross in you, cultivate the company of the best.

But now, the Apostle had found a fund of divine helpfulness in Jesus Christ. In Him he recognized a *timely* divine gift to meet the moral needs of men. Christ had proved wonderfully invigorating to him, and to thousands whom he knew. He saw in Him a precious provision of heaven for the needed reinforcement of men. This was his idea of Christ as a Redeemer, a Saviour—that He was a source of power; that He came not merely inculcating duties, but inspiring towards a better discharge of them. What was it that the law—the sense of right and of the glory of it—could not do, in that it was weak through the flesh? It could not beget a perfect obedience to its requirements. Well, St. Paul, observe, does not claim for the Lord Jesus that He could ; but his affirmation is that He has accomplished much in aid of a more perfect obedience, by having condemned sin in the flesh— by having, in the flesh of sin, condemned the sin which seems to belong to the flesh.

Let us try and understand. He speaks of Christ, you see, as having been "God's own Son in the likeness of sinful flesh,"—that is, here was a man with a nature like ours, including flesh like ours, the very flesh which in us is always bringing forth sin, always causing us to fail and fall short, in spite of our truer vision and aspiration, and the hindering, defiling influence of which we often deplore as irresistible and not to be prevailed against ; and this man was "God's own Son" in the flesh, without spot and blameless, exhibiting in it a sustained perfection of filial obedience. The thought is evidently, that the sinlessness of Christ in the flesh has condemned sin in the flesh to the help of those who are mourning over and struggling with it. Thus ; the tendencies of the flesh might appear to excuse sin—almost to justify it : might be regarded as an incubus, with which it was futile to strive. Men might say, "Who is to rise above them, and become what he would be? It is impossible not to be thwarted and frustrated by them; we must e'en be content with poor and low attainment while they continue to clog us;" and the effect of these feelings would be to discourage and dishearten for effort. But the sinless life of Christ in the flesh declares that sin is not necessary —that sin is not natural, because of the flesh ; and so encourages and inspires to persevering conflict with it. Such is manifestly the Apostle's idea.

I very much regret to see that the authors of the Revised Version have presumed to interpolate in the text, words of their own, by which St. Paul is made to represent the divine Son as sent to be an *offering* for sin, and as an *offering* for sin, condemning it—one of a few mischievous improprieties on their part, in the course of a noble work, nobly done, which inclines me to wait for some revision of their revision before proceeding to adopt it in the place of the old version. St. Paul says, that God sent His Son in the likeness of sinful flesh, and for sin—on account of sin, but there is nothing whatever in the Greek to indicate or suggest that he was thinking of a sacrificial death for sin, as condemning it. The whole verse, on the contrary, conveys that it was the transcendent purity of

Christ in our nature of which he was thinking as condemning it. On the one hand, he exhibits the flesh evermore rendering weak, and causing failure; to all appearance, hopelessly in the way of the law's triumph within us; and on the other hand, he exhibits One, who though in the flesh, like ourselves, was God's own Son, perfectly fulfilling His law; thereby condemning sin in the flesh, showing that it was not natural—that it was not necessary there. And this, in the Apostle's view, was God's blessed gift to cheer and inspire us in our seemingly vain war with the flesh, and to make us stronger for overcoming. Nor can it be otherwise than animating and helpful to any who are seeking to cleanse themselves, and to do the good that they would.

When depressed by repeated comparative defeats of our best effort, and consequently—for that is always the case—weakened for effort; when, depressed and weakened by such defeats, and ready to think that our difficulties are too great to be surmounted, that ours are circumstances in which success is impossible—when affected thus, we meet with another, who, under the same difficulties, and amidst the same circumstances, has succeeded gloriously where we have failed, if we be really in earnest, are we not stirred and stimulated by it? Yes; we look at the man, and say to ourselves, "Why now should we despair of ultimate victory? ought we not to be capable of doing what he has done? can we not discover his secret?" He delivers us from the despondency that had been creeping over us, and sets us hoping afresh; a new spirit enters into us, and we put forth new effort vigorously. Surely, surely, the thing is to be accomplished by us, no less than by him whose disadvantages resemble ours; and although we may not after all, equal his achievement; although we may still remain far below his height, and have to mourn our distance from it, we shall have come nearer to it with the brighter, heartier endeavour to which his example has moved us; we shall have advanced further than we should have advanced without its inspiration. To see one bearing bravely and beautifully some trial, beneath which we had been losing patience and staggering ignominiously, with the weak complaint that the trial was too hard to be borne—is it not to feel our behaviour condemned by him as not warranted, as not excusable? and if we be desirous of behaving well, is it not to be quickened to effort stronger and livelier than any we had exerted before; to effort which issues, not perhaps in our rivalling the superb endurance of that other, yet in our coming to endure more praiseworthily than we had thought we could?

How often has a youth, wishing to take part in some exploit, in some competition of strength or intellectual assay, but timidly hesitating from distrust of his ability—the result, maybe, of former unsuccessful attempts remembered with disgust—how often has he been kindled to try, resolutely and courageously, by witnessing the triumph of one of his companions—one of his own age and standing; saying to himself, " If he can do it, why should not I?" and forgetful of past failure in the animation of new hope, buckling to the task with a will, and a sanguine energy, which, though it may not have brought him alongside his crowned fellow, has enabled him to accomplish more than he had ever previously done, more than he had previously imagined to be possible for him.

To set a man seriously thinking that he *ought* really to do better in spite of his disadvantages, and might—to excite a baffled and desponding aspirant to some fresh eagerness and ardour in enterprise; *that*, is to help greatly toward higher attainment. Frequent defeat in aiming, takes the heart out of you, tends to dispirit you; and to become dispirited is to become enfeebled—is to have your feet lamed for walking, and your hands for climbing; you sink below the level of your own ability; which is what St. Paul meant, probably, in part, when he said that the law *killed*—that the law was unto death. An example of supreme success in one, bone of your bone and flesh of your flesh, and whose environment is similar to yours, assists to inspirit you, to awaken new hope in your breast, out of which increase of strength is begotten, which goes to ensure a nearer approximation to your aims. And when to those who, seeking and striving after a nobler life, sadly complain that the flesh is against them, that because of it they cannot do the good that they would—when to such, in their debilitating depression, Christ appears, with His splendid and perfect doing in their own nature, it serves to revive and excite them. "See," they say, "what man can be. Was He not one of us, a sharer in our burdens, tempted in all points as we are?" There may be, then, a true Son of God in the flesh, *it* need not prevent; why should *we* tamely consent to be held down by it? Let us re-gird ourselves, and try to follow him. Anyhow, with Him before us, it must never be ours to cease aspiring, to give up, or despair. So, to friends

D

whom he desired to urge on, the author of the Epistle to the Hebrews writes: "That you may not be wearied and faint in your minds, but persevere in the race, consider Jesus, the finished pattern of faith." Yes; such an one as He, once manifested in the flesh, is a divine provision in relation to sin, to help us against it, to encourage and stimulate us in conflict with it, since His spotless beauty condemns it in the flesh, shows that it is not inevitable there—that it cannot claim to belong there—that it is to be conquered and transcended there; declares that the dream of human perfection is no mere dream, but a foreshadowing and prophecy, and calls on us to pursue after it undismayed by continued frustration; stirs us, as with the sound of a trumpet, still to labour and to wait. For those who are craving earnestly to work out the beast and sin, is it not evermore fresh strength and hope to remember, that in the midst of the ages Christ has lived?

III.

PRAYER.

THOU who art the Lord of all, whose kingdom it is that ruleth, in whose hand we are held, who willed the world of mankind, and the inspiration of whom giveth us understanding, sustaineth us in being and in growth; we have come from Thee, in Thee we consist, at Thy mercy we lie, and we are moved at times to utter ourselves to Thee, we are moved at times to put our thoughts and burdens, our anxieties and aspirations into prayer to Thee, and cannot forbear though there is no sign whatever that Thou hearest us, though the skies send out no sound in token that Thou givest us audience, or that in following Thy eternal plan Thou workest aught for us with the breathings to which we are constrained. But it is borne in upon us that Thou meanest us to pray, and makest use of our praying in Thy secret government of us, in Thy secret flow towards us : it is borne in upon us that more things are wrought with it by Thee than we perceive or understand ; that we *are* heard, notwithstanding the deep unbroken silence, and do not cry in vain. We walk by faith and not by sight, believing that Thou hast made and fashioned us and that the instinct which prompts us is of Thee. To lift up the hand to the heavens is human, and being human must needs be divine, and to some fulfilling of the divine.

Thou Lord of all, whose kingdom it is that ruleth,—we have never looked upon Thy face to know that righteousness and goodness and loving care are Thine ; but there is that in our own nature, there are elements and features, dispositions and sympathies in ourselves which prevail to assure us that it is so. "He that planted the ear, shall He not hear? He that formed the eye, shall He not see? He that teacheth man knowledge, shall not He know?" Have we not received from Thee our moral heart, our sense of rectitude and justice, our holy aspirations, the fatherly spirit, the spirit of kindness and charity, the spirit that goes forth seeking to help and bless? Have we not received all these from Thee? and shalt not Thou, the Giver, be infinitely better than our best, infinitely more, in righteousness and goodness and loving care, than we at our highest and perfectest? Evil and selfish, unjust and malevolent, we often are, but then we confess with shame that in this we are not manly, that in this we are not as we should be; and there are other and opposite motions within us, other and opposite qualities displayed upon us, which we recognize and reverence as our true manliness, as constituting us worthy and noble; and are not these dim hints and reflections in us of a surpassing righteousness and goodness in Thee our Maker, a righteousness and goodness above our finest attainment, and above our thought, as the heavens are above the earth? We cannot doubt that Thou art indeed the very Father, the holy and merciful Father whom Christ our Prince and Crown, the man of supreme spiritual vision, declared Thee to be, in the faith of whom we worship and bow down, in the faith of whom we daily cast our care on Thee, and make our prayer to Thee as at this time. From the ends of the earth we cry and are relieved and strengthened, and in silence, in mystery, in ways past finding out Thou art blessing us; from the ends of the earth we give thanks and sing, and are made to rejoice anew in Thy works.

O God be near us, be with us, as we move through the days and occupy the lot appointed us, and meet the chances and changes of life, that we may know how to order our steps wisely, and how to find and receive the ministry that is hid for us in all things, the education to which all things are meant to contribute. Be near us, be with us, when our mood is low, that it may pass and not leave us permanently enervated or diseased ; when we are necessarily troubled and anxious and full of care, that the higher sensibilities may not be impaired by it, that nothing of coarseness may be engendered by it, nothing of sourness precipitated ; when the flesh wars against the spirit, and the world beguiles us with tempting offers to do the things that we would not, and the strength of the better heart is ready to fail, that we may be kept from yielding and made strong to overcome ; when we are about our work, the work assigned us to do, be it little or much, small or great, that it may be done always in unfeigned sincerity and truth, and that through the doing something may be ever added to us in furtherance of true being ; when claims are facing us, claims of friendship, claims of citizenship, claims of the family or of humanity, that we may be enlightened to appreciate them duly, and guided and strengthened duly to meet them. Be Thou near us and with us, O God, at all moments and in all scenes, to help us against whatsoever weakness we have, to save us from evil, to teach us under the various discipline of life, what we need to learn toward our slow meetening for the inheritance of the saints in light ; and so, in growing purity and peace, may we be ever coming nearer and nearer to Thee whose temple is the pure and gracious heart !

Lord and Father, we thank Thee for all divine truths to which Thou hast opened our understanding, and of which Thou hast persuaded us, and for all that Thou hast shown and art showing us of Thy wonderful works in successive discoveries here and there. As the divinely true is discerned, so may it win command over us, and may every acquired knowledge be sanctified. We bless Thee for Thy world, for the laws and the beautiful order thereof ; always beautifu we are sure, whatever difficulty, whatever confusion and suffering to us, it may sometimes involve. We bless Thee for all weathers—believing that Thou seest all to be alike good, whether we can welcome and rejoice in them or not— day and night, summer and winter, cold and heat, bright skies and dreary rain are Thine, fulfilling Thy word, and every word of the Lord is pure. Be merciful to those to whom bad weather, as we term it, may have brought perplexity and distress, and to all who are in any way severely stricken and afflicted through no fault of theirs; endue with patience and fortitude, where patience and fortitude are needed, for the endurance of manifold ills, and may the strong be ready to help the weak, the happy to sympathize with the sad. Be with those who are resting awhile in quiet places after long labour and toil, to sanctify the rest to their renewal and invigoration; and reinspire for the daily round of work and duty, those who are coming back to it, refreshed by change of scene and hours of idleness. Lord, the summer of the year draweth on toward autumn, and behold we all do fade as a leaf; feed Thou our roots that the good spirit within us fail not : behold, we all do fade as a leaf; help us, that by patient continuance in well-doing we may fade away at length through death, to glory and immortality and eternal life according to the resurrection of Jesus Christ our Lord, in the faith of whom we worship Thee, and hope to live and praise Thee for ever, world without end. Amen.

SERMON.

THE PROPHET'S LAMENT.

"The harvest is past, the summer is ended, and we are not saved."—JEREMIAH viii. 20.

THERE is no much sadder and heavier burden than the burden borne by him who is profoundly conscious of evils, and of threatened disaster, in some popular policy—some policy with which all around him are content and pleased, and of the happy issue of which they are confident; who, while his friends and fellows are entirely satisfied with things as they are, and flatter themselves that the course pursued will be surely productive of or conducive to good, carries about within him daily a deep conviction of existing serious defects, and of involved mischief and woe. Even such was Jeremiah's painful burden; the word of the Lord came to him amidst the reforming activity of the king and the priests, who were busily engaged clearing the land of idols, punishing obstinate idolaters, appointing religious fasts and sacrifices, cheerfully sanguine of averting thus the divine judgments that had been foretold against Judah—the word of the Lord came to him in secret amidst all this reforming activity, that was thought to be so fine and to promise so much, and he could not help feeling that the work was less sound and worthy than appeared, that it was too superficial, that a large amount of corruption lay untouched by it, and that under it, lay hid a good deal of false and worldly spirit; he could not help feeling, desire and strive as he might, to think otherwise, that the zeal displayed was not a pure zeal, that the ulcerous place was being only at the most, skinned and filmed, and that nothing done would suffice to turn aside the penalties which the past transgressions of the nation had incurred. His inspiration drove him, however reluctantly, to declare this, to hold aloof from the labours of the priests and the king, and stand testifying that they were utterly inadequate and vain; that they were not accomplishing at all what Heaven required, and that the lighting down of Heaven's wrath upon the country was inevitable. It was a bitter portion, a terrible trial,—especially for a tender, lowly, sensitive soul like his,—to be, as he sorrowfully complained, "a man of contention" to the whole community, to have to see and proclaim, in the teeth of universal derision, of universal opposition and reproach, the imperfectness of that which all regarded with complacency, central rottenness, where all were believing in recovery, impending destruction, where all were counting on redemption. There were moments, indeed, when it was almost too much for him, when he struggled wistfully to close his eyes and change his speech; but the spirit within him was not to be quenched or resisted; it compelled him to see and proclaim, against his inclination, the insufficiency of the steps taken, the vanity of the expectations cherished. Alone, in the midst of his friends and fellows, and in scorn-exciting, hate-rousing contravention of the prevalent idea and persuasion, he had to lift up his voice and cry,— "There is no real worth, no real healing, in these trusted efforts, these late hurried reformations: the harvest is past, the summer is ended, and we are not saved."

No hope, no hope! That was the peculiar burden of Jeremiah, that was the vision forced upon him, the message he was constrained to deliver, while the people and their leaders were nursing the assurance that all was going well, that a work was being prosecuted which would secure salvation. "No hope," was the testimony given him to utter; "the day of grace has fled; you have become too diseased, you have sunk too low to be restored, except through grievous crushing strokes of chastisement; desolation and ruin are not to be evaded; the house of Judah is infallibly doomed." Wha wonder that he was gnashed at and persecuted, and heard around him continually, "the defaming of many;" what wonder moreover, that he had often to wrestle with himself severely, in order to maintain fidelity to his mission, or that once and again he rebelliously whispered to himself, "I will not make mention, I will not speak any more," until "the word was in his heart as a burning fire shut up in his bones, and he was weary with forbearing, and he could not stay"?

Few things are more unpalatable and painful, than to feel it incumbent on you to say to any for whom you entertain sentiments of friendship and affection, what is calculated to damp and dishearten, to spoil the dreams of those who are dreaming pleasantly, deliciously, to destroy or disturb fond hopes; than to feel it incumbent upon you, instead of sympathizing with the joy of such hopes,—as you fain would, were it possible,—to shake your head and contradict them. We may have had to do this on occasions, with some eager child perhaps, reckoning blissfully of what we knew well could not be, or with some comrade blindly trusting in the success of what we well knew was destined to fail, in an approach of good fortune which we saw clearly was not to be realized; and we can remember the soreness of the task. It is a miserable thing to feel bound to try to take away from another, an anticipation with which his breast is warmed, to feel bound to tell him that the sweetness ahead on which his eyes are fixed, is but an illusion—that he must not continue to hope. There are cases in which it may be well, in which upon the whole it may be best, to refrain from meddling with hopes, the baselessness of which we perceive with pity, to let the possessors go on indulging them without any interference from us, until they shall awaken at length, in the course of events, to the chill of the disappointing reality. Unfounded and fallacious as their hopes are, and certain ere long to be painfully shattered, they may be less harmful, less fraught with mischief, than our present interruption of them might be. Their action and influence may be needed for awhile, and may be serving beneficial purposes for which the distress of their ultimate dispersion will not be too large a price to pay. We must take care often, not to rush in and smite down illusive hopes, before the time—they have often a useful work to do, the arrest of which by our rude and premature exposure of them, would be serious loss and injury. But cases there are, on the other hand, in which the right thing, the wisest and the kindest thing, will be at once to attack and scatter, or endeavour to scatter them, however unwelcome the task, and whatever suffering we may cause. The sooner the subjects of them can be shaken out of their hold, can be made to recognize their falsity, and be set face to face with the severity of the actual, the better. Comforting and comfortable as the dream may be, the sleeper, in his own best interests, must, if possible, be roused, since the dream is beguiling him perchance to courses that are wrong, and is misshaping and impairing him for what is at hand.

It was thus with the people of Judah in Jeremiah's time. Their hope that the reforms in progress were securing them against the rod that had been threatened, was not only a delusion but a snare; it was creating and fostering within them a false spirit, was preventing any true discernment on their part of what was really wanting in them, of their real unwholesomeness and corruption, and was unfitting them to bear the rod when it should fall, with the meek resignation, the humble submission, requisite to render it a purifying and chastening discipline. Nothing could have been a greater mercy to them than that the vision-burdened prophet should have succeeded in demolishing their hope with his cry, " The harvest is past, the summer is ended, and we are not saved."

But this cry of his over his country in the streets of Jerusalem,—by how many has something like it been breathed inwardly, with sorrow and bitterness, concerning themselves, as they have stood contemplating what they have, and what they are, after seasons in their history, seasons that had enfolded golden opportunity or shone bright with promise. Is there a day indeed beneath the sun, in which some human heart is not secretly wailing thus? Every day some are looking back upon circumstances and situations that had promised sweetly, upon resources, advantages, opportunities, that once were theirs, with the doleful reflection that these have been possessed, and are past, to no such resulting gain as they might have been expected to yield. Things have been seen afar off, and longed for, and perhaps patiently schemed and toiled for, certain placings, or conditions, certain acquisitions or experiences, which when attained were to be vastly serviceable to them, or beautifully operative upon them; then, would be their summer in which flowers and fruit might be freely gathered and abundantly stored; then, would come harvest, laden with sheaves of content and peace, or dropping richer aids, and higher and more favourable influences for the soul. And the things yearned after and sought with such confidence in their ministry, have been attained, the certain placings or conditions, the certain acquisitions or experiences have been won; and what is the issue of it all, but the dreary weary confession, We have got what we craved, and what we thought to derive from it, is wanting; it has failed to bring with it the effect of which we dreamed: "The harvest is past, the summer is ended, and we are not saved." How often has that been repeated, is being repeated around us, in various forms, from day to day; oh, the summers that have proved disappointing, the harvests looked forward to and relied on, whose ingathering has fallen sadly short of the calculated produce. Who is there, beyond the boundaries of youth at all, who has not had his seasons of promise, that have left him sighing orlornly over broken hopes? Infinite, in this respect, is the pathos of human life, crying dumbly, evermore for the infinite pity of God.

Or again, is it not frequently the case that bygone circumstances and situations are recalled with a sorrowful, humiliating sense of our not being the men in moral stature, in moral fibre and feature, which they should have contributed to make us, which they gave us in vain the opportunity of becoming—that remembering them, we feel with a pang of grief and shame, the good thing they might have wrought in us which they have not wrought; how we might have been disciplined by them, or stimulated to larger growth, to culturing action and endurance,—and were not? Do we not see regretfully, remorsefully, the smiling season that was afforded us in some former crisis of our history, in some former scene of responsibillty, of temptation or trial—a season from which we might have reaped richly in moral tempering and strengthening,—and did not? What a means of grace we missed then, accepting and utilizing! How we missed then, the tide, which seized and taken, would have left us surely, far in advance of what we are! The many who in moments of retrospect, have felt this, with sad soreness of heart, perceiving at length, that here and there in the midst of their days, days big with divine possibilities were given them, which they miserably failed to improve, for which they have nothing whatever to show; and these blessed days come back no more.

"Oh, could we weep," some are saying to themselves; "Oh, could we weep as once we wept, when similar situations and circumstances returned. If the recurrence now and again, of former scenes, of former contacts and conjunctures, could but stir in us the transient hopeful emotion which they used to excite, could but set us temporarily sighing, aspiring, resolving, as they used to do, when they always brought with them the promise at least, of our *going on* to better things; but the promise, alas! was never fulfilled, the transient hopeful emotion faded without producing aught; and now, the recurrence of the former scenes, the former contacts and conjunctures, ceases to awaken the emotion. The birthdays, the anniversaries, the quiet Sunday mornings, the hours of silence and solitude, that once agitated us with rushes of unwonted tenderness, with little wavelets of earnest thought, and higher impulse, which might have led to something further, to something of permanent effect,—they no longer touch us thus as they come and go; they have no longer the slightly quickening influence that they had: our harvest in them is past, our summer in them is ended, and we are not saved." Is not such the secret cry of some, who yet however, are not unsalveable by any means, since they are still *able* to weep that they *cannot* weep?

What is it, in conclusion, with the best of us, but failure? Are there any among the best of us, standing now in the autumn of life, whose feeling is other than this,—that life has not wrought with them, has not made of them what it should have done, and might have done; that the seasons, the seasons of discipline and opportunity, have not yielded in them duly? How very far they are below the summits which, with their means and advantages, they ought to have reached, and which they have dreamt of reaching; how poorly they have acquired in moral growth, in noble strength, sweetness, and quality, considering the educational circumstances they have experienced, the instruments of training with which they have been supplied. They have not worked out by a long way their appointed salvation—the salvation that was possible. They have not been, in their behaviours and endurances, in their posts, and spheres of labour, the half that they had thought and hoped

E.

to be. The high purposes and aspirations with which they started—what has been achieved to answer to these? Who is there, who is not conscious, mournfully conscious, of having failed? who is there, whom death when it arrives, does not find confessing upon his pillow, "The harvest is past, the summer is ended, and we are not saved."

Let the pity of the Lord our God be upon us!

And yet may we not believe, do we not feel to our solace, that at the least, something has always been reaped?—reaped for sowing, albeit with tears, in fields beyond; nay, that even in the mere lowly and penitent sense of shortcoming, which seems perhaps almost all that has been gained, we shall be carrying away with us from hence, a gathered seed-grain, to be for fruit, perchance for the fruit we have hitherto missed, "behind the veil."

IV.

PRAYER.

GOD, our Maker and Leader, who dwellest with us, and dost uphold us in secret, and we are not alone,—comfort us always with the conviction of Thy presence, and help us when the way is weary, and the burden is heavy, and the task is hard, to lean ourselves for spirit and strength upon the thought of Thee. We come to Thee in prayer, feeling our need of some stronger, deeper inspiration for the bitter-sweet trial of life ; of some stronger, deeper inspiration to assist us in bearing it well, than can be drawn from the circle of the visible ; and desiring earnestly to be made and kept freely receptive of those unseen realities of Thine in the vision of which lies might and reinforcement for the soul. The earth needs the sky. We are weak often to lift ourselves above ourselves, and seem to want for such achieving that door open in heaven which opened of old upon St. John as he stood among the confusions and mysteries of time. Show us, for our help, Thy glory. And whatever we may have been able to be and do that is praiseworthy, and on which we can look with satisfaction ; however brave and capable we already are, let us not miss reaching loftier heights that might be reached, through lack of spiritual sensibility and perception, through missing any inspiring influence that might be ours. If there be that in the region of heavenly things which we have not yet seen, in relation to which, as yet, our eyes are holden, and the seeing of which would tend to expand our heart and increase our strength, and make us doughtier in the battle, reveal that to us we beseech Thee. Hide none of Thy commandments from us, for we are strangers in the earth.

We thank Thee, O God, for the helpfulness of the faith, that love is over all—that love governs and reigns ; and although such faith is not always equally alive and vigorous within us ; though at times its hands grow lame and cannot grasp ; though there be many things by which it is apt to be enfeebled and deadened for a season, occasional moods due to physical causes, mental states arising out of temporary bodily states, in which it droops and ceases to live, and the glorious high throne, which we are wont to behold, seems to have vanished utterly, like a bright cloud at sunset—though the faith of the love that is over all be thus sometimes unavoidably stricken in our breast, may it never be ours to lose it, or fall from it, through our own decline from the spirit and the life of love, through our own infection with aught of hatred, malice, envy, or uncharitableness. Save us from that darkened vision, whose darkness is the shadow of a passion-clouded, cold, or selfish heart. We need the vision of the love that governs and reigns to sustain us in our lot, to aid us in standing bravely and acquitting ourselves nobly there. Keep us full of graciousness and good works ; keep us in love, that *it* may abide with us, and not grow dim and fade.

Teach us, O God, how to be thankful always *in* all things, even when we cannot be thankful *for* them ; thankful in difficulties and perplexities that vex us, because of the useful discipline they furnish, and the healthful exercise of gift and faculty to which they conduce ; thankful in grievous trouble and adversity, beneath which the heart is smitten and withered like grass, because of the many little alleviations that are always discoverable, the kindly consideration and sympathy that are shown us, and the possible sweet fruits of the bitter experience ; thankful in painful loss or privation of some pleasant things that we would like, and the absence of which is very hard to bear, because of the greater things which still are ours, and which the world cannot take away, nor the vicissitudes of life imperil; thankful in the presence of harsh and cruel mysteries belonging to the order of the universe, at the remembrance of Thy underlying law, to which both the good and the evil may be traced; thankful in the distressing failure of efforts which we had hoped would succeed, and in suffering severely from our mistakes and follies, on account of the lessons we are being taught thereby, and the instruction, the correction, which the Lord graciously intends; thankful, too, in finding others less worthy than we had deemed them to be,—less tender, and trusty, and true,—at the thought of what there is still in them that is good or promising, and of the more and better than we had looked for, which we have often found in some. Teach us, we pray Thee, to be thus thankful *in* all things, even when we cannot be thankful *for* them. We do bless Thee, O God, in our lot and portion, whatever it may be, believing in Thy goodwill towards us, and in Thy benevolent purpose concerning us, believing that Thou art giving us from day to day for our needed education, and that we might be much happier and much less burdened than we are, and should be, if only we were more heedful to govern and guide ourselves by Thy laws; and that if we be not destined to gain and enjoy some things of which we have dreamed, and which we would fain possess for our own, we have it at least in our power to be more serviceable to others than we have been—to be better messengers and ministers of good. May grace be granted us to act and strive in fuller accord with what we believe, and may they be enabled to bless Thee, out of like precious faith, to whom a heritage of trouble and grief is given, that the mournful heritage may not remain unblessed to them.

We remember at Thy feet, "all those who are any ways afflicted or distressed in mind, body, or estate," with sincere desire for their strengthening to patience beneath hardness and pain, and their eventual benediction through it. And at this time, especially, we commend to Thy fatherly goodness the great nation so heavily bereaved in the death, under such woeful circumstances, of their chief citizen and ruler. With them, we sorrow unfeignedly at the sad taking away from their head of the great and good man who had begun to fill nobly his high office, when, through wicked hands, his strength was ruthlessly weakened in the way, and it was appointed to him, after long months of suffering bravely borne, to be cut off out of the land of the living. We feel with them the pain of the mystery that a life so precious and important should have been permitted to be *thus* extinguished. May the heartfelt sympathy of all peoples assist to comfort and support them—them and the bereaved wife and family. May they cherish to profit, the memory of the just, which is blest. May the calamity be sanctified, and may right feeling influence, and wisdom guide, and grace govern him, whom this calamity, and not popular election, has unexpectedly called to the helm of affairs. O Thou who considerest the nations, and lookest upon all the sons of men, " and whose nature and property it is, ever to have mercy and forgive, receive our humble petitions." And may the grace of our Lord Jesus Christ, and the love of God, and the fellowship of the Holy Ghost, be with us all, evermore. Amen.

SERMON.

THE MEEK AND THEIR INHERITANCE.

"Blessed are the meek: for they shall inherit the earth."—
MATTHEW v. 5.

THIS was not at all original, this saying of Christ's. The thought is borrowed from the old Hebrew Psalm, which we read a few minutes ago. It had been lying there for ages, and there, generation after generation, devout souls had made acquaintance with it. They were not always new things that fell from Him when he opened His mouth to teach. Very much of what He said in grave converse with His disciples, and to the multitude on country roads or green hillsides, had often been said before. He drew freely, in His ethical and didactical utterences, from the wisdom of the ancients—from the inspiration of saints and sages who preceded Him. But what a debt we owe frequently, to those who do but repeat for us ideas that have been long in circulation, and with which we are already familiar; what fresh revealings have they contributed; what fresh inward stirrings and quickenings, when old things which they have taken in and assimilated, have come forth from them, spoken with new emphasis, clothed in new form, exhibited in new lights and connexions! And again and again on the lips of Jesus, old things became new, acquiring new force and energy from the spirit of Him who rehearsed them, or new significance and suggestiveness from the frame in which He placed them. As He taught what perhaps the scribes of the nation had often previously taught, the people were astonished at His doctrine, sensible of a power, an authority in it that was strange to them—a power and authority which they had never felt in listening to the scribes; and this sentence from the song of a former prophet in Israel, incorporated by Him here in His own series of beatitudes, is in some sense another and a deeper word.

"Blessed are the meek: for they shall inherit the earth." And who are the meek—whom, at least, would He be intending by the term? You know how it is generally applied. He is meek, we say, who submits uncomplainingly and with gracious resignation to inevitable ills; or who bears silently without passionate resentment, without seeking to retaliate, insult and injury; or who is ready and willing to receive advice, to be counselled and instructed by others, who is capable of taking patiently and sweetly adverse criticism or reproach. But if we would understand what it was especially, that Christ meant by the term, we ought perhaps to look back to the Scripture from which He is quoting, and see how it is employed there. He would be most likely thinking of what it represented in its original setting. Now, the starting-point of the Psalmist, is the prosperity which at the time of his writing, was being enjoyed by the wicked—the good fortune that pursued and crowned them, the success of their schemes, the high positions they had won and were allowed to retain, their continued exaltation in the country above the righteous; and he is occupied in exhorting the latter not to fret themselves because of this, not to let it discompose or distress them, and never to be chafed by witnessing it, into any deviation from the straight path of rectitude, into any decline towards the wrong courses that were seen to bring worldly enlargement and gain, but to go on calmly and quietly trusting in God—calmly and quietly persevering in goodness—for the day will surely come, he asseverates, when the triumphant evildoers shall be cut off and waste away, and the meek shall inherit the land. The meek, then, on his page, are those who, in spite of what is calculated to irritate, to unsettle, to stagger, to dishearten, or to draw aside from adherence to the true, are found calmly, quietly persisting in their allegiance. And would not such be the meekness which Christ was contemplating?—the meekness which, believing deeply, serenely holds on, in fidelity to its best vision, whatever there may be to vex or beguile; neither fretted by obstruction and opposition, nor cast down by disappointment and failure, nor made to halt by encountering misconceptions and frowns, nor tempted to swerve an iota, by the prospect of moving more smoothly or achieving faster; the meekness that can suffer unrepiningly, can relinquish and forego many a thing tranquilly, and, instead of consenting to *descend* for the sake of gathering something *at once*, can wait long and patiently, with little or nothing to show, that the highest and the noblest may be at last secured. Such was the very meekness which He Himself exemplified in His course, whom no persecution shook, no hostility unnerved, no slander or reviling stung to bitterness; on whom contact with prejudice, dulness of discernment, and stubborn unreceptiveness, had no exasperating or distempering effect; who could endure in still resignation, to have His friends grieved with Him and offended at Him, rather than tone down the sharpness of a felt true word, or vary in the least from a felt true method of procedure with a view to soothe; them who would never be enticed or driven to stray a step from divine principle, from the path divinely marked out for Him, in quest of offered immediate success. Not in mere *outward* lowliness and mildness of demeanour, but in this strength of imperturbable staying, and tenacity, of unruffled forbearance and long-suffering for the kingdom of God, He was the Prince of the meek.

Meekness, you will find, although perhaps you may not have noticed, is frequently indicated in our sacred Scriptures as a prominent trait of the ideal teacher and the ideal governor; while we may think of it mostly in connexion with pupils and with subjects, these Scriptures are found connecting it again and again with teaching and with governing. "The servant of the Lord must not strive, but be gentle toward all, apt to teach, in meekness instructing those that oppose themselves." "Who is a wise man and endowed with knowledge among you, let him show out of a good conversation his works with meekness of wisdom." The erring are to be pursued and restored by the enlightened, in the spirit of meekness. The quality in which Moses—the lawgiver, the leader, the guide—is said to have excelled, was meekness. Christ is represented as inviting the weary and heavy-laden to come and learn of Him, because He was meek; and the distinction ascribed to His royalty is the distinction of meekness: "Behold, thy King cometh, meek."

Now, meekness in teaching, is the opposite, not of resentment, proud unreceptiveness, or rebellion and defiance, but of impatience, and false accommodation, and selfish haste. It bears untiringly and graciously with ignorance and folly, and slowness to understand; it makes allowance readily and sweetly for the failings, the stumblings, the mistakes, the unresponsiveness of its scholars; it pauses and considers to adapt itself, with whatsoever circuitousness and self-restraint, to their condition and capacity. It can wait and hold back, and refuse to snatch at certain speedy and showy results, in order to work long and laboriously for the best; and it will not be lured to court any effects, though ever so desired and desirable, through aught of unfaithfulness. So, also, meekness in governing is opposed to the arbitrary, the despotic spirit, which hurries to shape and arrange all, according to its ideal, at once, regardless of the material with which it has to deal, and the amount of preparedness in the community; which cannot tarry to educe little by little, but rushes recklessly to impose—as the famous Peter the Great hastened to civilize his empire—without staying meekly to make a people, meet for civilization,—to endeavour to regenerate and educate. The meek governor is he who can be content to move slowly, to bide his time, to continue quietly steadfast in the apparently barren labour of laying sure foundations, that the building, however delayed, may be stable and firm —in which sense God Almighty is the meekest of governors.

But what, now, is the inheritance of the earth promised to the meek? What it means in the Psalm from which Christ quotes is clear, namely, that possession of the land in social position, in rank and power, which was being usurped for a while by the wicked. At present, theirs were the honours and the high places; they were the successful men; they stood exalted; but it would not be so always, sings the prophet-poet; sooner or later they would be brought down from their elevation, would sink into obscurity and shame, and consume away like the smoke, and the meek would be seen enthroned. They who had held on calmly in the ways of righteousness, in silent, unshaken fidelity to principle, notwithstanding all that existed to annoy and disturb and seduce, would come to the front and obtain the pre-eminence; it was the writer's faith that *they* would rise ultimately to prominence and prime station in the land; and this, I dare say, was something of what Christ meant. The people around Him were sighing, pining, to have the country in which they dwelt for their own. Hence most of their anxiety for the manifestation among them of the promised Messiah. They were counting on getting the country for their own by force of arms under His banner, by contending for it under His leadership, in insurrection against their oppressors; in opposition to which He declares that it was destined to fall into the hands of the meek, of the quiet, uncomplaining, undistracted followers of truth and goodness; meaning thereby, not indeed that it should be theirs in the coarse, earthly sense in which the people around Him were dreaming of gaining it, but that they would become kings there in moral might, in widely quickening, widely moulding influence; that they would be felt there, extensively and profoundly, as rousing, constraining, healing powers. And do we not know, how, in His patiently faithful disciples the prediction was fulfilled; how, at last, in their steady, unswerving loyalty to the heavenly vision that was granted them, they began to be great in the land, and went on to shake the world? Nor does such meekness as theirs ever fail to impress itself, and sway and command, in the end.

But suppose that we take the land, as we well may, to represent what is most solid, substantial, and enduring; and is it not true that meekness tends to inherit *that*? How often, in teaching and in governing, for example, has *that* been missed, through lack of *it*? There has been an inheritance of some kind, of early and flashy results, perhaps; impatient haste, eagerness to achieve quickly, by super-imposing, instead of tarrying to evoke, by dragging forward, instead of lingering to lead— these, may have produced apparently grand effects, but they were not real, they were not vital, and shortly they crumbled and shrivelled away. The thing was too much a surface work; things were hurried on too fast, faster than the taught or the governed were capable of bearing, or were prepared for; there was no root, and after a time collapse and decline set in, all that had been done was undone, and the last state, perhaps, was worse than the first. Meekness, on the other hand, found fault with, and possibly despised and derided for the poverty and paucity of its immediate results, has, through its tenacious, contented determination to accomplish slowly, and its resignation to suffer the odium of seeming failure, inherited at length, a genuine and durable work.

Or, again, have we not seen in society, a loud, blustering, ambitious self-seeker, laying himself out by all means to win attention, observance, influence, and winning it abundantly for a season; while another beside him, neither striving, nor crying, nor lifting up his voice, but simply intent on being worthy, has been nowhere, has been comparatively ignored, until by degrees the former has lost entirely the standing he had struggled for and won, and the latter has grown to be permanently esteemed and valued? One man, in connexion with some public function, say, has gone in for gaining popularity, has studied, and planned, and, when necessary, has not been able to avoid stooping to the dust and defiling himself, for it—and he has got it. A comrade in the same public function, has started seeking only, and has continued seeking only, to be true, has persevered, unmoved, undisturbed, when such seeking has threatened and entailed loneliness, obloquy, and ill repute; neither envious of his fellow's exaltation, nor teased, nor soured at the contrast, and never led to diverge from his line for the sake of mitigating somewhat the harshness of his portion. The end has been that, while the popularity of the first has waned and vanished, to the second has come, although late—too late, indeed, perhaps, for his own eyes to see it—yet to him, eventually, has come an inheritance of homage and reverence, in comparison with which the transient, flimsy popularity of the other was but as the flash of a lighted match to the sheen of the constellations. This kind of thing has often happened: the meek, missing much, maybe, for a while, are endowed after all with the land.

And then, again, it is theirs emphatically, *to inherit*. What they get in amount, may not be equal to that of others; they may secure considerably less of the world, and the good things of the world, but something more is possessed by them in what they get; their little is better than the riches of many. It is not what you have in your hand, but what you *find* in what you have, that determines your real wealth ; and what you shall find in it, will be determined by what you *are*. Two men go forth into the same morning sunshine, visit the same historic scenes, have the same great thoughts uttered in their hearing; but how different may be the yield to the two of the same experience; and the spirit of quiet, patient fidelity, possesses more in what is gathered, than the opposite spirit. We are often too coarsely heated in our seeking, to enjoy the daintiest flavour of our gains.

A man sets himself to get on in life, and in his hunger to get on, learns gradually to strive *anyhow*, not only fights for it, not only toils for it, but consents to crawl a little for it, consents to be false for it to the better soul within him ; and he gets on famously, and is proud and happy under it, has pleasure in the full harvest he has reaped ; and yet, does it render to him as sweetly, as finely, as another's comparatively scanty harvest, who was content to get what could be got truthfully and righteously, and who has not distempered himself by worrying to grasp, nor soiled himself, however strong the temptation, with unclean means ?

And is it not a fact, once more, that to meekness there often comes, without seeking, the very good which restless, reckless ambition laboriously pursues, and only thus overtakes ; that, while the latter may wrest it for itself with much straining and sweat, the former just encounters it—is just visited and embraced by it ; even as estates that were originally acquired by violence, or at a great cost of prolonged effort and hard struggling, are now, by the gentle descendants of rough, rude ancestors, peacefully inherited. Oh, the force and the craft that are wasted often in labouring to obtain what meekness lights upon, and has freely given it by the way! Men exhaust themselves, wear themselves out, in anxious devisings, and weary working for things—for pleasure, for influence, for repute, for standing—when, if nobly at rest from impetuous self-seeking, and surrendered to calm, undistracted persistence in truth and duty, they would wake to find themselves presently, in ample possession of these ; for "Blessed are the meek : they shall inherit the land."

V.

PRAYER.

FATHER of fathers, and God of our fathers; Thou who art of all fatherliness the reason and fountain, in whom are the springs of all the parental grace and tenderness and self-giving to be found among us, and which the world of man has contained from the beginning until now. All the true love, with its sweetness and patience, with its kindly cares and gracious works, that breathes to-day, and has ever breathed upon this earth of ours, all is of Thee. How unsearchable the depth of the riches of His love from whom it comes! What must be the fervour of the sun itself, whose rays we know and bask in! Oh, the love behind, divine and infinite, which we seem to behold afar off, and are moved to worship, in every example of noble human benevolence or affection, in the beautiful generosities or the self-forgetting devotions, which from time to time we meet by the way! Of these, too, we are constrained to sing: "They are but broken lights of Thee, and Thou, O Lord, art more than they." We men and women are manifesting—are we not?—things of Thee, which forests and mountains, stars and firmaments, do not and cannot manifest. Thou breakest through a little in us, as in them Thou dost not and art not able. We think of Thee as struggling to show in us, hidings of Thy power; and, in the gradual ascent of man from high to higher, in the gradual growth of his moral nature, of his loftier sensibilities and sympathies, we seem to see Thee more and more succeeding, until at last Thou shalt shine out upon us as Thou wouldst, and then, with the glory that has been veiled and covered, revealed, Thou wilt have finished Thy work, and wilt enter into Thy rest, and we shall rest together with Thee, being filled with all the fulness of God.

Thou Father of fathers, who art also the God of our fathers; we bless Thee for fathers of our flesh, who trusted in Thee, who taught, and—what was more—helped us their children to trust in Thee; at whose knees we learned Thy name, and in whose love and holy lives we found suggestions of Thee. They have left us, perhaps, and their place knows them no more, but we remember with gratitude and reverence their virtues, their wise and beneficent nurturings, and how bravely they feared Thee, how faithfully they bore and laboured. We bless Thee for parents, the memory of whom is inspiring, and a means of grace for ever; for mothers whose precious influence followed us far out into the world, and because of whom, all women have since been sacred to us; for homes in which it was good to be brought up, to the atmosphere of which we owe much, where lessons of worth were learned that are not lost upon us to this day. Receive, O God, the hearty thanks of all who can heartily thank Thee thus, and give strength to such to walk within their own houses in the steps of their fathers, that *their* children may likewise rise up to call them blessed.

We praise Thee for the divers manners in which Thou dost visit us, Thou who art the unseen, and present; for the divers manners in which Thou dost visit us, to provoke to better things, to quicken, instruct, or refresh; for the many media through which Thou comest to us, for inward stirring, enlargement, or correction; for the great names of history, and the lessons taught, the warnings furnished, by its pages; for the mighty in noble faith, and good deeds, of whom we read or hear with a glow of admiration, which while it fades, is not finished, but leaves us somewhat purer and higher in tone; and for the people we have met by the way occasionally in casual and brief encounter, who have given us new food for thought, or from whom we have learned some new thing worth knowing and treasuring. We praise Thee for the new light which life has sometimes thrown for us, strangely enough, upon subjects that had perplexed, or upon truths which before we had but seen in part and dimly, and also for the news, the often useful, and fruitful, though perchance painful news, concerning ourselves, that has been brought to us by circumstances, which, while seemingly but troublesome and unfortunate chances, were thus, true messengers and ministers of Thine. We praise Thee for things which the great sea has said to us in summer loiterings by its waters, when we have heard it yearn as if in baffled yet persistent aspiration, or moan as if in patient pain, or thunder as if it were a soul in conflict with itself, or murmur softly after storm, as if it were prophesying the low, sweet song to be sung by those who, striving faithfully, shall at last overcome and be at rest. So have we heard at times the voice of the Lord upon the waters, and have gone away with new hope and strength in our hearts. We praise Thee for summer nights or winter nights, when we have felt "the silence that is in the starry sky;" and for rambles by day, when we have been soothed and awed with "the sleep that is among the lonely hills." We praise Thee for summers that are past, for harvests that have been gathered, and for autumn, with its precious fruits, its red afternoons, its beauty of decay, and the sadness of the falling leaf that is not wholly sad. We praise Thee for all precious things, for the dear hearts that love us, for the teaching of sorrow, the uses of pain, for the healing touch of time, and the wider thoughts it brings, for the helpfulness of Christ and the inspiration which He continues to be; for the sense—the assurance—that life even at its hardest and sharpest is worth living, for the growth and spread of benevolent sympathy, for the struggles of men to be wiser and better than they are, for the hope that looks beyond death, and for the faith that Thou art leading us through the mystery of evil toward issues that shall be amply elucidating, toward an inheritance more perfect than our best dreams have whispered. For all precious things we praise Thee; and good it is to give thanks unto the Lord, to show forth His lovingkindness in the morning, and His faithfulness every night. Nay, do we not come nearer to Thee sometimes, and more deeply receive of Thee, in just singing at Thy feet over what we have and enjoy, than in pouring out our prayers and requests to Thee; for what we most need often, is not some fresh gift or supply from above, but some fresh and truer reception of that which is already ours—a reception promoted by meditating thereupon with thanksgiving. Hear Thou, then, our thanksgivings this morning, and answer them; and may the grace of Jesus Christ our Lord, and the love of God, and the fellowship of the Holy Ghost, be with us all evermore. Amen.

SERMON.

SAMSON'S GIFT.

"And the woman bare a son, and called his name Samson: and the child grew, and the Lord blessed him. And the Spirit of the Lord began to move him at times in the camp of Dan."—JUDGES xiii. 24, 25.

THIS Samson, as you know, was one of the fifteen more or less notable persons who, prior to the establishment of the Jewish monarchy, successively obtained power and command in Israel, at least, over some portion or other of the land; attracting some tribes to look up to them, and lean on them, and exercising among these an amount of rule and authority by virtue of certain strong qualities, or superior abilities, that distinguished them.

He, whose birth and beginnings are recorded here, was the last but two of the fifteen judges, as they are called, and the scene of his so-called jurisdiction seems to have been the country of Dan and Judah, where, for a score of years, he stood supreme, and made himself famous through his remarkable bodily strength, with which he was constantly harrying and discomforting the neighbouring Philistines, to whom, at that time, Dan and Judah were in subjection. The story of his exploits is familiar to us all (and a story of curious, strange marvels it is), there is no other in the Hebrew annals to compare with it; we are reminded rather, in reading, of what we have read of the heathen Hercules: very noticeable indeed are the points of resemblance between the achievements and the characteristics of the two heroes. The picture preserved for us of the Scripture hero can hardly be deemed, in all its details and particulars, historically true; it is doubtless highly coloured, full of exaggeration; drawn ages after the period in which he lived, it exhibits the shape which he had then taken in the popular imagination, and the legends that had gathered around him, and attached themselves to his name; within and behind which, however, there lay, we may assume, this basis of fact: that a Samson had once reigned in Dan and Judah, whose corporeal might was extraordinary and who with it, wrought wondrously to the bruising and affliction of the people's oppressors: that his exceptional powers, moreover, were regarded by himself and his contemporaries as God-bestowed, and were believed to be bound up with the maintenance by him of a certain exceptional simplicity of habit and consecration of person, to which he had been devoted from his birth. Such, we may conclude, was the actual Samson, to be found embedded in the chapters of the Hebrew story, and to glance back at whom, for a little, may not be wholly unprofitable or unsuggestive.

First, then, here was a man of surpassing physical strength. His distinction was, that in splendour of muscle and sinew none could approach him, and hence his popularity and the high position he acquired; hence the sway and influence he wielded; because of it, the chief place was accorded him, and he was allowed to rule. In a later age and a more advanced state of society it would not have enthroned him thus. In times less rude and wild, he would not on account of it have produced the impression or commanded the homage that he did. But these are the earliest masters, these are the primitive heroes—the men of transcendent brawn and thews, the men who can do great things with their limbs. Afterwards, the dominion is taken from them and given to the largest brains; and the more civilization increases, the smaller is the admiration they excite, and the smaller their importance grows. The stronger hands deliver up the kingdom to the stronger heads, and become meek followers and servants of the latter. "The weak things of the world" in bodily capacity, in brute force and courage, confound with vigour of mind "the things that are mighty."

Now, Samson was simply mighty in muscle and sinew; a big, burly fellow, who to a giant's strength united something of a giant's slowness, indolence, and easy good nature, but who, dedicated from his mother's womb to the work of contending against the Philistines, and taught from his childhood to detest their yoke, gave himself to employ his singular coarse endowment in worrying and tormenting them. Unlike most of the other judges, he does not appear to have possessed the slightest military genius or enterprise, nor any power of combining his countrymen in opposition to their enemies, or inspiring them with spirit and desire to fight for liberty. There was no generalship in him, and no gift for leading. He never collected an army or secured a following; of the discontented and distressed, none rallied around him, to be led by him to battle. He was just from first to last, a huge, lone pugilist, capable of dealing tremendous blows: he could just smite, rend, crush with his two hands marvellously, and that was all; and, like a wise man, he attempted nothing more, but stuck contentedly and determinedly to what he knew he could do better than anybody else. Instead of straining to emulate the judges who had preceded him, instead of trying to organize troops and conduct campaigns, *because* they had done so, he recognized the kind of ability that was his, to exercise in the service of his tribe, and set himself to make the best use of it in their service. He had but massive, magnificent limbs, and went in, straightway, for applying them to the help of Israel without caring or aiming to be more and other than heaven had qualified him to be. And is it not a grand thing always, to see clearly what our special work is—the work for which we are fitted, to which we are called, and to be giving ourselves to it, undistracted by the vain wish that we were capable of something else, and untempted to reach foolishly after what is beyond us? Is it not a grand thing always, to perceive the line along which we can minister, and to be willing to pursue it, and able to keep to it, however narrow or relatively inferior it may be, intent only on striving to accomplish the very perfectest ministry along that line, and with no poor anxiety or ambition to stretch toward another and a loftier? Not a few would be more successful, and more useful than they are, were they but more bravely content to be themselves—did they but accept more unreservedly, the talent committed to them, and study more simply and independently to be faithful to it.

Samson's gift was not much, was not of the highest kind. It was far below that of other judges in Israel, nor did it produce any great results; the country was never emancipated by his single-handed, desultory blows; nevertheless, he did, and did earnestly, what lay in him to do, and it served some purpose. If the tribes remained undelivered, at least their despondency must have been lightened, their broken, cowed spirit in a measure revived, and the hold of the Philistines would be a little weakened and loosened: The man was useful in his time, as many things have been in their time, which later on, have come to be despised, being superseded by better things; they once fulfilled a ministry, although no place may any longer be found for them. And then see. Since it would be certainly, during the period of Samson's activity, and while his fame was spread abroad, that the child Samuel in Ephraim, was dedicated to the

Lord—is it not possible that the reported mighty deeds of the redoubtable Nazarite of Dan had something to do in moving Hannah to set apart her boy, the boy for whom she had prayed, to be a Nazarite from his birth? Can we not imagine that the impulse which led her to resolve on consecrating her little son, and having him brought up altogether for Jehovah and the nation, may have sprung from what she had heard of the consecration and the exploits of Manoah's son; and that thus, unconsciously, and unsuspectedly, Samson may have contributed to give to Israel, the greater Samuel? "I, too," he had stirred the woman in Mount Ephraim to say to herself—"I, too, would fain have a son devoted to work wonders in the cause of God's people; let me make sacred for the purpose, this new-born babe of mine!" and out of that, came, not a mere repetition of the same wonder-working strength, but something infinitely superior—even the wisest, noblest, and most powerful judge the land had ever seen.

And so, often, they who are doing faithfully, in quite a small way, on quite a small scale, may be secretly conducive to the awakening and inspiring of grander actors than themselves. So, often, a lowly and very imperfect work, faithfully wrought, may be secretly quickening and stimulating toward the accomplishment by others of far higher and more perfect work. There are those who, with their rough and crude performances, with their honest yet blundering attempts, with their dim guesses and half-discoveries, do prepare the way, and furnish the clue for subsequent splendid successes on the part of some who come after them. *They*, and their inferior things may not be much regarded or remembered; yet, but for them, perhaps, *these*, and their finer achievements might never have been.

But observe, secondly, what Samson's countrymen thought of his amazing physical strength, and how it impressed and affected them. They ascribed it to the Spirit of the Lord; when they witnessed, or recalled and recounted his surprising feats, they said to themselves, with some reverence and awe, "The Spirit of the Lord came upon him." That was how they looked at it. That was how they understood and estimated it; according to their habit of recognizing in all phenomena the presence and power of God—His operation, in all human gifts and endowments. Their mountains were to them more than mountains, they were the mountains of the Lord, and the might of their mighty men was the might of the Lord. It is worth having, and cherishing, this old Hebrew sense of the sacredness of things; this old Hebrew vision and worship of a divine secret in every manifestation of force or faculty; it helps to make the world a grander place, and to enhance and elevate one's enjoyment of all skills and powers displayed by men. Whether the great strength of Manoah's son did much or little for the Danite tribesmen against their foes the Philistines, there would be blessing for them at least, and no small blessing, in the way in which it spoke to them, in what they felt it to represent and signify—a new incoming of God around them, a new arrival and expression of God in their midst. They heard in it, the pulsing of the Spirit of the Lord. It said to them, "See, the Lord is among you, down here in your camp, visiting richly and working mightily in one of your brethren;" and was there not, irrespectively of any serviceable deeds that might be wrought by the strong man, a real and a great blessing for them in the purifying awe, the comfort and hope, the stirring of heart, which this would induce?

Samson's chief value lay, perhaps, after all, in the one inspiring thought which his prowess awakened,—the thought that God was there; for it is a blessed thing to be the means of starting in any human breast, in any sluggish, despondent, or earth-bound human breast, some inspiring thought; to be the means of raising another, in his inward lowness, to a higher key, of helping him to feel for a time, more healthily, more nobly, to perceive with kindling conviction, loftier aspects of life that had been hidden from him, to see the sacredness of duty, the beauty of truth, the flaming of the bush, as he had not seen it. Good work it is, and great, to be the instrument of putting another, for a while, into a better and holier frame, of leading him to be more tender, more patient, more finely sympathetic, or more believing in the divine government of things, and in the reality of the kingdom of God. And such work is done, not alone, not mainly, by those to whom is given "a mouth," with wisdom, who can discourse, earnestly, and impressively. How many of their words, indeed, are waste, and effect nothing? Ay, and how simply wordy *they* grow at times, with whom the gift and office of speaking, tends to wordiness. The work is done often, by quite dumb souls, who, "mute" but not "inglorious," are themselves inspiring, and again and again, perhaps, without meaning it, or being conscious of it; again and again assisting to quicken or worthily animate some one whom they touch, with the spirit that is in them, and exhales from them; with their own brave and gracious lives, assisting to lift him up to a sense of higher things, or to revive his half-lost faith in goodness and in God.

Oh, prophets of the Lord are they, whether the tongue of the learned be theirs or not; prophets of the Lord are they, who are heavenly enough in their tone and deeds, to be daily bringing heaven down to earth, and ever and anon making it visible and vocal to earthy, or earth-depressed hearts beside them—hearts moved thus, by them, to look up, with some throb of purer thought, or flutter of nobler sigh.

But there is one other thing to be noticed with respect to Samson's strength, and the way in which it was regarded by the people. They received the impression that, while having its source in the Spirit of Jehovah, it was somehow, intimately connected with the Nazariteship of the man, and depended for its continuance upon his maintenance of that Nazariteship. Such was the general belief, and the belief, apparently, of the man himself. The strong son of Manoah, had he not been a Nazarite from the beginning, and was it not concurrently with his breaking of the vow that he began to weaken? Now the Nazaritic institution among the Hebrews, meant this—the special consecration to God, of a layman. The proud theory was, that all Israel were consecrated to Him, forming in the midst of the great world a holy nation; within this holy nation, however, a class—the priests—occupied the same relation which the nation held to the world—they, were the specially consecrated ones, set apart from the rest, to the Lord's service; but any private Israelite, if he were moved to desire it, or if his parents desired it for him when he was a child, might be specially vowed to the Lord; not, indeed, to officiate as a priest, yet to be considered, either for his whole life or for a specific term, as belonging in a peculiar sense to the Lord; and the consecration of such an one was outwardly denoted and expressed by certain strict observances on his part. Since, for example, the priests while engaged and busy about the tabernacle, were required to abstain rigorously from all wine and strong drink, he, as if always on holy ground, as if always waiting upon Jehovah, had to practise perpetual abstinence; and since, upon the altar of Jehovah in the sacred place, no tool of any kind could be lifted without desecrating it, he, as being himself a living altar, was inhibited from using any tool upon his person, and must e'en go with hair and beard unshorn.

This was the Nazariteship to which Samson's mother had devoted him; in continuous submission and adherence to which, he had been seen putting forth a giant's strength and performing wonders, and his ultimate recreancy from which, was known to have been followed by loss of power. Hence the conviction that his gigantic strength from the Lord, was due to his Nazariteship, and hung upon his loyally abiding therein : and so, here was another fine use which he served, infinitely more important and valuable than anything he did for the people against their enemies, with his Herculean arms and hands. He served withal, to remind them forcibly, that their might and their hope as a nation lay in their fidelity—in their fidelity to the consecration to which they had been chosen, to the separateness from heathen morals and manners to which they had been called, to the God and the divine ideas revealed to them. Such was the lesson he exemplified and left behind him; and which, as often as they remembered him, what he was, while maintaining his Nazariteship, and how he fell in falling from it, would be uttered to them afresh, in tones of mingled encouragement and warning,—that to be strong was to be faithful, and that with faithlessness came weakness and decay.

A grand lesson to have been the innocent means of impressing and exhibiting vividly, and one of eternal application, nothing being truer to-day, and for ourselves, than that simple faithfulness is evermore full of heavenly promise, and that without it, we can expect no abounding toward us, of the Spirit of the Lord.

VI.

PRAYER.

O GOD, the everywhere present, the everywhere quickening and inspiring Spirit, whom none escape, from whom none can flee, whose is the beautiful strength with which bad men work evil, as well as the strength with which good is wrought, in whom we live here, our little lives from morning until eventide, and to whom in dying we shall come. When we say, on bended knee, how great and wonderful art Thou, how unspeakable the majesty of Thy glory, it is not, Thou knowest, that we mean to applaud Thee, or that we think it needful to tell Thee of Thy greatness, and to proclaim to Thee our sense of it. We may say things sometimes that seem to savour of this; we may sometimes seem to indulge in a foolish waste of adoring words; but Thou understandest what it means; even the involuntary cry of the heart under the burden of Thy felt immensity, the cry with which the burdened heart relieves itself as it meditates of God, and His marvellous works. What can we do else but pour ourselves out in syllables of admiration, when oppressed with the knowledge which is too wonderful for us? Oh, the mystery of that awful power which we feel to be over and in all, the invisible secret of things that do appear, the informing soul, the ever-sustaining, ever-renewing life of the world. And, oh, the mystery of that Fatherly goodness toward us, which we feel to be hidden and shining in the darkness, and cannot prove. It awes and greatens, comforts and stills us to believe that we are not our own, but Thy creatures, whom Thou hast made and art upholding ; Thy children whom Thou lovest, and art redeeming. And when Thou dost perplex us in our thought of Thee, and our musings upon Thy travailing creation, travailing in pain even until now ; preserve us ever, behind and beneath, all our perplexity, in the peace of Thy Son Jesus, the peace which passeth understanding. Give us always, we pray Thee, the peace needful for living well, helpful to wholesome growth and brave doing. We would not crave enjoyment as our end, would not hunger and sigh to be at rest, for in turmoil and distress what education we often receive ; but such inward rest we do desire, as shall set us free for duty, and assist to make us wise and alert, and strong to fulfil it—such inward rest as shall enable us to be good workers, to be heroes in sorrow and pain, to be capable of giving our best attention to the things that claim it, and standing steadfast and immovable in assaults of temptation. For how often are we meaner and faultier than we should be, less faithful, less courageous, less patient, less pure, less just and considerate toward others, because we are not inwardly at rest ; should we have erred, and strayed, and lost ourselves sadly, as we have sometimes done, if in the soul there had been peace? Lord, evermore guard and garrison our hearts with that unspeakable gift of His who said, " Peace I leave with you ; my peace give I unto you." Fill us with the comfort of a wise and gracious content. May we know how to accept, without impatience or repining, and without envying the lot of others, the things that must be, the heritage appointed us, the discipline provided for us, while discontentedly reaching forth from existing things that should not be, toward things before us, which it should be our ambition and passion to overtake. And if we are called to engage in work, and to be bound to work, that we like not, and from which we would fain be released, help us to pursue it, not reluctantly and sullenly, but cheerfully and willingly ; and, yet more, to force ourselves to be interested in it, and to resolve on performing it with the utmost pains as thoroughly and as perfectly as possible, that so we may come by degrees to love and take delight in it. Forgive us, O God, in Thine infinite mercy, both our wrong discontents and our unworthy contentment, and work in us more of the quiet and happy acquiescence that grows from faith in Thee, and in Thy providence, and to which unexpected treasures are revealed, with more of that divine hunger and thirst which Thou must needs satisfy, and for which is laid up corn and wine of heaven. Thou who speakest within us, in every one of us, in the "I ought" of conscience—whether our ideas of the right and true be absolutely correct or not, and however these may have changed, and may yet change,—Thou who speakest within every one of us, in the "I ought" of conscience—help us to be always loyal and obedient to this voice, and whereunto we have attained in vision of the right and true, may we walk by the same rule, and mind the same thing, that if in anything our vision be defective or false, Thou mayest enlarge and rectify it in due time. Strengthen us to do faithfully as we see, that we may learn to see more and more perfectly. O Lord, Thou seest from Thy throne, how we are growing down here, under the pressure of our earthly environment, under the circumstances and influences to which we are subjected; our gradual shaping beneath it all, is not hidden from Thee, as it is hidden in part from ourselves; and this is the all-important thing, not what we meet by the way, but what we are becoming in the encounter, not what surrounds us, but what is being made of us. Lord, let us not be developing aught of hardness, where we should be increasing in sensibility and tenderness, nor aught of weakness, where we should be waxing strong, and stronger. Let not the fierce gales of winter twist and maim us, nor the burning heat wither us. And, let not any virtue or faculty be growing in us at the expense and to the suppression of any other, that should be growing with it side by side; but may we progress altogether, and symmetrically. And, if, while our special circumstances and pursuits, our daily necessary contacts and absorbing occupations, may be affording plentiful exercise to some graces or good susceptibilities in us, there should be some, or one, which they are not calculated to call forth, but are rather calculated to weaken and impair; help us to look carefully after that, and to make careful provision for its exercise, to the end, that we may be preserved in healthful balance and proportion, growing up in all things unto Christ our Head. O Lord, wholly sanctify and save us, that our life and influence in the world may be to some sanctifying, and saving; and unto Him that is able to keep us from falling, and to present us faultless before the presence of His glory, with exceeding joy, to the only wise God our Saviour, be glory and majesty, dominion and power, both now and for ever. Amen.

SERMON.

THE ELECTION OF GOD.

" For the children being not yet born, neither having done any good or evil, that the purpose of God according to election might stand, not of works, but of Him that calleth. It was said unto her, The elder shall serve the younger. As it is written, Jacob have I loved, but Esau have I hated."—ROMANS ix. 11–13.

THIS passage belongs to a certain argument which St. Paul is pursuing, and sets forth one of the historical facts to which he appeals in support of it. His argument, viz. against the complacent persuasion of the Jews, that they must always be the people of God, and could never be lost through refusing to accept the Christ whom the Apostle preached—*because*, they had Abraham for their father. Even so, they did flatter themselves, and the whole chapter before us is occupied with his endeavours to expose and shatter the delusion; to convince them that the descent of which they boasted, and in which they trusted, was not enough to save them from coming into condemnation—

would not hinder in the least, or stay for a moment, the judgment of their unbelief. While admitting, amidst his grief at the doom which he felt they were incurring by their unbelief—while admitting, all the distinguished privileges they had enjoyed and inherited as the children of Abraham, "to whom pertained the adoption, and the glory, and the covenants, and the giving of the law, and the Mosaic ritual, and the promises"—his position is, "they are not all Israel, who are of Israel." He undertakes to show, that it was possible to have sprung from the loins of their great progenitor, and yet not be numbered among his heirs, that there were actual cases in which offspring of his had been excluded from his family; and the first example is presented in the words, "In Isaac shall thy seed be called," a quotation from the Book of Genesis, which declared that Isaac, and not Ishmael, should bear his father's name, and carry on his line; that though both were sons of the Patriarch, the former only, with his posterity, should be reckoned as belonging to him, and the latter, with his posterity, should be shut out and counted strangers. If, then, says the Apostle, Ishmael's natural descent from Abraham did not preclude his being cut off from participation with

Abraham's natural descendants, how can your mere natural descent from him, be relied upon to protect you against any divine excommunication? It might be said, however, in reply—and be deemed by those who said it, a sufficient answer —that Ishmael, after all, was but the child of a bondwoman, and not worthy therefore to share with Sarah's child. Hence, St. Paul hastens to adduce a second example not open to such objection. Remember, he adds, the stronger and more striking instance of Jacob and Esau, the two sons of the son of the promise, by the same mother, Rebecca. Was there not the most perfect equality between these two, in their relation by birth to the father of the faithful? Yet, were they united in constituting with their posterity the chosen seed? No. While Jacob was designated to obtain the blessing, Esau, in spite of his equally pure birth, was debarred; and not because of any misbehaviour on his part, deserving, and demanding it,—although he did misbehave himself,—since, before the brothers had done good or evil, the verdict of excision had gone forth against him. "Of the two nations, in thy womb, the one shall be stronger than the other, and the greater shall serve the less." Seeing then, says the Apostle, that history records cases in which patriarchal descent has not sufficed to insure a place in the patriarchal line, when the Almighty determined on appointing otherwise; in which, when He determined on appointing otherwise, patriarchal descent, without the slightest shadow of a flaw, and unaccompanied by aught detracting in moral character and conduct, did not avail to preserve in patriarchal connection—seeing that it has been thus, what warrant has the Jew of to-day for the proud confidence he displays in the shielding power of his descent from Abraham? How can he flatter himself that, in consequence of it, he need not fear losing the Abrahamic standing with heaven, even though he should be found rejecting heaven's own Son?

Such was St. Paul's argument, and it was an argument that could hardly fail to have some effect on Jewish minds; they could hardly help feeling, in listening to it, that the ground on which they built, the ground of their sacred ancestry, was not quite so solid and secure as they had been accustomed to consider it.

But, now, the text speaks of a separation made between Jacob and Esau, with regard to inheritance and future destiny, irrespectively of, and antecedently to, any merit or demerit attaching to either, and represents it as exemplifying the election of God. You all know, of course, what the doctrine of election was in the old evangelical theology—the doctrine, viz. that out of the human race, lost and ruined by sin, the Creator had from eternity, predestinated a certain number to attain salvation, leaving the remainder to perish, or to shift as they might. Surely a horrible thing to have been attributed to Him by His creatures; and they thought, forsooth, to justify the supposed way of the Lord, with the reasoning, that He had an entire right to do as He pleased with His own; to select from the ranks of the guilty and fallen, some for redemption, and to let the others sink to everlasting hell; forgetting that having brought all into existence, He owed equal duties to all; and that, whatever his *power*, it could give Him no *right* to abandon any to the awful perdition from which He resolved that a portion should be rescued, and might have resolved that all should be.

But, our text was always claimed as supporting and illustrating the doctrine referred to. It was always prized, indeed, as furnishing one of the chief Scripture proofs. "Here," they said, "is an inspired Apostle's affirmation of the election which our creed declares; Jacob chosen, Esau rejected, before they were born, that the purpose of God, according to election, might stand, not of works, but of Him that calleth." The writer's object, however, as we have seen, is really to demolish the position of certain predestinarians, who maintained that, as the children of Abraham, they were ordained to be for ever the blessed children of God —an object which he aims to effect, by showing how, in one and another instance, descent from Abraham had not been sufficient, even to keep within the Abrahamic family, and could not therefore be held to carry with it infallible continuance in the favour of Abraham's God. And while such is his object, the separation between Jacob and Esau, to which he points, was not a separation in regard to spiritual inheritance and eternal destiny, but simply the choice of the former to constitute, with his descendants, the Messianic seed, and the denial to the latter of a place among that seed. St. Paul was quite innocent of any thought about what has been termed, unconditional election to everlasting life.

But, then, you will say, he *does* intimate, at all events, an unconditional election to something. Here were a couple of men, twin-born, and nursed at the same breast, who, according to him, were divinely elected in the womb, to very dissimilar portions—the one to a goodly heritage, to be the father of a highly-favoured people, "of whom concerning the flesh Christ came;" the other to a much inferior heritage, to be the father only of the rude, red Edomites, inhabiting a country of fire and sand. Yes, truly, and the Bible is full of such election; it begins with the record of the call of Abraham, to whom alone, in Ur of the Chaldees, came the word of the Lord, whispering to him of a God whom his fathers knew not, and summoning him out from his father's house. Then, we have Israel, specially visited, and made the recipients of a special moral and religious training, having educational ideas and experiences granted them, to which the surrounding nations were not admitted. Then, again, among the lost sheep of the house of Israel, Christ appears, and among them displays His heavenly visions, while the Gentiles sit in darkness. And, you remember how He himself preached election, to the annoyance and anger of those who heard, saying, "Many widows were in Israel, in the days of Elijah, but unto none of them was he sent, save unto Sarepta, a city of Sidon, unto a woman that was a widow. And many lepers were in Israel in the time of

Elisha the Prophet, and none of them were cleansed, saving Naaman the Syrian." Was not St. Paul, moreover, constantly reminding the cities of the heathen world, to which his course had been directed, that to the blessing of acquaintance with the glorious Gospel, they had been elected?

The mystery of unconditional election to good and sweet things runs through the Bible. And does it not run also through human life? Is the story of Jacob and Esau any more than an illustration of what is perpetually going on before our own eyes? Is not the fact daily, hourly repeated, that some are chosen and some rejected, not of works, but of Him that calleth? We all start to build, to build for eternity, upon foundations already laid for us, which we have had no hand in forming, and are powerless to change. However earnestly we may labour, or whatever we may attempt, we can only build on *them*. They must needs, more or less, define and regulate the structure; and how widely they differ in different persons—*here*, how spacious and splendid the foundations are, *there*, how comparatively narrow and mean; *here*, what advantages are inherited, in physical constitution and temperament, in parental example and influence, in the atmosphere

H

of the home, and in the whole environment to which the child is committed ; *there*, what immense and remorseful disadvantages. *This* man has received a frame, and a nervous system, electing him to a strength and decision of character, and to consequent happy achievements, which his neighbour's congenital weaknesses doom him to fall short of, and to be incapable of, desire and strive as he may. One enters on the race, bearing within him the refinement, the sensibility, the grace of a long line of noble ancestors ; upon another, his ancestors lie, a heavy, laming weight. One is sent hither to acquire truth, and to learn wisdom, with a strong and healthy brain ; another with a brain deficient or malformed. One is launched amidst conditions most favourable to beautiful growth, to attainment of knowledge, or to his preparation for great visions and ideas ; another is plunged from the first, in conditions severely unfavourable. There are elections to wealth, genius, station, and fine opportunities, and there are reprobations to idiotcy, penury, obscurity, and meagreness or privation of opportunity. Contrast the child born to-day in some happy English home, to a heritage of tender care and Christian culture, with the child born in some loathsome den, to a heritage of neglect and misery and shame. See how *these* are shut out from good things to which *those* are chosen, and not of works, but of Him that calleth. And where much of what is possessed and enjoyed, may be due, to the man's own seeking and effort, in which he has surpassed others, and apparently deserves more than they; to what is much of his own seeking and effort due, but to conditions within him, and around him, that were determined for him, without any will or choice of his—conditions to which he was appointed, while others were denied them. Some are made to have, or gain, what some are made to be void of, or to miss.

Well, now, this fact with which we may be often teased and perplexed; which seems to savour of unfairness and injustice in the ordering of things; what can we say about it? What does it mean, under the rule and government of an Almighty Father? The old Bible throws some light upon it, suggests something, at all events. In reading, for example, its account of the call of Abraham, we get at once an illumining idea. He *was* chosen, say the ancient Scriptures, out of his countrymen and the world of his day, to be specially instructed and enlightened; to hear, on still, starlight nights, a divine voice, inaudible to others, and to realize a divine communion, more elevated and purer than theirs. And why? Did it denote that Heaven cared for none but him; that he monopolized its regard? Had those who were left in the dark no part in its thoughts and purposes? Was his election a mere piece of favouritism toward him, to make him richer and more blessed than his fellow-mortals—to exalt him above them? No, no,—say the ancient Scriptures; he was elected for *their sakes*,—in him, thus specially visited and quickened, all nations of the earth were to be blessed. Then Israel, again; why were they chosen to be in certain respects, as they were, a peculiar people, to receive exclusively, the adoption and the covenants, and the Mosaic law and the promises? Was it simply for themselves, and their own aggrandizement? Many of them may have fancied it was, but their sacred writings show that some of them had different ideas of what it meant.

You find there, now and then, an old prophet reflecting that the Lord was blessing them and causing His face to shine upon them, that through them, His ways might be known on earth, His saving health unto all nations. This, indeed, is the Biblical view of election to superior possession and privilege; that it is the method by which the wisdom of God proceeds in purposing and working for the good of *all;* that determining good for the many, it endows the few, in order, by their endowment, to prepare the way for it and bring it to pass;—preference being shown them in the interest of the many. And have we not witnessed and experienced the beneficial issue of such preference? Have we not seen how it is made to serve by degrees, the welfare of the excluded crowd?

Christ was sent only to the lost sheep of the house of Israel, and to them, His first messengers were strictly charged to confine themselves. "Go ye not into the way of the Gentiles, and into a city of the Samaritans enter ye not." But, lo, what a river of water of life has rolled out into all the world from the gift of Him to Judea; as He himself said, "Salvation is of the Jews." And, any great and beneficent ideas now diffused among mankind,—how came they to be the general property? Had they not their rise and beginning among some elect people, and in some elect individuals or individual of that people, from whom they slowly crept forth abroad? Is there not always some elect people, or individual, in whom any new and enriching idea has to be first hidden, in order to its unfolding and dispersion for the blessing of humanity? The many are constantly inheriting from the inspiration or investiture of the few, who for the time may seem to be chosen to the stern rejection of the former. The elect obtain, and the rest are blinded; yet the obtaining of the election is for the ultimate profit of the rest. What benefit has accrued to society in various ways,—in the shape of more knowledge conducing to more comfort and happiness, in the shape of useful discoveries and inventions, in the shape of widely serviceable action and enterprise, from some having been born to brilliant genius, or special advantages, to greater wealth, leisure, brain, than their fellows. Could such an one, and such an one, have contributed as they have done directly, or indirectly, to the furtherance of the whole, had they not been preferred before us to some peculiar gifts, or resources? Not always consciously, and intentionally, often, quite unconsciously, and without intention, the elect in endowment, are ministering beautifully to the multitude. They have not set themselves, perhaps, to minister; in using and putting forth their distinguished powers they may be moved chiefly by selfish ambition, by thirst for fame, or by the mere pleasure they take in the exercise, by their passion for certain pursuits; but out of it, come gradually manifold meliorations or augmentings, for the multitude.

Look at the investigations and discoveries of such men as Pasteur, the famous French chemist. Had they been born, as thousands of their fellow-creatures are, to abject misery and poverty, or with mean faculty and small brain, such investigations and discoveries would never have been made by them. And how largely they are calculated to add, and will doubtless add, to the general well-being and happiness. As somebody said in the "Nineteenth Century" this month, "It would be impossible to find in the records of human industry, a work of more promise to the world than these contributions to the knowledge of disease, and of its cure and prevention."

The election of some, signifies the divine purpose of advancing all, and is the divine method of fulfilling it. And what does it mean, that there are daily disappearing from hence, "behind the veil;" on the one hand, elect souls who have been chosen, not of works, but of Him that calleth, to discern and enjoy inspiring religious truth, and to reach high moral and spiritual attainment, together with a greater number, on the other hand, whose birth and circumstances have operated to keep them outside such truth, and below such attainment? What does that mean, but that the former have been enlightened and quickened in *time*, for ministry to the latter, in *eternity*? It is not that *those* are chosen, and *these* for ever excluded, but that through the choosing, now, of *those*, *these* are to be hereafter, blessed. Every election from among men, carries within it the promise and prophecy of good things for mankind ; and whatever of good may be given *me*, to my enlargement and exaltation above others, is given me, not for my having, but that by means of it, in some way, others may be served.

VII.

PRAYER.

GOD, our Father, whose will has enlightened us with the light of the living, who hast caused our eyes to behold the sun, who hast blessed us with the unspeakable blessing of being, and given us our place for a while here upon the earth, with the wonder of the starry heavens above us, and the voice of the moral law in our hearts ; Thou hast made us, and appointed the bounds of our habitation, and our holy and beautiful house, we believe is full of Thy glory, wherein the secrets that have been laid up from the beginning, and that are being searched out more and more, are secrets of Thine, with which Thou meanest us to be enriched and profited, and to hear, withal, the music of Thy wisdom, the thunder of Thy power. Thou hast made us, and we believe that a beautiful purpose of Thine with regard to us, is in progress, and is slowly, yet surely, fulfilling itself, a purpose in the ultimate accomplishment of which, we shall be more than comforted for all the years during which we may have seen evil, and Thou wilt be justified and glorified. On the morning of our leisure day, a day in the midst of the days that we are thankful for, and would not lose, we come together again from our several homes, from our several rounds of work and care, to unite in glad worship of Thee, as the Lord of our lives and the Father of our spirits, as the unseen love, whose government we own and trust ; and to join in thinking our thoughts, and wishing our wishes, and uttering our burdens at Thy feet, in the sanctuary of Thy presence, remembering

Him who of old spoke comforting and inspiring words of Thee, which we feel to be living and true words for ever; and rejoicing, that with Him, who often turned aside to kneel, and look away into the heavens, *we* are able to behold the face of Thy glory, and to pour out our souls to Thee.

O God, this house in which Thou hast made us to dwell becomes at times rather a painful place. It puts us sometimes to trouble and grief; with lightnings that wound or slay; with ship-devouring seas; with upheavings and convulsions that scatter ruin; with sharp smitings of windy storm, and tempest; we are strangely bruised and hurt in it, often. Thou art often strangely cruel to us with Thy world-order. Forgive us, for we speak as children, even as in the days of our childhood, we were wont to speak to ourselves concerning fathers of our flesh who mysteriously vexed and afflicted us; yet, while suffering under their perplexing severities, we gave them reverence, and trust, and love, too; and shall we not much rather accept with reverence, and without loss of faith, Thy perplexing severities, the seemingly blind cruelties involved in Thy world-order? O ye winds of the Lord, that rend and lay waste; that shake the forest, and break the cedars; whose mighty gusts bring pain and misery to many, and harm capriciously. O ye winds of the Lord, praise ye the Lord.

And we will praise Him the while, for the sweet pity, the sympathy, the love and benevolence, found in his great handiwork, Man, amidst the ruthlessness and remorselessness of material nature. We will praise Him, too, for the manifold good things which we are conscious of owing to many dark and evil things; for the useful teachings which these have yielded, and the blessings that have unfolded from them, like flowers of spring from ugly winter roots; for what we have seen in our time, and do see, of sorrow's beneficial work; of profit through loss, of richer life out of doleful destruction and death.

O God, lead Thou us still in the way that Thou choosest, and give us grace, in that way, to be evermore learning, of

Thee, toward our true creaturely progress and final perfecting. Keep us in good heart for all patient endurance, for all earnest research and inquiry, for all brave effort, for all philanthropic enterprise, and for all the recurring duties of the day, both great and small, with the faith that Thou *art* leading us, and that with Thee is the calm of eternity, whatever turmoil and travail may be ours, because Thou seest the beauty of each stern necessity, and the glory of the beatific end which we see not ; as, "we say, in under breath, all our life is mixed with death ; and who knoweth which is best. May we smile to think Thy goodness flows around our incompleteness, round our restlessness Thy rest." We pray to Thee for the comfort and succour of those who are suffering to-day. Many are in pain as with a sword in their bones ; many are eating with wry faces bread and water of affliction ; many are struggling to soreness, with hard circumstances, and all things seem to be against them ; some are bowed down and broken in heart, because Death has come into their house and taken away their head from his place ; some are weary with long sickness, and well-nigh weary of seeking health in vain ; and they are troubled for dear ones who watch them anxiously, and for whose sakes they would fain grow strong, but, alas ! strength will not come. Some in the midst of long ease and prosperity are suddenly plunged in great sorrow—sorrow that blots out for a time all brightness, and spoils for them the taste of their pleasant things ; and it is as though they must sink utterly in these deep waters, except they be holden up. Some are walking in the shadow of sad forebodings, they are full of fear, dreading the fiery trial with which circumstances seem to be threatening them, which seems to be approaching to try them ; and their hearts faint and fail at the prospect. "How can I bear that?" they cry ; "Oh, that Heaven would but spare me that ! " Such sufferers, and all others, we cast upon the mercy of God, craving for them divine support, the patience of faith, the resignation of trust, strength to carry their load without being wrung or crushed thereby, and if it may be, to some exercise and calling forth of grace within them, to some inward correcting and sanctifying.

Receive, O Lord, the thanksgivings of the happy, of those who are glad to-day because they are quiet, because Thou hast healed their sicknesses, because Thou hast filled their houses with good, because Thou hast given them the desire of their hearts ; and accept the repentance and confession of those with whom is the consciousness of having done wrong, and whose soul on account of it, is humbled within them ; and accept the work of those who, by Thy help, have done well, who have been aiming and endeavouring worthily, who have been engaged in seeking the benefit of others, and in aiding that which is good. Direct and prosper in their labours, every wise-hearted ruler, every gifted statesman intent upon serving his country, every religious discourser anxious to speak faithfully his vision in words that shall quicken and edify, every honest student of science, every worker in art, every divinely-sent evangelist with the Gospel of the Lord Jesus upon his lips, every teacher of babes. Direct and prosper, we pray Thee, the instructions given in the Sunday-schools of our land, may their management be wise and wiser, and their influence increasingly beneficial, with less and less of alloy. In them, may good seed be sown, the fruit of which shall be found after many days ; and through prayer *with* them, and *for* them, as at this time, may the hearts of those who go forth to sow, be comforted, and encouraged, and inspired anew.

" And unto Him who is able to do exceeding abundantly, above all that we ask or think, according to the power that worketh in us, unto Him be glory in the Church, by Jesus Christ, throughout all ages, world without end. Amen."

SERMON.

UNCEASING PRAYER.

"Pray without ceasing."—1 THESSALONIANS v. 17.

IT often happens that men are awakened on a sudden, in one way or another, to a vision of deeper meanings in familiar words than they had before suspected in them; to find therein enshrined ideas or allusions of which they had never dreamt. They have been using these words in daily intercourse, without imagining for a moment that aught was contained in them beyond what they were accustomed to express with them, taking for granted that they knew and understood all their significance; and then, some day, the words have been laid open to them, disclosing hidden thoughts, or hidden images, that have made them henceforth to their eyes and ears quite new things, charged with new force and power. So, also, a writer or public speaker will occasionally emphasize or apply a common word in such a way, will occasionally place it in such connection, as to throw upon it a wholly fresh light, as to reveal a depth in it that had not been previously felt; or we are arrested by it, and set brooding over it, with a sense that more lies in it than we have hitherto discerned—that to the utterer, at all events, it says more than it has been wont to say to ourselves. Now, for thousands—for the large majority, perhaps—what does the word "prayer" represent, but the act of supplicating Heaven on bended knees? To pray, is with them, to ask of the Almighty for desired blessings, for "things requisite and necessary;" or else, perhaps, without any asking, to bow down before Him in adoring worship. That, is just what they understand by it. Well, now, suppose that one of their number, reading attentively and thoughtfully, should come for the first time across our text; would he not be detained there in some little wonderment and perplexity? And as he questioned and pondered, would he not be led to think that prayer must needs have meant more for the Apostle than it meant for him—that the Apostle's conception of it must needs have been somewhat different from his own—since asking and worshipping, he would reflect, *can* only be occasional exercises, they cannot be carried on unintermittingly, neither, indeed, should we be justified in attempting it, even were it possible? There are tasks and duties claiming us that would have to be neglected. Prayer may be too much indulged in—too much for faithfulness, as also for the soul's health. What, then, could be the praying which St. Paul saw might be maintained, and should be maintained, without ceasing?

I remember meeting, many years ago, with a story of some devout domestic servant, who when invited by the teacher of the class of which she was a member to say, if she were able, how the exhortation before us could be obeyed, replied, modestly enough, but promptly and confidently, that she not only knew, but was herself in the habit of obeying it; and to the inquiry how she managed, answered at once after the following manner: "On rising in the morning, I lift up my heart for grace to rise with Christ from the death of sin to newness of life; dressing, I pray to be clothed with the robe of righteousness; washing, to be cleansed from fault; as I light the fire and arrange the room, that my soul may be kindled and adorned by the Holy Ghost from heaven; as I sit at meals, that it may be mine to be fed and nourished with heavenly bread;" and so on through all the scenes and business of the day. The girl's answer, I recollect, was much commended and admired. What she described, however, was not praying without ceasing. Assuming that the description was ever in any case actually realized, which one is constrained to doubt, it would be merely the employment of successive circumstances and situations as incitements and suggestions to a passing prayer; and the Apostle, we may be sure, would scarcely have recognized in it an embodiment of his idea.

What was his idea? If we could but be shown the very picture that rose before him as he penned the words of the text! Anyhow, asking God for things, or engaging in the exercise of worshipping God, could not have been in his view essential to prayer, often as it might take the form of such asking and worshipping; often as it might thus find vent and pour itself forth. These necessarily intermittent acts, must have been to him but intermittent expressions of something behind, in which lay the real essence of prayer, and which might go on throbbing still during their suspension, throbbing continuously, in their absence. What was his idea of unceasing prayer? There happens to be a passage in another of his Epistles, in which he seems to me to have hinted it—in which, while not fully explaining himself, he gives us at least a clue to follow. "Praying always," he writes to the Ephesians, "praying always with all prayer and supplication in the *spirit*,"—as though he had written, "Whatever you may be saying or doing, however head, heart, hands, may be occupied, be praying always in the spirit of your sayings and doings, in your pervading temper and disposition, in your central animating principle." Asking God, and worshipping God were regarded by him, then, as the utterance at intervals of a certain spirit, a certain spirit which might be otherwise and variously uttered; and to live in that spirit, to have it constantly pulsing and ruling within you, would be his idea of praying without ceasing.

And now, we are left to answer for ourselves the question, What is that spirit which constitutes prayerfulness, and which may be, and should be, habitually ours? To me—if you care at all to listen for a while—to me, it is a compound of three elements. First, Aspiration. In all true praying we have the cry of an inward hunger for better being and doing. It means a soul looking onward and upward to an ideal which, seen afar off, is yearned after; it means a soul discontented with itself, with its present attainments and perform-

I

ances, unable to rest in things as they are, and craving more and nobler. "Thy kingdom come: Thy will be done on earth, as it is in heaven." There is the wistful reaching forth toward something higher and more perfect. Wherever, then, improvement is being desired and sought (not, of course, improvement in our surroundings, but ourselves; not, of course, improvement in what we have, but in what we are and do), there is prayer, even though it may not be breaking out at the time, in any cry to God; since, there is the very same spirit which breathes in the cry of prayer. You know the picture which underlies those words of St. Paul,—"Not reckoning myself yet to have laid hold, I press toward the mark for the prize of my high calling,"—the picture, namely, of the Grecian racer in his agony of effort and hope, as with eye fixed on the distant garland, he throws himself into the struggle to win it, his body leaning forward, his chest heaving, every muscle strained, every vein starting, the sweat-drops beading his brow. That, might stand for a pictorial representation of prayer—he is ever praying in the spirit, who is ever aspiring. Well, here is a man, an artisan in his workshop, or an artist in his studio, engrossed through the day, from morn to eve, in striving to realize his idea of what would be fitting and fine ; anxious to overtake, if possible, or at least, to get nearer than yesterday, to his vision of the truest and the best, in surpassing what he has hitherto done—trying to succeed, disappointed, dissatisfied with the result, and trying again, altering, rubbing out, touching, and touching anew, intent upon executing his noblest, until the night falls ; and, "behold, he prayeth," and has been praying unpausingly, the livelong day. Now, there is such a thing as an aspiring *temper*, in contradistinction to the negligent, self-complacent, abject temper ; when it may be said to be the wish and aim of one's life to go on improving—to be growing out of conscious defects and faults, into a figure less faulty and defective, to be learning ever, a little more excellence in work, a little more thoroughness, and faithfulness in duty, a little more grace of behaviour in all spheres and relations : when an ideal of goodness is cherished, in the light of which our best is never wholly satisfactory, and which is evermore urging us to transcend it ; and do we not then, pray without ceasing ? Under the burden of our abiding wish and aim we may be moved often to look up to heaven—with a cry, a cry of entreaty for the better thing that we seek, and for strength to make better progress toward it; but whether we be crying or not, is not that constant burden, itself, the very soul of prayer? Yes, instinct with prayer is he, in the sight of the omniscient Seer, who, though he kneel not to supplicate, is all the while, worthily aspiring.

And again, what is praying but the utterance Godward of a holy and benevolent love—love for divine things and for men? When the heart withdraws at seasons from the activities and occupations of daily life, from the customary round of work and duty, to commune with the beauty of the Lord, with the infinite perfection of the All-Father, and to make request of Him for light and guidance, for reinforcement and renewed inspiration, what is it but the uprising and forthgoing of the heart's love for the great things of being, for those realities which, while most real and substantial, most precious and enduring, may have but comparatively little charm or attraction for the many? Is it not affection for them, temporarily sighing and suing at the feet of God? When, then, a man is seen devoted, for example, to the pursuit of worthy knowledge, pursuing it simply and sincerely for its own sake, caring more for it than for material comforts, mere worldly success, or fulness of gold, content, and willing to deny himself for it in some respects, and finding delight in the witnessed progress and diffusion of such knowledge;—when a man is seen, eager in search and inquiry after truth, ready, if needful, to follow it through storms, to incur trouble, and suffer sacrifice for it; or concerned to keep a good conscience rather than keep or gain, at its expense, a good name, more solicitous infinitely for honour and righteousness than for pleasant place and smooth circumstance, giving the supremacy always to moral considerations, always sympathizing strongly with what is just, and pure' and true;—when a man is seen living thus; is he not exemplifying from morn to eve the very holy love of prayer, that love for the best things of which all real prayer is the expression? There it is possessing him permanently, and in being permanently possessed with it, he "prays without ceasing."

But who prays really, for himself alone? who can begin to call upon the great Father of the world, to enter with his burdens into the presence of the eternal goodness, and not begin to throb with desire for others? You hear the prayers, the repeated prayers of the Church, in its assembly, "for all sorts and conditions of men," for the sick in their chambers and the workers at their toil, for them that struggle and them that weep, for the heavy laden and the weary; and in so far as these are genuine prayers, what are they but Love crying? Let love, then, be abiding in you, a spirit prompting to kindly thought and generous action, to unselfish considerateness and timely helpfulness, ready always to offer sympathy and afford what succours it can, to feel with those around it in their joys and griefs, to study their interests and charge itself with their needs; a spirit of willingness to serve, and that seeks and seizes opportunities of serving; let such love be abiding in you, constraining you to be ever recognizing duly, and answering graciously, the appeals to you, that may lie in the state and condition of others; and are you not in spirit and deed praying unceasingly, in spirit and deed, still praying, when you have risen from your knees, and though you should never kneel again?

"Abou Ben Adhem (may his tribe increase!)
  Awoke one night from a deep dream of peace,
  And saw, within the moonlight in his room,
  Making it rich and lily-like in bloom,
  An angel, writing in a book of gold.
  Exceeding peace had made Ben Adhem bold,
  And to the presence in the room he said,—
  'What writest thou?' The vision raised its head,

And with a look, made of all sweet accord,
Answer'd, 'The names of those who love the Lord.'
'And is mine one?' said Abou. 'Nay, not so,'
Replied the angel. Abou spoke more low,
But cheerly still, and said, ' I pray thee, then,
Write me as one that loves his fellow men.'

"The angel wrote and vanish'd. The next night
It came again with a great, wakening light,
And show'd the names whom love of God had bless'd,
And lo! Ben Adhem's name led all the rest!"

I do not say that praying may not aid you greatly in loving well, nor that love may not require it, towards its richer sustainment and its finest growth; nevertheless, love to man, where it beats, and while it lasts, *is* prayer; and he whom love has kept busy through the day, whether it has been love for his fellows in their necessity, or love for truth and righteousness,—he, need not be careful to bow his head and clasp his hands, before sleeping, to save the day from being prayerless, since in the love with which it has been filled, it has been full of prayer.

Then, once again, all true praying has its root, has it not, in trust, and means trust? If it be anything, it is the casting of the soul on God as its all —as its refuge and support—and is the outflow of the soul's confidence that He is mindful of us and cares for us; that the world is under His government, and that we are His children. In praying, we commit ourselves to Him, with the faith that His is the kingdom, and the power, and the glory; that His wisdom and goodness are ours, in exercise for us; but, if it be so, how sadly unprayerful is the general spirit, the prevailing temper, and mental attitude of many who are not unaccustomed to pray! How sadly wanting they are in anything like divine trustfulness; indeed, what actual distrust their conduct often indicates! "Therefore," says the Apostle to his friends at Corinth, in speaking of the pledges and promises which he found in God, "therefore, we are always courageous;" but scant courage is *theirs*, whenever loyalty to the right looks dangerous, or inquiry after truth threatens trouble and confusion. When the path of principle lies through deep and rough waters—instead of following without hesitation, with bold and calm abandonment, they "linger shivering on the brink, and fear to launch away;" and, unable to dare, unable to throw themselves upon the Lord, as they seem to do in their prayers, you find them creeping for safety into some mean shelter of expediency. They are afraid, how frequently! to abide with principle; or afraid, again, to trust the light within them—the light, perchance, for which they have supplicated upon their knees—because it points, maybe, to a lonely road, where they will no longer walk surrounded by troops of friends, and will be parted from the multitude; or afraid, again, of speculation, of discussion, and of the free telling of all men's dreams, lest, forsooth, the interests of the truth should be imperilled thereby; or else, are afraid to adhere exclusively to worthy means in the pursuit of worthy ends, and to reject peremptorily the crooked policy that appears to offer swifter or better success, lest, forsooth, the Lord's aims should be retarded and fail of their due accomplishment. Such doubting, suspicious, timid creatures they are, and so painfully care-burdened, as though the right-doer were not in safer keeping than his own, and no wise throne above them were ruling all. This is the prayerfulness in spirit and life of some who pray; for prayer is *trust*, trust in a reigning rectitude and benevolence, and in its invisible things; trust in conscience, and in moral principle, and in the kingdom of God; and he who is thus habitually trustful,—able with tranquil courage to resign himself to duty, and fearful of nothing but unfaithfulness thereto,—he, "prays without ceasing."

VIII.
PRAYER.

O GOD, the Spirit ; whose breath is our life, upholding all things with its power ; we live because Thou livest, who art the source of every precious thing. In Thee we live as in our vital element ; Thou lightest our lamp and feedest the flame thereof, and the spirit of man is the candle of the Lord ; all our springs are in Thee ; we look not back across untold ages, and cycles of ages, to a distant might that once quickened and created ; we look on ourselves and the universe as the daily, hourly expression and effluence of Thy present might. In the march of things we hear the sound of Thy going, whose goings have been ever of old ; in the mystery of things we hear Thy purpose moving on, dark through exceeding depth, bewildering with unfathomable skill. Thou art in the dying leaves of these autumn days, making beautiful their decay, and with Thy fresh coming from behind Thou loosenest and scatterest them. Evils that vex us are hidings of Thy love ; and while we feel their ugliness, and lament and struggle against them, on their other and invisible side they are bright—bright as clear morning or cloudless noon, with Thee.

O world of God, how great and good thou art ! O beating heart, within our breast, how divine thou art ! The earth is full of the glory of Him who makes winds and flames His ministers, and we—we are the temples of the Holy Ghost. Let us be brave and not profane, humble and not fearful ; let us reverence ourselves and one another, and work at our work as those whose calling is sacred, and study to keep mind and spirit pure. We thank Thee, O Father of Lights, for all Thou hast given us to think of Thee, and to believe concerning Thee, which is inspiring; for all the thoughts of Thee that visit us, and are not able to explain or justify themselves, and will not be questioned or examined, and which, yet, we are constrained to entertain as Abraham did the angels, and do find to be, as Abraham found the angels—guests brightening the house, and bringing with them blessed gain. We thank Thee for the filial sense, and for filial aspirations after obedience, and filial efforts to attain to it, which are full of revelation, and come back to us again and again with whispers of heavenly things that are not seen, with happy reports of a land belonging to us which no man has beheld; whispers and reports that commend themselves to us as true, and in listening to which we are inwardly animated and made strong. May we learn to feel our rank, our divine heirship and relations, in learning to be lowly and holy, useful and large-hearted. May we reach the hill of vision, in climbing with bent head and earnest steps, the ways of Thy commandments; and may our stumblings in those ways, and our errings and wanderings from them, be issuing ever in that broken heart and contrite spirit, toward which the heavens bend down, and into whose tenderness they can freely flow.

O God, never let our repentance be bitter, however bitter our punishment may be, but sweeten it always, when, through the heaviness of the stroke, and the sharpness of the pain, it tends to become embittered, with the balm of that faith in Thy holy love, which takes from the rod its embittering sting. May our sorrow for chastised sin be the sorrow of those to whom it is granted to feel the goodness of the chastisement, the infinite mercy which it signifies and means; and when, in the truest, deepest sense, it is well with us, when duty is bravely done, when evil is overcome with good, when conscience is satisfied, when unworthy weakness is resisted and fierce temptation conquered, may it be to us Thy strength which has wrought in us mightily, and Thy love which has given us the victory; so shall our best accomplishment seem better than its best, as being not our own merely, but Thine in us, and so shall we be saved from that spirit of self-worship with which often noble triumphs are marred, and the soul is hurt to sickness by its own noble deed. Lord, come Thou to us inspiringly, when the will is weak—weak to follow the vision, and carry out the ideas of the good mind—when we are not inwardly impelled as we would be, to do the thing which we feel should be done, but are inclined to neglect, or postpone, or evade. Help us, then, to shake ourselves as from sleep, to throw off the clinging languor, and struggle to be true; rise in us, then, to sweep on to performance,—instant performance,—that we may not have to look back upon that day with humiliation and remorse, and the consciousness of added weakness incurred in it, but may be able rather to remember it with satisfaction and with joy, as marking a victory over the flesh, with which we strengthened ourselves; thanking God, from the bottom of our hearts, that we did not yield then, to the inclination which had well-nigh led us captive.

Be with us in all our honest and laudable strivings for whatever object, that whatever they may bring us, whether little or much, that whether the result be gratifying or disappointing, that whether we gain what we seek or miss it, we may be blessed and enriched by the striving. Be with us in the various intercourse of life, that to "all sorts and conditions of men," so far as we mingle with them, our behaviour may be true; that all may receive from us as they should receive, servants and children, inferiors and superiors, neighbour and friend, and the stranger within our gates. May nothing of evil be encouraged or provoked by us in any, but rather may the better nature of each be aided and drawn out by our touch.; and may no cynical minds be able to infect us with their tone, no impure or uncharitable ones to depress us to their level. Be with us in health and strength, for which we thank Thee, that we may make the best use of them ; and in sickness and pain, that these may not be without secret ministry to us, and may leave some benediction behind them. Help us, O God, to be heartily concerned for the cure of remedial ills and evils that we witness around us, and for the furtherance of what is good and right ; heartily concerned that sound knowledge should be diffused abroad, that grievances should be redressed and justice done, that all earnest and patient efforts for the benefit and the better weal of the community should be guided to success, that our national policy should be honourable and righteous, and our rulers be directed with true wisdom, especially in times of difficulty and perplexity ; that as at this time, when the burden is heavy upon their shoulders, the counsel of the Lord might be theirs, even to the ultimate establishment, in the place of confusion and strife, of healthy and happy peace. We pray for reconciliation, wherever there is painful estrangement and division ; for the calming of angry passions that tend to warp the judgment and blind the eyes ; and for the growth of a mutual spirit that shall conduce to mutual understandings, and to the re-knitting of broken relations. And may the grace of our Lord Jesus Christ, and the love of God, and the fellowship of the Holy Ghost, be with us all evermore. Amen.

SERMON.

THE REJOICING OF CHARITY.

"Rejoiceth not in iniquity, but rejoiceth in the truth."—
1 Corinthians xiii. 6.

"The heart knoweth his own bitterness, and a stranger doth not intermeddle with his joy." So wrote the wise ancient, among his many proverbs, nor did he ever write anything more true. It is not merely that there are limits—strict limits—to human sympathy, that no one after all can, by any exercise of imagination or instinct of affection, put himself exactly in another's place, and feel with him wholly his very rapture or pang. That is true enough, for between us and our nearest and dearest a gulf is always fixed, across which we do not and cannot pass each to each. We are always, to a certain extent, alone in our emotions, with whatever close friendships we may be blessed. The deepest sympathizer who is able to watch with us while the rest are overcome by sleep, whom love and experience combined, admit to the most intimate fellowship with us when we weep sore or jubilantly sing, he, still falls short of sharing with us perfectly, and though entering the inner court whither none penetrate but him, is still outside the innermost; complete participation with me in my sadness or gladness is impossible.

But what is also true, is, that to the stranger—to one who, being, perhaps, a familiar associate, and a kinsman according to the flesh, is yet alien in mental habit and disposition, and wanting in spiritual affinity—that to such an one our griefs and pleasurable thrills, our woes and ecstasies may be alike an inscrutable mystery, something that he is quite incapable of comprehending, and can no more conceive than a man born blind can conceive the charm of colour, or born without the sense of smell, the misery of foul odours. The joy which some persons taste in certain pursuits, in certain scenes or encounters, is a thing which some other persons beside them are altogether powerless to understand; nay, it is incredible to them that the former *can* be enjoying themselves. They are actually pitying them maybe, thinking how flat, and tame, and lustreless life must be with them, how vacant of warmth and glow. We think thus often, from our superior height, concerning those who are below us, whose surroundings are so much coarser and meaner than ours, whose occupations are so sordid or vulgar; and they think often the same of us, wondering what enjoyment we can find along our line—in the subjects and objects that engage us. The common multitude are ready to acknowledge, probably with respect, to some loftily absorbed, or heroically devoted soul, that he is of nobler quality than they, that he stands, in his aspirations and sympathies, upon a level considerably higher than theirs; they are constrained, perhaps, to admire him, and in observing his course are touched, perhaps, with a sentiment akin to awe. "It is very fine, is it not?" they whisper among themselves—"it is very fine, is it not?" and yet it seems to them, withal, that it must be rather cold and cheerless up there, that there can be no real pleasure in that kind of thing; their reverence for his altitude, is mixed with *a little shiver* at the thought that, however grand to dwell thus upon the mountain, the mountain air is surely chill, and the mountain comforts few.

And as St. Paul depicts the features and behaviours of his divine charity, are there not many whose feeling would be, that while beautiful and sublime enough, it could hardly have much to do

The Rejoicing of Charity.   129

with joy. She suffereth long, is slow to assert herself, or insist upon her rights, seeketh not her own, refuseth under grievance to be easily provoked, beareth all things, endureth all things. "Ah, splendid conduct to be habitually pursuing, but what room can it leave for enjoyment; a splendid life to lead, doubtless, but dull and heavy, and throbbing with no exhilarations;" so might selfish souls reflect—strangers to charity—for they would be unable to imagine any pulsings of delight in connection with such a life: and then, in the midst of the Apostle's description of what love does, and how she comports herself, comes the word "rejoiceth." Yes, unloving men may not understand it, unloving men may not credit it, but the love that can be always forgetting itself, always studying and considering others, always alert to share their burdens, and suppress or deny itself in their service, is far from being a joyless thing. Great joy waves visit and sweep it, great joy swellings rise within it, that are all its own, and which no man knoweth save he in whose breast it rules; while in the very heart of its painfullest yearnings and solicitudes, and its hardest sacrifices, a secret bliss lies smiling, like green verdure beneath the snow.

But now, when, in his admiring portrayal of

charity, St. Paul writes first, "Rejoiceth not in iniquity," we may be inclined to murmur, "Well, that is not saying a great deal in its praise; there is nothing specially excellent in that; what does it amount to after all, that a man should be able to avow, I never rejoice in iniquity? are there not thousands who could, truthfully, make such a declaration, and who, at the same time, are not much to boast of, are not particularly estimable creatures? to go through the days without rejoicing in iniquity is not surely indicative of high worth." Yet, let us think for a little. How many are the gains won, the ends accomplished, the successes achieved, the smart things said or done, by men of fair character and repute, on which men of fair character and repute congratulate themselves, over which they rub their hands and stroke their beards with pleasure, and, which have involved more or less of iniquity, in the shape of injustice towards others. Somebody has been wrongfully neglected —overlooked, unfairly used, hurt, wounded, defrauded—in these victories, by these clever exploits or utterances of theirs, with which they are charmed; in connection with that which gratifies them so, some have received a measure of unjust treatment, some have been sinned against. Here, now, is one, recognized as an extremely respectable and thoroughly upright man, rejoicing without stint in a life of ease and luxury, a life which is emphatically "laden with iniquity," since there are claims upon his compassion, his sympathy, his interest, which are daily ignored and left unresponded to; to live, as he does, with his election to such endowments and resources, doing no more than he does in the way of ministry and help, is injustice, foul injustice, to those whom he has been elected to serve, and fails to serve; and yet, how he rejoices in his life, how sparklingly happy he is in it! And what comfort, what pleasure, we can and do often find in personal habits, in activities, in conditions or circumstances that carry with them the wronging of some, some infraction or contradiction of the law of righteousness! You may say that "if it be so, we do not think of the iniquity; we are not alive to it;" that "the evil which may be inflicted, or precipitated, is not present to our mind"—which is probably true enough, since you may not seldom see men—apparently honest and right-hearted men—who, while shrinking from certain iniquities, and incapable of consenting to them, are perfectly undisturbed by certain *other* iniquities, and can allow them to go on, can allow them to exist, without the least touch of compunction or concern ; but then, this is the condemnation, not that we mean to rejoice in iniquity, or that we are conscious of rejoicing in it, but that our eyes are holden to the iniquity of what we do rejoice in— that it does not occur to us, is not borne in upon us. You may not be aware that you are unjust at all to your fellow ; but how much of shame it may be to you, that you are not aware—what ugly unsusceptibility, what inward, low, coarse quality the fact may proclaim !

Now, it is the distinction of St. Paul's charity that its moral sensibilities are too delicate and acute to admit of its rejoicing in aught that covers any iniquity, or bears any taint of it ; that, where others can be satisfied and happy because the injustice of the thing is not apparent to them, does not strike them ; it, discerning at once, and deeply feeling the injustice, *cannot* be content, or pleased. The secret of the difference lies in its superior fineness and purity of nature. I remember a schoolmaster of mine, years ago, a highly cultured, fastidious man, whom we boys took with us one day for the purpose of showing him a certain exquisitely executed inscription upon a building in the town, the execution of which had excited general admiration, and I remember vividly how, when we were counting on the admiration which he would express, he astonished and disappointed us by turning away abruptly, after the first glance, with a gesture of disgust and contempt, saying irritably, in reply to our wonder, "No, gentlemen, I can rejoice in nothing—I can admire nothing, however beautiful the workmanship, in which there is anything ungrammatical." He saw in a moment, the slight stain of bad grammar that had escaped our notice, and it spoiled for him the whole thing. *We* had been rejoicing inwardly in a violation of the rules of syntax, but *he* could not; and such is the divine sensibility, the open-eyed fastidiousness of St. Paul's charity, that in that which betokens or entails the slightest iniquity, it can never rejoice. "My harp is turned to mourning," said Job; and how often would discontent and sadness be found, where now, men laugh, or lounge at peace, if only they were nobler than they are?

But see now, when the Apostle proceeds to exhibit the joy of that love whose withholding from joy has been noted, what do we find him placing over against iniquity as its opposite? We might have expected that it would be rectitude or integrity, instead of which he writes, "rejoiceth not in iniquity, but rejoiceth in the truth." "*The truth.*" And how came this word to flash from his pen in the instant of his mind's recoil from the thought of iniquity, rather than the word which we should have guessed would be dropped, and which it may seem to us would have formed a better antithesis? Ah! what a story a man will sometimes tell about himself, in his way of putting things, or in little expressions that escape him, in little peculiarities of utterance! "Thy speech bewrayeth thee." And have we not here, a revelation concerning St. Paul?—are we not shown here, what his religious ideas were, and what, the faith he cherished? The same contrast is made by him in other passages; in the Epistle to the Romans, for example, where he pronounces judgment upon those "who obey not the truth, but obey unrighteousness"—the truth and unrighteousness—iniquity and the truth. These were fundamental contraries with him. And why? The reference is, of course, to the truth of Christ. That was the truth which absorbed him—the truth that fell from the lips, and breathed in the life of Christ; and in it, he saw the inspiration and the strength of all goodness, a divine power for the purification of man and society, the grand instrument of moral quickening and nutrition; he opposed it, in writing, to iniquity, out of the fulness of his persuasion that it was pre-eminently a righteous-making force, mighty above all else to cleanse and rectify. Such was his continual teaching—not by the works of the law are men to be justified, but by the hearing of faith. Let them drink in, and vitally embrace the truth, as it was in Jesus, and iniquity should gradually wither away before the birth and reign of righteousness.

And here you see, what Christ really meant for him—why he loved, and worshipped, and devoted himself as he did, to the work of proclaiming Him. It was because he believed intensely that His *truth* was calculated to promote and to produce, the highest form of goodness, or, as he would have phrased it, to redeem from sin, and to reconcile to God. What led him to extol and enthrone the grace which rejoiced in the truth, or more correctly, I suppose, with the truth—with its advances and triumphs? What led him to esteem and declare it a mark of worth, a lofty excellence, to rejoice in the spread and progress of the truth? Was it that the truth just signified his own fond views, and its spread and progress, the victories won by a name to which he was enthusiastically attached, or by a cause in which he had embarked his all? No, it was the conviction of the moral value of this truth for the world—that it was the prime organ and energy of Heaven towards curing the disorder of iniquity, and constraining and inspiring to righteousness.

The Apostle's wonderful passion for the crucified Nazarene, was his passion for the purifying and ennobling of mankind. "Wherefore we labour, teaching every man and warning every man, that we may present every man perfect through Christ Jesus." Theology was to him the most practical and sweetly useful of sciences—even the science of raising men to truer, purer life, through the knowledge of God, in Christ Jesus the Lord. Hence, the joy of the love that could not abide iniquity, and mourned over it, must needs be found, his heart told him, in the diffusion of the truth; for him, to rejoice in it, was to rejoice in the opposite of iniquity; and can we doubt the beautifully transforming effect it would have upon society, in proportion as society should come to be really imbued with the living religious faith of Mary's Son, and governed and swayed by His ideas? Is it not the tendency of that faith and those ideas, where they capture, where they inwardly lay hold, to refine and elevate, to create and nourish a loftier moral sense, to scatter fear and cowardice — the root of so much that is crooked and base, to quench selfishness in love, to develop

> " The valiant man and free,
> The larger heart, the kindlier hand " ?

If we *could* most surely believe—as thousands upon thousands do not, who yet profess and avow what is called the Christian creed—if we *could* most surely believe His doctrine of the divine fatherhood, and the human brotherhood, and feel the circle of invisible things that were vividly present to his soul ; would it not prevail to loosen the bonds and chains of many a wrongness to which we are now in bondage, and to bring forth upon us something of lovelier feature than we have yet displayed?

St. Paul does seem to me to have been right in thinking, that nothing is more threatening to the dominion of iniquity, and more conducive to the growth of goodness, than our learning to believe Christ, and to believe *with* Christ. If, however, any are unable to share his grand faith, and to accept his religious ideas, may Heaven help such, to do the best they can without them ; and, in any case, let us be diligent in seeking to acquire, and in co-operation to disseminate, all true knowledge ; and in every extension of all true knowledge let us rejoice, for there is no true knowledge gained and communicated, that is not more or less against iniquity, that is not assisting to contribute, directly or indirectly, to some furtherance of righteousness.

IX.

PRAYER.

MIGHTY FATHER, in whose perfect goodness, conjoined with power, we humbly believe,—help us now and evermore to worship the goodness, the self-giving love, which Thou art; may it be charming to us, may its praise be in our hearts; and since there is no homage like the homage which he receives, whom men imitate—whose principles they adopt, whose ways they follow, the spirit of whose life they catch and reflect—help us to magnify Thee, the holy and the gracious One, in seeking to be imitators of what we acknowledge and feel Thee to be, in all merciful justice, in all righteous benevolence; let us be drawn after our confessed Ideal, and be still panting towards it, like some anxious and eager swimmer towards the bright shore which he sees afar off, still panting to attain, however a contrary tide may retard progress and baffle effort—however the distance may seem to stretch, unlessened, and our strenuous strokes to be in vain; for if an Apostle could say with quiet assurance, "We know that we have the petitions which we desire of Him;" may we not know, that in trying we do succeed, even when nothing but failure is apparent; that every worthy endeavour does bring forth fruit, after its kind, even though there be no taste in our mouth but the bitterness of disappointment. God, help us to be confident, that we have never thrown away one striving of ours heavenward, let it have looked as futile as it may, but that in some future height of being to be reached by us, we shall find hidden, each earnest aiming of the present, over which we may now mourn as barren. The true things that we fain would find in their effects, and do not find, they are not lost ; and, alas ! neither are the false things that we could wish might never be found—they, too, are effectual according to their quality, so inexorably effectual ; our past iniquities remain with us, and take hold upon us ; our indolences, our idle words, our careless neglects to redeem the time, to seize the opportunity ; our occasional mean yieldings, our tarryings to listen to the flesh, our thoughtless infidelities to the spirit ; these have not perished in the waters of our repentance, nor has Thy forgiving mercy extinguished them. We bear about within us marks of them to-day, and the attainment of to-day, in which we are able to rejoice as the result of labour and prayer—does not this bear witness of them, and exhibit their working, for how much greater, how much loftier, might it be had they never been ? Oh, those weak and foolish descend-ings in former times, by reason of which, certain ascents are now impossible to us, however high we may manage to climb ! If we perceive not all that we are *gaining* with our aspirations and holy industries—aspirations and industries which seem often to produce so little—we also perceive not all that we are *missing*, and shall always miss, through past follies and wanderings.

And we thank Thee, Lord, that much of what Thou seest with respect to ourselves, is hidden from us ; such darkness is better, doubtless, for us to learn in, and grow in, than a full light would be. We might see too many things for the due working out of our salvation—too many things for the one thing needful, even our due education in filial grace and righteousness. We thank Thee for the darkness of exclusion from the Father's vision concerning ourselves—an outer dark-ness which is not for weeping and gnashing of teeth, but for the children's learning and growth, until they are made meet to be partakers of the inheritance of the saints in light.

Let us be content, and earnest, to do what day by day presents itself to be done—to do that faithfully and well, whether we like it or not—whether we see the use of it or not in relation to any divine purpose for our training ; let us be content, and earnest, to gather what knowledge we can of men and things, and of the works of the Lord; to cherish and follow what, after sincere inquiry, seems to us true; to obey what speaks to us with authority in our higher moods—in our best frames; to strive to shape our lives according to the dictates of these, and to contribute something by our action and influence toward the bettering of the world, and the happiness of others. Let us be content, let us be earnest thus, in the faith that Thou art leading and teaching us the while, who art in secret, and that in this way we are coming through the night, to the dawn, to a city of foundations, to a city of light which is preparing for us; and that some time and somewhere, we shall awake to find ourselves rejoicing in Thy finished work concerning us. O God, pitiful God, forgive our wanderings, our misspent days and powers, our waste of breath in vain complaint, our often dimness of perception through a little disorder of heart, our fearfulness through unbelief, our timid compliance with felt wrong ways, in submission to general custom, our feebleness of interest in what concerns the good of society, the progress of mankind—our unbrotherly acts, and our unbrotherly inactions. Forgive us that impatience with ourselves, and with our faults and infirmities, in which there is more of Saul's anger with himself that he had played the fool, than of David's contrition at having sinned against Thee. Forgive the poor self-complacency in which we sometimes linger, when we should be hastening on to things before; and the self-attention which sometimes detains us from due attention to others, and leaves us feeding withal, on dust and ashes. The Psalmist prayed, "Lord, satisfy me with Thy mercy;" and we, too, would pray with him that prayer, for what so satisfying as Thy mercy, when it is upon them that fear Thee? Yet we would that Thy mercy might so be upon us, and so fill us, as to bring forth within us a mercy of our own, with which we should be satisfied. Oh, for more of that divine blessedness, that fulness of life, which is found in being given to the exercise of mercy, which is realized in living not unto ourselves, in occupation with benevolent cares and generous sympathies ! May we enter into the joy of our Lord by entering a little into the spirit of His cross ; may we learn of Him to be inspired with a passion for use.

Be with those who are devoting themselves to works of charity and labours of love ; who are seeking in any way to be of help in the world—of help towards lightening burdens and furthering peace and righteousness. Be with those, a great multitude, who have no time to give ; whose hands are full of necessary toil for daily bread ; that such a heart may be nourished in them, as shall make them unconsciously, involuntarily influential for good ; that with their character and the breathing of their spirit they may silently bless, whatever their employment may be. Be with those who are set in families, that they may learn there, to be thoughtful for others —to be unselfish, and considerate, and kind ; and save, of Thy mercy, those from contracting a cold and narrow heart whose lot it is to dwell alone, or in whose houses no voices of children are heard. God, our Father, make us all somewhat paternal, by working in us the filialness of Thy Son, our Saviour ; and unto Him whose offspring we are, unto Him be the praise of our thankfulness, and the worship of our trust and obedience, both now and evermore. Amen.

SERMON.

CHRIST LEANING BACK ON GOD.

"And yet I am not alone, because the Father is with Me."—
JOHN xvi. 32.

"AND yet." It marks the coming-up from behind of the second better thought; it ushers in the correcting, consoling after-thought with which the clear soul swiftly answered the wail of forlornness and despair—"Ye shall be scattered, every man to his own, and shall leave Me alone." He saw, with an inward shiver, the bleak solitude impending for Him—the solitude unrelieved by a single friendly face or lingering comrade. Already, in anticipation, He stood forsaken; all, to the last beloved disciple, had fallen away from Him; and to a nature like His, the pain of it was exquisite, for His was no cold hermit-nature, with leanings towards a lodge in the wilderness or a cave upon the mountain, rather than towards the social circle and the place of concourse. On the contrary, He had always sought to be among the people, had always been at home in the street, in visiting men's houses, in watching the ways of the children, and talking with them; and when at times, He would fain escape for a little from the crowd, it had been His wont, generally, to take with Him two or three of His followers. In His hours of mental distress or deep depression, He had desired, generally, to have some of them near Him; their presence was a comfort and support to Him, even though He might not be able to share with them His secret. He was helped a great deal by the glance of loved eyes, by the touch of brotherly hands. His heart went out after sympathy— "Come apart with Me into the desert, and rest awhile"—"Tarry ye here, and watch with Me." To such an one, the prospect of being deserted by all, would be terrible; but, as He stands contemplating it, filled with the doleful prevision, in the midst of its dolefulness, the thought rises like a star, that *the Father* would be with Him. Suddenly, the sweet reality of His presence and nearness, flashes upon Him, and gradually possesses Him. There was a moment of miserable darkness—"Ye will leave Me alone"—and then, the next moment, came a burst of light—"The Father will be with Me."

Do we not know that kind of experience,—the angel visit of some soothing remembrance, or happy suggestion, when we have been wrapped in a black cloud of anxiety or dread; the opening of the eyes to a well of water in the barren burning sand, as when Hagar lifted up her head and saw? We have been sitting disconsolate, seeing nothing but gloom, feeling nothing but hopelessness, and all at once an idea has glided in, a reflection has occurred to us, which, if it may not have turned our night to radiant noon, has softened and cheered it; the whole aspect of things is changed, we awake as from a hideous dream, in which some actual trouble of our life has been grimly exaggerated, to say, with a sigh of infinite relief, "Oh, it was only a dream; thank God, that though troubles exists, it is not so bad as that."

"And yet," said Christ,—reaching after and seizing the invisible Reality, of which, for an instant, He had lost sight, in confronting the bitterness of the visible. The latter was very vivid, very sharp and penetrating; it laid hold upon him fiercely, and bore Him down; for an instant it detained Him from the sense and impression of the Unseen. For He who lived in such close habitual fellowship with the Father, into whose soul the heavens were always flowing, even He knew what it was to have those heavens occasionally hidden from Him by lurid vapours from below and around, however brief might be the interval of obscuration; as, when, blinded upon the cross, He groped in wondering darkness and cried, " My God, why hast Thou forsaken Me?" And now, and here, in looking forward, shudderingly, to the dreary destitution that awaited Him, He does not straightway grasp the comfort of the Father; it is not immediately enjoyed by Him; He has to feel for it—has to recall the fact of the Father's abiding nearness. There is a moment during which all that lies within His view is the loneliness with which He is threatened, that He is about to be left to endure with no human friend beside Him; and then, He bethinks Himself of the unseen company that will remain to Him, of the unseen sympathizer whose arms will be around Him—He begins to remember the Father.

Is it not thus with ourselves; that we have, again and again, for our spiritual succour or defence, to reach after invisible realities, which, while they have always been acknowledged and believed by us, yet, in certain crises, in certain experiences, when the sense and impression of them is most needed, do not hasten to offer themselves ? In temptation, for example, the higher considerations that are wanted to strengthen and restrain us, have to be summoned and brought to mind ; we are not at once visited by them ; we see the glittering bait with which evil allures, our ears are filled with its syren promises ; and it is not until we turn to seek them, that those higher considerations draw near, and steal in to save us from yielding. Honour, the claim of principle, the majesty of duty, the smile of God, the ugliness and disgrace of that to which we are tempted, these have to be recollected ; the thought of these has to be courted ; and sometimes, how slow they are to enter in and take possession, how difficult it is, amid the enticing voices and witcheries, to realize them as we would, and as at other times we have realized them! We have succumbed often, and gone wrong, just because invisible things of our faith were not borne in upon us ; the earthly thronged the field of vision, and the heavenly would not shine. " Could I but have felt that invisible thing at the moment "—many an one has said, in mourning remorsefully over his broken integrity, or his wretched weakness and collapse under trial—" could I but have had it present with me at the moment, I should not have failed and fallen thus." Did he, however, go in quest of it; did he make any effort to call it up before him, as when Christ roused Himself from His shivering dread to think, and say, "And yet I am not alone, because the Father is with Me"?

You see what He is doing here. He is leaning back on God. All are about to forsake Him. Bare and desolate grows the outward scene; the trees beneath whose shade He has sat, are withering; the wells at which He has been wont to drink are running dry—

> "Around Him lies a loveless land
> Without lair or rest on either hand;"

and He retreats for refuge into God. It is a blessed thing to have something to take shelter in, and be at peace, when our external world is ravaged or spoiled; when the sand comes up over our garden, and where until lately roses had gladdened us, we look forth on desert; when the days have lost their sunshine, and faces that smiled are missed, and we are no longer pleasantly attended as we were. It is a blessed thing to have then, something behind on which to stay ourselves and be at rest—some inner reserve from which we can draw consolation and sustenance. There are men with whom it is not so. Adversity leaves them quite naked and destitute. Their animal gratifications, their comfortable and bountiful surroundings, their money and houses and friends, and the popularity they enjoy: these are their all; let them be deprived of these, and they have no high tower into which to flee, no resources in themselves, to save the heart from famine, no thoughts and ideas to live upon, no good conscience with which to find sanctuary, no holy and beautiful faith to nestle in. What poor, miserable creatures some men are when they are left alone, when their prosperity is shattered, when the outward garnitures of life to which they have been accustomed are swept away, when of the approving or applauding people who were once with them, none remain! Jesus had always the Father to fall back upon.

We are surprised occasionally, by the way—we are surprised occasionally, by the sustaining stores revealed within us under calamities that we may have fancied and feared would crush us utterly. We had thought, perhaps, that such calamities we should never be able to bear without sinking, yet, when they have befallen us what unexpected strength we have found in ourselves, what unexpected nerve and courage and powers of endurance; how we have seemed to be upholden by a might, and inspired with a spirit greater than our own! How old truths, too, which before had never stirred us much, which before, maybe, had lain afar off, and looked dim and pale, have then drawn nigh, and shone out to us with a wonderfully vivid, and a wonderfully helpful light! How the heavens, maybe, that had been dumb and distant, have then stooped toward us and spoken with us, until their word was in our heart as a new spring of life! We should never have dreamt of being so sustained and enlarged in circumstances so distressing. Nevertheless the secret of it lay, doubtless, within us—all within us; in what we had been, under previous and different circumstances. In our prior soul-growth, we had been preparing, without observation, to *be* thus sustained and enlarged; for nothing is produced in us except from seeds in us, and that which comes to meet us— whether from above or beneath, whether it be angel or devil—is always a refluence and return upon us of ourselves. We are creating silently in our every-day action, and breathing, the radiant company, the grim hauntings, or the black void, for our loneliness.

Christ found His way so easily and readily into the Father's arms, when the storm struck, and refuge failed Him, because He was habitually, in His ruling temper and sympathy, with the Father. God yielded Him comfort in comfortlessness, because God was His constant hidden life, and daily law. We must be rooted and grounded in the heavenlies, amidst the earthly pleasantness and plenteousness, to be able to retire into the heavenlies, and feel them warm about us, and draw from them with joy, when the earthly is roughened, and blighted. The little brook continues its liquid song in the drought, though it misses the rains, because, while the rains had ministered to its volume, its springing was not in them, but in the fountain that wells always. Men who acknowledge and confess, grandeurs unseen, maintain, often, too little intercourse with them, are too little in subjection to them during the satisfying brightness of the seen, to have them nigh and clear for soothing or stay, when the circle of the seen is darkened. Their beautiful beliefs have never been sufficiently vital in them, have never sufficiently occupied and suffused them, to be of much comfort, or help to them in desolate hours. They are not at hand then, to rest in and lean on. We believe, perhaps, in certain great invisible things, but, like those who, with a number of mere acquaintances, have made no real friend, we have not been intimate enough with our invisible things, to cast ourselves upon them for relief and succour, when the heart is sorrowful, and the trial of life is sore.

There is a sense, however, in which they who have not been living in God at all, as Christ had, are yet given to turn to Him, and seek shelter with Him, under stress of trouble; when the world has disappointed them, when the world has grown barren and hard. So used He is to this—to have men stretching out their hands to Him, and running to find solace with Him when the days are drear, and all else has failed them! Oh, the prayers of the prayerless in their misery! the creeping to His feet of those whose cisterns are broken, whose field yields no meat, who, because, where they have been wont to feast merrily, nothing remains to them but husks, say to themselves, with the son in the parable, " Let us arise and go to the Father"! And, do you know, what strikes me here as very beautiful, is the instinctive confidence felt in His great generosity—the childlike trust with which, after having all through their lives forgotten and slighted Him, they are able in their time of destitution to sue to Him freely—that, selfish as they are themselves, mean-souled, perhaps, incredulous of any tender magnanimity in their fellows, they can and do thus take for granted His openness to their appeal, His availability as a last resort for them when other refuge they have none. Yes, it is beautiful; the fact that even in the most graceless human breast, there seems to be left, generally, the power of believing in One, at all events, who is infinitely generous, to whom—though hitherto neglected and flouted by them—they may venture to bring their nakedness and wretchedness. What faith we do retain at the worst, in a wondrously good God; with what involuntary assurance we can cry to Him, whom we have ignored until we are forsaken, Lord, have mercy upon us!

But, now, what is it upon which Christ falls back in His loneliness, and finds Himself not alone? There are invisible things that have been precious company, often, to earnest and noble souls, when their lot has been bitter and forlorn, when lover and friend have been put far from them; when honour and sympathy have been denied them; when the people have passed by on the other side, suspicious of them, disapproving them, sneering at them, and their dreams and visions. The deep conviction that they are right in the thoughts they think, in the course they choose, though society condemns; the clear, happy consciousness of duty done, of fidelity and truth persevered in; the calm, firm confidence that time will eventually vindicate them, that their unpopular and opposed ideas must sooner or later commend themselves, and win universal acceptance—these, and such-like invisible things, have been with them in their loneliness, and, they have not been alone; on these they have leaned, and they have not fainted. And these, doubtless, were with Christ, for His comfort. He was satisfied of the rightness of His cause; He knew that He was faithful and had not swerved; He saw afar off, the Cross blossoming and all men coming to Him; and herein, amidst the scattering from Him at length, even of those who had hitherto clung to Him—herein He was not alone.

But there was something more in His case—there was something more in which He sought and found support—an Invisible Being who, while of the people there were none with Him, cared for and loved Him,—understood, approved, sympathized with Him. He wanted the Father; in His desertion by every earthly friend, He felt wistfully after the Father. He could not say with entire content, "I am not alone," until He could say, "the Father is with Me." If all are to be driven away, *He* must e'en stay by Him to give Him balm, to help Him to endure. Some natures might have been capable, in His circumstances, of doing without this, but He could not, and most of us could not. There are trials, in which it would be hardly possible for most of us to stand wholly resigned and patient and still, unless we could believe that there is One above, at whose feet we may unburden ourselves—a real, living goodness, who looks down upon us, and sees and appreciates our pain, the sincerity of our purpose, our struggle to be true. Who of us, left alone in our uprightness of spirit and purity of aim—misconceived, suspected, scorned, and with no single friend to cheer us—who of us would not need then, in order to courageous, tranquil persistence, the sense of the Father with us, knowing and judging all? Oh! life would have been a yoke, unbearable to some, at times, had they not possessed and cherished that sense; but for it they would never have borne so grandly as they did. You may be inclined to ask, perhaps, whether it would not be grander really, to be independent of it, to be finding sufficient company for serenity and peace, in ourselves, when all things are against us, or when all men forsake us—whether it would not have been grander had Christ been equal to the noble endurance of His loneliness without nursing the thought of the Father's nearness and sympathy? But, assuming the reality of the Father, it seems to me the truest thing, and, therefore, the grandest, to lean like a child, and, like a child, to be strong through leaning

Anyhow, was there not a certain charming sweetness, a certain exquisite tenderness, in the heroic firmness with which Christ bore His lot; and was not the peculiar sweetness and tenderness which distinguished His staunch endurance all through, attributable largely to the source from whence He drew His courage and His strength, namely, to His faith in the invisible Father? One has seen lips grandly knit in suffering, which yet were scarcely beautiful, though not a groan or a plaint escaped them; and, again, one has seen lips knit in suffering, which, though equally close-set, were softly beautiful the while. There are different ways of bearing bravely: there is the hard, cold, stoical way, to which you may attain, if you are made for it, without the Father; and there is the way of smiling gentleness, which is likely, I think, to be best learned and exemplified by those who can say to themselves, as they enter into the cloud, 'We are not alone, because the Father is with us."

X.

PRAYER.

O GOD, who art holy, and hast written Thy law in our hearts, giving us the knowledge and discernment of what is good, of what we should seek to cultivate and attain to as Thy children, and withal, some aspiration after it; we thank Thee for the man, the better and nobler man than ourselves, whom in visions we see before us, and admire, and wish that we were, and do somewhat strive to resemble, and to whose figure, we think, that One who made us means us to grow; may His radiant form never fade from our eyes; may His beauty never cease to trouble and attract us; may He never shrink to smaller proportions, but rather greaten and increase in stature as we reach toward Him. Thou who hast shown us what is good, and what the Lord requires of us,—make us more seriously and earnestly bent on trying to raise ourselves to this, and more willing to be exercised and disciplined in any way that Providence may choose for our furtherance in the direction of this. Let us not succumb to difficulties, nor allow adverse influences to check and relax our efforts. And let us not be impatient of any severities of temptation or trial that may perchance be the means of contributing to our training. May we feel that all our good aspirations are of Thee, and not from ourselves merely, and that in the circumstances of life, from day to day, we are being schooled by Thee, to the end that the glory which we behold and sigh after, may be gradually realized in us. Smile Thou from Thy throne on every sincere struggle of the spirit against the flesh, however little it may accomplish; pity Thou our defeats and disappointments; accept our victories and advances; receive and sanctify to us our convictions of unworthiness, our confessions of negligence and culpable shortcoming, our repentance for sin.

We thank Thee for what we have learned concerning ourselves, now and again, in times of great misery or happiness, of great trial or enlargement; for the further deeper insight into our real character and our fundamental dispositions which we have then acquired, for the discoveries we have then made of what lay hid in us, whether of latent strength or weakness, evil or good. Ah! the new self-knowledge that has come to us at such times; occasionally, it has been gratifying perhaps, and perhaps it has been painful and bitter; but in any case we thank Thee for it, for what ignorance is so much to be deprecated as self-ignorance? Better, far better, to be made to perceive, at whatever cost, if in any respect we have not perceived, what manner of persons we really are; and while sometimes, the developing solution of circumstance may have brought out unsuspected stains, and shown us that we were rather feebler, rather meaner, than we had thought, sometimes, on the contrary, it has revealed unexpected lines of beauty; but who ever sees all that he is, or can be, and who must not be content to say with St. Paul, "Yea, I judge not mine own self; He that judgeth me is the Lord"?

O God, let us not think that we are Christ's while we are not; let us not assume pleasantly that we are His because we have eaten and drunk in His presence, and He has taught in our streets, because His doctrine is on our lips, and we sing hymns to His name; when, if He were here in our midst He would be unable to own us. May we consider that we belong to Him, only so far as we are like-minded with Him, and that they who are wanting in His Spirit are none of His. May we understand and lay to heart that if we would be His disciples indeed, we must live His Word, and not merely repeat it—must take up our cross and follow Him. And teach us, we pray Thee, how to apply and act upon His principles in working the work which the Father may have given *us* to do ; how to carry His Spirit into the common life of to-day, and have it exemplified by us in occupations, and in modes of activity other than His. Nor let us think for a moment that our modern situations and necessities are such as will not admit of this, that in the present day we must needs be content to live below His level, to take, at least, in some conjunctures, a less lofty line ; let us not think thus, but be strong and firm in the conviction that while the form of His life was a local and temporary thing, and peculiar to Himself, the spirit of love for truth and righteousness, of love to God and man, which inspired and shaped it, is the true eternal spirit in which we *all* may offer ourselves to Thee, in which we *all* are called to fulfil our course, and to do whatsoever our hand findeth to do ; and that though sometimes, it may make things difficult and hard for us, and oblige us perhaps to forego gainings and successes that we would like to enjoy, it is none the less the highest glory and honour and blessing to be led of this spirit.

God, our Father, we do believe in Thee and in Thy kingdom : help Thou our unbelief. We are not always confident, Thou knowest ; there are moments and moods in which we are full of doubt, when the heavens seem to us empty, and Thy face does not lighten on us—we strive to see it, as at other times, but we cannot see it. Our heart and our flesh cry out for the living God, and He appears not to our cry. We are haunted by gloomy shadows of mistrust ; it is whispered and whispered within us that the world has no Head, that men are orphans, that the Invisible is but a dream. Lord, Thou knowest that it is thus with us at seasons ; we stretch out lame hands and are unable to lay hold upon Thee, grasping instead only dust and chaff. Hold Thou us with Thy strong hand in these seasons of darkness, binding us still, in unmovable steadfastness to duty and charity, to faithful work and self-forgotten love, until through such sustained steadfastness, we be brought back to hope and faith. At least keep us pure and true ; then, Thou wilt be coming to us and making Thine abode with us, wilt be dwelling and working in us divinely, even while we are groping to find Thee in vain, and are wondering dismally whether Thou art, or not; keep us pure and true, so shall all good things be ours, and ours too, the good which evil hides; so shall be given to us, amidst whatever seeming want and poverty may be ours, Paul, and Apollos, and Cephas, and the world, and life and death, and the present and the future, and Christ and God.

O Father of our spirits, whom not having seen we believe in and trust, fortify our hearts with Thy holy comfort, that we faint not. Rest us when we are weary, strengthen us when we are weak; when we are calm and glad, consecrate and guide Thou our force; when we are in grief, control and sweeten and sanctify our tears; and at last, in the hour of death, when the earthly task is done, and we have passed through the school of time, albeit perchance with few honours—fewer than we might have gained—then, receive us to the place prepared for us, and give us the clearer light for which we may be fitted, and let us still be praising Thee, who art worthy to receive glory and thanksgiving, and worship and blessing, both now and for ever. Amen.

SERMON.

THE JUDGMENT OF THE FATHER.

"And if ye call on the Father, who without respect of persons judgeth according to every man's work, pass the time of your sojourning in fear."—1 PETER i. 17.

IN saying "if ye call on the Father," the Apostle did not mean for a moment to express any doubt; the "if" simply introduces a premiss on which a conclusion is to be based, as when St. Paul wrote, "If ye then be risen with Christ, seek those things which are above." There was no uncertainty as to whether the readers of the Epistle—Christianized Jews scattered abroad—were calling upon the Father, or more correctly, as to whether they were calling Him Father, who, according to the belief in which they had been brought up, reigned on high, the righteous and impartial Governor of the world. That was just what they were doing, having learned to do so in their conversion to the Christian faith. They had always believed in a righteous, impartial Governor of the world—

in a God who, unlike most of the heathen divinities, was the perfection of purity, and perfectly equitable toward all His creatures—the God, namely, of Moses and the prophets, who was supremely the just One, and who judged the work of every man without respect of persons; and now, since their surrender to Jesus as their Master, and their acceptance of His Gospel, they had come to name this God, the Father. Such was the idea of Him to which they had attained, the aspect in which they were regarding Him. He whose throne was in the heavens, who hated iniquity and ruled with faultless justice, He was the Father. "And if He be," says the Apostle, "pass, I pray you, the time of your earthly sojourning, in fear.

A true word, a word spoken in utter sincerity, and representing what is fact, may yet prove very misleading—may convey or suggest something contrary to truth. It may create an impression the opposite of that which you intended and desired to produce, and be the means of leading astray where you are seeking to enlighten. For a word can only communicate to him who hears or reads it, in accordance with his capacity or preparedness for receiving. What it shall say to him will be determined, not by the speaker's thought and purpose in uttering it, but by his own mental condition and culture. It is a word, perhaps,—an old word—which, owing to his personal circumstances, his previous training, the influences amidst which he has lived, has become clothed for him with a significance quite different from the significance which it bears for the speaker. They are not at all similar images which it starts in his mind. He has been accustomed to attach to it other ideas. How surprised, and how disappointed we might be at times, were we able to follow words of ours whither they go, and to descry their exact import, their particular excitations there! How often we might find them failing to deliver the message with which we had charged them, and even mischievously twisting and belying it! If language be a vehicle of thought, it is far from being always an adequate or a safe vehicle. The contents are apt to get spilled and spoiled by the way, and there is an unloading, possibly, of something altogether at variance with what we wished and meant to transmit. Language indeed, is an awkward and uncertain carrier; one cannot rely upon it; and many are the mistakes and confusions, the misunderstandings and deceptions, which it causes when we want it to tell honestly or declare plainly. Two men quietly assume that they are agreed upon a subject, that their conceptions entirely harmonize, because they are using the same words; and all the while, maybe, an unsuspected gulf yawns between them—they are using the same words in divers senses, with divers visions and impressions lurking behind.

Now the word, "Father," we might anticipate, would speak alike to all. The relation which it designates is common enough. We have all made acquaintance with it, have all had to do with it intimately, either in the way of subjection or action. Yet how differently the word may affect different individuals, what different pictures it may conjure up before them! As to what it shall express to any of us, much will depend upon the kind of domestic experience we have had, upon the kind of home with which we are most familiar, in which our childhood and youth were spent. *You* cannot hear the word, perhaps, or at least cannot pause to dwell on it, without thinking at once of self-forgetting love, of wise counsel and patient teaching, of combined firmness and tenderness in rule. It recalls to you one of dear and revered memory, who was your happy refuge in all trouble and difficulty, to whom you always looked, and never in vain, for sympathy, who made what he considered your best welfare, his careful study, and for the sake of promoting it would brace himself to incur or inflict any necessary pain; whose judicious, conscientious, administration, and whose affectionately applied, though often apparently severe discipline, you remember to-day with reverent thankfulness. Oh, the world of grand and sweet meaning for *you*, in the word Father! What a solemn, noble, gracious sound it has! But here is another, upon whose ear it falls with no sound of music, in whose mind it is associated with harsh and tyrannical exercise of authority, with the suffering of unjust blows, miserable neglect, or capricious and foolish indulgence. It brings to his recollection a testy, passionate, wrath-provoking man, whose ways were hard to bear; or a man, cold, stern, austere, whose presence chilled and rather discomforted, whose coming caused depression, and his departure relief; or one who, while protecting and ministering, was uncertain in judgment—now weakly lenient, now unreasonably and unwholesomely strict—and who betrayed often, feebleness and self-love, in yielding where he should have been firm, in sparing correction from which benefit would have ensued, the loss of which is now felt and lamented. Father! it is not a beautifully pregnant word for *him*.

And there are those to whom, in consequence of their past home life, or of what they are themselves as parents, the word may say out less than it would otherwise have done, to whom it may not be suggestive of some things which it should suggest. Signifying for them much that is pleasant, much that is good, it yet may fail to utter to them all that it ought to utter—the picture flashed by it before their eyes will be wanting in certain important features. And St. Peter would seem to have apprehended that it might be thus with his readers, that in calling the Divine Governor, Father, they might scarcely be alive to all which the name implied, might scarcely be entertaining the full idea; for he proceeds to indicate to them how it behoved them to be moved and affected by the sense of God's Fatherhood. He is seeking, apparently, to awaken them with his grave exhortation, to the perception of something more and deeper, in the fatherly relation, than they had hitherto discerned, or been much impressed by—" Since you worship as the

Father, Him, who without respect of persons judgeth according to every man's work, pass the time of your sojourning *in fear*." And it is very likely that this conclusion of his rather surprised and staggered them. "In fear!" they would exclaim, perhaps; "should he not have written, on the contrary, 'in comfort and peace,' 'in bright courage and hope.'? Has it not been always with us, and must it not always be, a consoling, cheering, animating faith, that the Ruler of the world is the Father?" To which the Apostle would have replied, "Yes, yes, most surely; but then, it should inspire you also with a great awe, and if it do not, the whole meaning of the word Father cannot have been grasped by you; if it do not, your conception of what it is to be a father is sadly narrow and defective, for the true Father is not merely the gracious Protector, Succourer, Provider, but the constant, persistent, earnest, unsparing Educator, also, whose love deals closely and inexorably with each child of the family, in desire for his due training and his best development."

Now, as may have been the case with the people whom St. Peter addressed, we perhaps, are possessed with too poor and low an idea of fatherliness, and, more or less blinded by that idea, need to be reminded of what he saw and sought to inculcate, namely, that the Fatherhood of the Almighty is a very solemn reality, and serves to render life very serious. There is, I think, a widespread tendency to repose in it as involving rather less demand upon us for moral care and earnestness, as allowing us to be rather less particular about the cultivation of righteousness, rather less anxious concerning our spiritual condition and quality. They who may once have been taught—as in their earlier years many were—that God was the Father of some only, of some few religious and scrupulous folk, while to the rest He was simply Ruler and Judge, and who now hear and accept the contrary teaching that we are *all* His children, from the beginning and always—many such, I fancy, are led to feel and cherish a little relief—a little unworthy relief—saying to themselves in secret, that with the Ruler and Judge of their earlier years transformed into the Father, disobedience to His laws is not quite so dreadful or grave a matter as it was; that they may well be somewhat easier than they used to be, in respect of ill-doing, and may expect to be treated more leniently, more indulgently, and not to be visited exactly, according to their transgressions. "Let us not be troubled greatly," they say to themselves—" let us not be troubled greatly if we are negligent and unfaithful, and do not amend or improve as we should; is not the Judge and Ruler the Father, and will He not therefore be gentle with us; may He not therefore, overlook much, and make things considerably pleasanter for us in the end than we deserve?" Are there not those who reason thus from the thought of God's Fatherhood? Yet did they consider and understand, the very thought in which they find relief, would rather set them trembling—would rather oppress them with a sense of unescapable divine inspection and besetment—of unescapable divine chastisement and pursuit; they would feel, in fact, that they were shut up to stricter judgment, and could only hope for peace and quiet, in learning to be good.

For, see, what government is so close and penetrating as the government of a true father? Is there anything in existence to compare with it? How very much it takes cognizance of, to frown upon, and rebuke, which no other government notices! Parents will often punish severely, where the police would never interfere. Yonder lad, with his companions, engages in some boyish mischief and folly that brings him into trouble. You, a stranger, passing by, will stop to extricate him from his trouble with a slight and, perchance, half-smiling reproof of the mischief and folly indulged in; or he is charged with it before a magistrate, who, with a few words of censure and warning, releases him; but *when he goes home*, then it is that he is sternly dealt with. *There*, how much more is made of his fault than you or the magistrate made of it! *There*, what agitation and concern it excites, and what penalties it incurs! The man whom the lad has to fear, when others show lenity, is his father, and because he is the father. Oh, the strictness of paternal love to mark iniquity—iniquity which another than the parent might scarcely recognize, or be ready enough to wink at and condone! A father's rule, again, a true father's rule, consists not merely in legislating and in punishing when laws are broken, but in studying to train toward obedience—to school and discipline, with the object of eliminating or checking what is wrong, and guiding and helping to the formation of right habits. He not only commands good conduct, and visits the opposite with his displeasure, but endeavours in every way, and by every means, to influence to goodness, and to educate the child on all sides, with whatever exercises and appliances may seem fitting, to the best of which he is capable. To this end, he watches over and pursues him; and with what patient persistency,—never retiring offended or disgusted, with any amount of obduracy, or trying indocility, and intractableness, but persevering with the work in defiance of every discouragement; and with what unselfish and brave devotion,—never neglecting it, never evading it, to escape trouble and distress, nor shrinking from what must needs cause pain and wear an appearance of cruelty, in order to prosecute it. Do we not acknowledge, that to be at all careless about the training of our children, and their culture by us to better things, is to be unfatherly, and that the fondness which passes by a fault demanding c rrection, rather than draw forth tears and put to grief, is not true paternal love?

If then there be a Divine Governor of mankind, all-holy and just, the principle and spirit of whose government is really paternal, is it not a profoundly serious thing for us men, in our state of confessed imperfection, with so much in us which as yet falls short of and is contrary to holiness, with so much in us that is morally defective and out of order? What does it mean for us, but that our moral lack and wrongness cannot be lightly allowed or lightly treated, cannot be suffered to go on and linger in any, unopposed, and must be met by all sharp measures required to effect a cure? What does it mean for us, but that we are doomed to be disturbed and troubled with a view to our rectifying, and are not to be let alone until our rectification is accomplished? What hope can there be of rest or happiness, what hope of acquittal, for unrighteous souls, if God, the infinitely righteous, be the Father? Can He ever be content to tolerate them as they are, to leave them as they are, unvisited, unmeddled with? If He be indeed the Father, what chance can there be for one of us, of our not receiving according to our works? Do you not perceive the certainty, the inevitableness of due punishment upon the supposition of His Fatherhood? Do you not perceive how impossible it is, assuming the truth of the idea concerning Him, that any future, or future world, should find us at peace, unless we have learned to be good? When I see men advancing in years unimproved, and unimproving, notwithstanding the lessons and the warnings which the years have supplied; notwithstanding the various teaching and discipline to which they have been subjected, growing more selfish and carnal, rather than more loving and spiritual, stifling still their higher impulses, instead of fostering and following them, and passing at length from hence in unrelieved bondage to a number of evil habits and false sympathies; then, in proportion as I believe that God is the Father —the Father of the living and of the dead—I cannot help being burdened and dismayed for them. I think of the suffering that must yet be in store for such; for without suffering, how are these habits and sympathies of theirs to be worked out? and I know, methinks, that they will have to be worked out; that the great paternal Love will not be able to refrain from them, or stay its hand until they are. Oh, sirs, there is nothing, when you consider it, that makes life and death and the prospect of the world to come more serious for us unformed and faulty creatures, than the thought that the Divine Lord on whom we call is the *Father.*

XI.
PRAYER.

HOLY and blessed God, who hast blessed us with faith in Thy name and kingdom, in Thy constant immanent presence and Thy ruling will. Thou movest us to utter ourselves at Thy feet; and such self-utterance before Thee, in filial humility and trust, will not be in vain. In many ways thou dost fulfil Thyself; and Thou fulfillest Thyself, however secretly and untraceably to us, in our prayers, in our groans of desire, in our sighs of supplication, when we are inwardly constrained now and again, to pause amidst our work and look up to heaven with a cry. Thou art with us when we put forth effort in labour, to strengthen and uphold; Thou art with us when we sit apart and fold our hands and think seriously, to give power and to guide our thoughts; Thou art with us in our worthy and sincere inquiries, to enlighten our darkness by degrees, to reveal to us according to our receptiveness and need; and Thou art with us when we pray, to hear and answer. It is not for nothing, it is not without divine purpose and divine working, that we want, and are led, to pour out our souls to Thee. In our reaching to lay hold on Thee, Thou stoopest to lay hold on us; in our aspiring Thou art inspiring. The cry that breaks forth from the burdened breast—burdened with benevolent solicitudes, with holy longings—and seeking to unburden itself before the Lord—is not this cry one of the many servants of the Lord, through which He executes His will and does His pleasure? Father of Spirits, Thou hidest Thyself; but Thou art present on the right hand and on the left, where we perceive Thee not.

Prayer. 175

We do not see the invisible scene, but we humbly believe that "more things are wrought by prayer than men wot of." Give us liberty of heart and of utterance, and may we feel the heavens of Thy love about us while we kneel.

We come to-day, from hours of labour, to bless Thee that brain and hand have not failed us, and to be replenished from above, if it may be, for more faithfulness and truth in labour. We come from hours filled with various secular cares, with various agitations and anxieties, to be calmed and quieted from these; to have any wrong-heartedness which they may have wrought in us, corrected, any unwholesome temper of mind, healed and chased away. We come from thoughts of many things, to learn through fresh chastening and purifying of soul, where thought has been unwise or false, and to be guided where we may have erred, to truer and juster thinking. We come from our homes—from our happy homes —that, receiving anew in communion with the Father of All, we may go back to them with a more perfect spirit, stronger and readier for our duties there, and, being made capable of more unselfish affection and truthful action, may exert a healthier influence, and minister better to the happiness and the highest well-being of those with whom we dwell. We come from fresh mistakes, fresh failings, fresh sins, to be forgiven afresh out of the fulness of Thy mercy, to find in the light of Thy countenance a place for repentance, and to be "endued with the grace of Thy Holy Spirit to amend our lives according to Thy Holy Word."

O God, we are weary—weary of our recurring faults, faults repeated again and again, in spite of contrite tears and right resolves; but let us not be weary of contending with them, even until they are overcome, and we can walk with Thee in white. May we be still pursuing until we achieve, encouraging and comforting ourselves the while with the word of promise, "Be thou faithful unto death"—faithful in aim and effort—" and I will give thee a crown of life"—a crown of life, we think, at last, far off, so far, but yet at last. Lord, we are weary of the misery, the suffering, the manifold evil and wrongness around us, that goes on for ever and for ever, and ceases not. Our eyes fail with watching for the morning, for more light than the light of stars ; but let us not be weary of trying to mitigate and relieve a little as we can, of seeking to help as we are able, toward a little rectifying here and there, believing and assured that the night will ere long melt before the day, that a harvest of peace and purity is in store for the earth, and that each labour of love, however small, and seemingly vain, is the sowing of a seed contributing thereto. May our endeavours to do good, such as they are, be blessed to ourselves, if they should not effect much in the way of ministry to others ; if little or nothing should be done by them for the benefit of others, may they be so blessed to ourselves the while, as to be fitting and preparing us for greater use hereafter. Let us consider that the strength spent in labouring fruitlessly, is never really wasted ; let us reflect that in labouring fruitlessly, we may be gathering and acquiring for future success, and that so, only to *try* to serve, is truly to serve, in the end. Father, Almighty, be making something of us with these present experiences of ours, under the action of these present earthly circumstances. Be training us for something in Thy kingdom. We would not be a vessel marred and broken in the hand of the potter, which the potter must throw away ; but then Thou wilt *never* throw us away, however marred and broken we may have become —however we may have mis-shapen ourselves, Thou wilt bring us yet, with pains, and through pain, to some shape for Thyself, although it may not be the grandest or the fairest. Help us to cry with sincere surrender, with sincere desire, " Lord, work on us and in us as Thou wilt, until the best is done with us that can be done, and in Thy great House, in which are vessels of gold and silver, and also vessels of wood and earth, we be found, whether of this kind or that kind, a vessel unto some honour."

Come to us, O God, as we need ; with just the touch of Thy hand, with just the whisper of Thy Spirit that we need— to the young in their fresh vigour and lightness of heart, with their natures yet unfixed ; to the busy men, so busy, with buying and selling and getting gain, absorbed in " the chase, the competition, and the craft ;" to the bent with years, in whom passion has cooled, and expectation grows drowsy, while they remember the former times ; to those who are encamped just now at Marah, where the waters of life are bitter ; to those whose portion is sweet, and their souls are comforted ; to the sufferer in secret ; to the perplexed with doubt ; to the thinker in his solitude ; to the philanthropic in their labours ; to the sentenced criminal ; to the little dreaming child. Come still, with Thy teaching, to the world, for its further learning ; and with ever-renewed inspiration to Thy Church, until it shall come to Thy perfection. May the grace of our Lord Jesus Christ, and the love of God, and the fellowship of the Holy Ghost, be with us all evermore. Amen.

SERMON.

THE IMPORTANCE OF SELF-RESPECT.

"And he said unto me, Son of man, stand upon thy feet, and I will speak unto thee."—EZEKIEL ii. 1.

OPPRESSED and overwhelmed by his vision of the glory of the Lord—the great vision described in the previous chapter—Ezekiel had fallen prostrate; the marvels and majesties beheld, smote him with an awe so profound that, unable any longer to sustain the burden of the spectacle, he had sunk face forward to the ground, and lay there deadly still, deadly faint. But he was to be the bearer of a Divine message for the correction and moral rousing of his countrymen, and in order that Heaven may impart to him its secret, and inspire and instruct him for the work to which he has been chosen, he is called to rise and stand upon his feet. The same thing occurred at another time. A little later on, he was again lying prostrate before the blaze of the glory of the Lord, and again had to be raised up that the Spirit might speak with him, and put its words into his mouth. It was just thus also, you will remember, with the prophet Daniel. Of him, we read how, in gazing on certain invisible realities, his "comeliness was turned to corruption, and he retained no strength," and how the celestial agent, sent and waiting to communicate with him, stirred him to a kneeling posture, and, not satisfied with that, bade him stand upright, to listen and comprehend. So too, in New Testament days, with Saul of Tarsus at his conversion—struck to the earth by the mystic sheen, and beneath the piercing reproach of the Jesus whom he persecuted, it was only when he had risen and stood erect, that the purpose of the Lord was declared to him, and he received his commission as a minister and a witness thenceforth among the Gentiles.

Here then, in the very Book in which humility and lowliness of mind are constantly inculcated—in which we are always meeting with injunctions to *bend and bow*, if we would be divinely visited—here, are instances of men summoned to get up from the dust of conscious littleness and unworthiness, that they might be divinely spoken with—of men, prone upon their faces in the presence of God, who were required to place themselves upon their feet before He could say anything to them, or make any use of them. Yet, we may be quite sure at the same time, that their prior prostration was equally indispensable. When Jehovah would charge Moses with the task of delivering Israel, and called to him out of the midst of the bush, the shepherd of the Midian desert went forward calm and unabashed, answering "Here am I," and *he* was straightway commanded to halt, and remove his shoes, and the sacredness of the spot was impressed upon him, until he grew afraid and fell to the ground. He had to be taught to tremble. The word to him, was not "Stand upon thy feet that thou mayest hear and be invested from above," but, "Fall upon thy face." When however he had been deeply awed and humbled, to begin with, and had learned to feel under the mighty hand of God, his weakness, his nothingness—then, he was bidden to uplift his head and believe in himself; and his slowness to do this, his continued timidity, and self-distrust, in spite of all the encouragement afforded him, drew down upon him, according to the ancient story, the anger of the Lord. It was needful, that as Saul and Daniel and Ezekiel were, he should first be deeply awed and humbled;

but like them also, he needed to become erect after depression for the Heavens to be intimate with him, and to make him their mouthpiece and organ.

Now the son of the priest Buzi was designated to a great and arduous enterprise—he was wanted to go among the Hebrew captives settled along the banks of the river Chebar, and tell them truths that would not please; it was to be his to expose, and denounce false hopes with which they were deluding themselves, and to endeavour to warn and wean them from corruptions of heart and habit into which they were sinking. They were being depraved by adversity, in conjunction with the insidious action of the heathen scene, the heathen atmosphere, and must be awakened to righteousness. Many of them were nursing the vain dream of a speedy termination to their exile, and must be undeceived with the stern tidings that, notwithstanding the apparent consolidation of the broken kingdom in the hands of Zedekiah, and the expectation of help from Egypt, their country was doomed to suffer still more terribly in coming days, and that no redemption from bondage would be possible until the seventy years predicted by the prophets were fulfilled. Here was Ezekiel's mission—to undeceive and awaken, to assail the refuges, and to rebuke the sins of an infatuated and stiff-necked people; and no one ever does any great thing in the way of moral ministry, as teacher or reformer, who has not had visions that have laid him low, and left him for a while without spirit or strength—who has not at moments, been weighed down to faintness, almost to despair, under a sense of the magnitude of his work, under a sense of responsibility and inadequacy. He will have thought, and thought sometimes in secret, till his heart has well-nigh died in him—will have known what it is to groan and stagger in secret, beneath the burden laid upon him, crying, "Lord, spare me—I cannot carry it, I am not worthy." Once and again, Ezekiel fell upon his face, and if he had not, he would never have accomplished what he did. Had he not been made weak thus, once and again, he would never have been the strong prophet that he was, mighty in word and deed.

But then, it is quite true, on the other hand, that no one ever does any great thing in the service of truth and humanity, unless he has superb confidence in himself—unless he can feel that *he* is divinely called and qualified. He must be conscious of knowledge and power; and must be able to trust his own ideas, his own principles, and to believe in his own methods against the most discouraging delay of success, against all ridicule, and adverse criticism, and fierce opposition. If he be not self-satisfied and self-reliant he will be no servant of the Lord—no polished shaft in His quiver. So Ezekiel, with his face in the dust, was lifted to his feet and made to stand upright, before the Spirit could commune with him, or work through him. And for healthy living, for beautiful action and endurance in our place, whatever it may be, we all require to have these two united in us—awe and assurance—prostration and erectness—the recognition of our insignificance—our dependence—and the recognition of our worth and dignity. We need to be both lying down in felt emptiness and helplessness, and rising up in brave self-sufficiency; and while it may be the fact that Heaven will reveal nothing to those who are not humble and lowly, it is equally the fact that Heaven never has anything to reveal to those who are not duly reverencing, and manfully leaning upon themselves.

Now this is what we may find for ourselves, in the angel's address to the prophet of Chebar—the importance of self-respect; an importance which is frequently implied, and much recognized in our sacred Scriptures, more so, indeed, than some of you may think. Moses begins it, with his ritual of offerings and lustrations for transgression, instituted by him in connection with the numerous laws he promulgated—offerings and lustrations that were understood to absolve from guilt, and to rehabilitate, to reinstate those who had disgraced and defiled themselves through disobedience—removing the stain they had incurred, and enabling them to start afresh, as clean creatures. So, while imposing upon the people a number of severe rules and commandments, he provided, in his wisdom, for the restoring of their self-respect whenever they should have failed or fallen, by delivering them from the burden of shame and despair, by giving them back their name and their place in the society. He must have felt very strongly—Moses must—the moral benefit that would accrue to men, the wholesome influence that would be produced, in saving them from self-contempt and self-despondency, when they came under condemnation; in helping them, on confessing and repenting, to rise again to their feet, and stand once more, well themselves, as those whose misdeeds had been washed away. It is

The Importance of Self-Respect. 185

the loss of self-respect after sin, that assists to make men such sinners as they are, that operates to hinder amendment, that contributes often to plunge into further and worse sin; and I say to you, beware of undue humiliation of soul, on account of wrong-doing. Beware of lying overlong in the dust of penitence. Forget the things which are behind, in reaching forth to things that are before. Contrition is all very well, but contrition beyond a certain point, is distempering and depraving. We must be careful not to scorn or despise ourselves, if we would learn to do better. The sense of our unworthiness must not be too much with us, or we shall be weakened for growing worthy. And let parents take heed that in noticing and reproving the faults of their children, they do not so wound their self-respect as to render all the harder for them the conquest of their faults.

But coming from Moses, to the New Testament, we meet continually, in its pages, with the same recognition of the importance of self-respect. Jesus Christ was always saying something in aid of it—something to encourage and support it. When He would strengthen his Apostles for cleaving to their convictions against the opposition of the world, for brave and fearless prosecution of the work to which they were called, He talked to them of their worth in the eyes of the Almighty Father, telling them that the hairs of their head were all numbered, and that they were of more value than many sparrows. When Simon Peter, overwhelmed for a moment with the feeling of his manifold imperfections, fell down at the Master's feet, crying, " Depart from me, for I am a sinful man, O Lord," how was he treated ? The Master dropped at once, a hint of the great capacity which He saw latent in him, and waiting to be developed, of the great use which he was destined to be in the service of the kingdom—" Fear not, Simon ; from henceforth thou shalt catch men." When again, Christ mingled with the degraded outcasts of Judea, of what did He speak to them ? of their worth, of how Heaven missed them and wanted them. They heard from His blessed lips of the shepherd's concern for the *lost* sheep, of the housewife's eager search for the *lost* piece of silver. There is nothing more conducive to healthy self-reverence, against the influence of felt poor quality, and low desert, than the assurance that we are dear to some one who is superior—that some one who is superior, cares for us, and clings to us, and considers us capable of much better and greater things. And this was the strength which Christ brought to the weak—the Gospel with which He raised the self-despairing. You are the child of a God, who thinks on you, and yearns over you, and to whom, in your worst vileness, you are a prince in bondage, worthy of being sought after and redeemed. And what again, did He make to be the turning-point in the history of the dissolute youth of the parable, on what did He make his recovery and salvation to turn, but on his awakening to some self-respect, on his beginning to feel his dignity? "How many hired servants of my father have bread enough and to spare, and I perish with hunger! I will arise and go unto my father." True, he saw and confessed that he was not worthy to be called a son, nevertheless he was a son, above those hired servants, and it was the recollection of that, which revealed to him his unworthiness, while at the same time, emboldening him to go home. He began to be saved, according to the representation of Christ, when he began to be self-respecting.

Well then, look at the Epistles—the Pauline Epistles especially; in them, how constantly are the readers reminded of their high estate, or of the great things that were imputed to them, of the great things that were assumed with regard to them; of the lofty *idea* of their condition and character, which His perfect manhood involved, whose members and brethren they were. "Ye are bought with a price,"—" Ye are all children of the light, and of the day,"—"Know ye not that your body is the temple of the Holy Ghost?"—" Reckon ye yourselves to be dead indeed unto sin, but alive unto God, through Jesus Christ our Lord." The Apostle would have them understand and consider how grand they were—how ideally pure, and contemplated their being strengthened thus, to vanquish lower tendencies, and to aim at and ascend toward what was noble. The whole tenor of Scripture teaching is suggestive of the importance of self-respect. Gentlemen, let us see that we are not wanting in it, that we do not expose it in our breast, to injury, that we do not drift away from or sink below it. Let us be heedful to guard and maintain it. We cannot be men, we cannot be sons and heirs of God, without it. In order to its best preservation, be true, be faithful, live sincerely, obey conscience—you need not be faultless to keep it and refuse to be deprived of it by any painful sense of weakness, culpability, or sin. Be humble:

bow the head in penitence, but withal "Stand upon your feet," assured that the present and the future are still yours, and that divine possibilities sleep within you.

But you will say, "When are we *not* self-respecting?" Well, he is not for one, who craves and courts the approbation of others, and sets himself to gain it—who wants it, wants it to comfort and uphold him—who can be strong and happy enough while others are praising or smiling on him, but when they are not, waxes feeble and melancholy. We may value approbation when it is given us, and be cheered and encouraged by it, without losing self-respect; but to be dependent upon it, to be anxious about it, to make it a motive of action, that is degradation. If it come to us, let us, with the consent and amen of conscience, readily accept and freely enjoy it, but do not let us look out for it; do not let us go in quest of it. "And how can ye believe who seek honour one of another?" Nothing tends more surely to deaden those higher sensibilities, to which the angel speaks.

Again, he is wanting in self-reverence, who gives himself at all to imitate another, who, in any work which may be laid upon him, tries to repeat the greatness of another, to copy his distinctions rather than to evoke and cultivate his own, to strain after his dimensions, rather than to be as perfect as he can, within his own. He is guilty of irreverence toward himself; and the result is, that Heaven never communicates to him what it waits to communicate—that the special good thing which should be his to receive and contribute, is withheld from him, is debarred from coming forth in him; his own peculiar gift, little or great, is lost. Many a man, it may be, has lived and died without being spoken to from above as he might have been —without saying or doing just that which he could have said or done as no one else could, because, instead of consenting to be *himself*, he has foolishly repressed and thwarted himself in striving to be something that others were. They were noble words of the new Dean of Westminster in his first Abbey sermon last Sunday, when, referring admiringly to the unique work of his famous predecessor, he remarked, " To attempt to continue *it* would leave the world no richer. Let others carry on in their own way, and in their own measure, such good work of his as falls within their powers, and find such other work as suits their gifts and experiences—not waste their energies or misdirect their efforts in dreaming of prolonging him." There breathed true self-respect, enfolding the promise of some individual fruit and achieving.

Then again, he is not self-respecting, who hesitates at all, to go with his convictions, who fears to trust and follow the light within him, when the many are moving in the opposite direction; who, when careful and honest inquiry seems to be carrying him to conclusions that will separate him from the multitude, and perchance from those who are deemed great and wise, becomes afraid—afraid to abide with what commends itself to him as good and true. We may well pause to reflect afresh, and re-examine, on finding ourselves parting company with the chiefs and princes, and standing comparatively alone; but if further reflection and examination have the same issue for us, and will not allow us to think otherwise, we should have the courage to surrender to our vision, to cherish and utter our thought, though all voices be against us. So only can we hope to receive and retain the Spirit of Revelation. Dare to listen to the whispers of your own sincere soul, and to be guided by them, however at variance they may be with prevailing opinions and ideas. Do not be ready to mistrust what you, with an earnest and single eye, may see, because it is not what others see.

And one word in conclusion. Beware of losing self-respect through living dramatically—with a daily appearance put on, which is not true to the reality—with the frequent assumption before spectators, of that which does not belong to you. Beware of losing it through leading an idle, aimless, useless life, a life without any high or worthy purpose. Beware of losing it, especially, through for ever failing to obey your higher promptings, and for ever regretting and bemoaning the failure, while never seriously endeavouring to improve. There are men with whom it is thus, who are always grovelling in the dust of self-abasement for faults and follies of theirs which they are still always repeating, with no resolute effort to avoid or rise above them. Miserable creatures are these, depraved instead of purified, by their perpetual remorse and shame, and over and around whom the heavens of God must needs lie shut and dumb. Let such rouse themselves from the bondage of habitual indulgence, to strive. One strenuous determined struggle against their baser nature, even although no immediate victory should be won by it—one strenuous determined struggle, would serve to restore to them the blessedness, and to inspire them with the strength of some self-respect.

XII.

PRAYER.

THE Lord is a God of judgment; His wisdom is infinite; there is no searching of His understanding; He knows our frame, for His hands fashioned us, nor does He fail to remember our frame when He takes account of us, and of our doings. A Discerner is He of the thoughts and intents of the heart; all our need lies clear before Him; all our secrets His eye penetrates; whatever is good for us, of trouble or rest, of pleasure or pain, He knows how to give, and we are never neglected by Him, nor mistaken and misconceived. In His balances our faults and our virtues are unerringly weighed, and who can comprehend our merit and demerit like Him? His laws are fixed, steadfast, and immovable, and with them He works for us and ministers to us, according to His wise will. Because He is, and we are all in His hands, we shall all have our rights, shall all receive our due portion, and are receiving it now, from day to day; none suffer from short measure, however, to their own calculation, it may seem to be otherwise, and none get what they ought not, however at times their bruised hearts may cry, "Oh, why for me this cruel wrong;" none are forsaken, though they perish miserably; and none are mocked by life, though life disappoint and deceive them ever so bitterly, even until they are driven to say, "It were better for me that I had not been born." We plague ourselves with doubts and fears, with worries and alarms, and all the while we are children at home. For each human soul there is a Father, and it is not lost in the crowd, and its own place is being prepared for it, its meet inheritance is sure. So we meditate, O God; and would fain stand bravely, patiently, uprightly in our lot, and be true to one another in all mutual communication and aid. Make us happy with Thy countenance, that we may find thereby, how many bright things there are around us, and how much happiness waits for us in life; that our eyes may be opened thereby, to see the sun between the clouds, to see the gleams that come and go during the wintry day, to see the bits of sky in the wayside puddles, to see the flowerets under the hedge, and gathering them, feel that the dull lane is not without its beauty and joy. Make us happy with Thy countenance, that with our inward smiles we may kindle smiles, and be able to perform a better work, and to succour better those whom we wish and seek to succour; for they hear most music by the way, who go singing by the way, and their task is best done, their service is the deepest and finest service, to whom God, their Maker, giveth songs in the night.

We ask not for the joy that is pursued after, but for the joy that overtakes. Grant us, we pray Thee, not the joy for which a house is built, and swept, and garnished, and which so often leaves the house waiting for the expected tenant in vain; but the joy that steals into our own poor house as we sit at work there, thinking of no such visitor, too busy to look out and desire. Grant us the joy that comes in, to those who go forth to serve, and which, whether they know it or not, whether they be glad because of Thee or not, is the very joy of the Lord. And make us dutiful always, and in all things,—dutiful to the claims of each hour, with whatever temptings to the contrary we may be assailed; dutiful to the truth that is revealed to as, however hard and exacting its demands may be; dutiful to the higher principle that seeks to lift its voice above the clamour of the lower impulse, to the sober judgment that beckons us away from the heat of passion; dutiful to our inferiors, and dependents, and servants, according to that which we owe them; to the ignorant the poor, the miserable, among whom we are cast, or whose cause waits close by, to be searched out by us ; to the friend who trusts us and lies in our bosom ; to the enemy who thinks he has something against us ; to those with whom we share the family life, and to the children who are ours to care for and train, whose interests need our best wisdom, our greatest patience, and all sympathetic understanding and imagination. Make us dutiful always, and in all things, and may a true, single, loving heart be evermore our guide. We thank Thee for the way in which a holy simplicity has often illumined and led us ; for the light we have met often, in going forward as far as we were able to see, in taking, amid the darkness, the one step which we saw should be taken ; for the less difficulty and roughness often encountered than we had expected to encounter, in venturing at what we felt was the divine bidding, upon what seemed to us a wilderness, wherein would be much hardship.

We thank Thee for every inspiring thought with which we have been comforted and strengthened ; for every helpful friend we have found, whose counsel and influence, whose sympathy and love have done for us great things ; for such high aims as we have learned to cherish, and are still pursuing; albeit with little achievement, and sometimes with lame feet ; and we thank Thee for all pleasant refreshings, and quickening, stirring ministries which we are permitted to find in social converse, in intimacies of affection, in books, pictures, music, in dreams of the poet, in facts and marvels of science, in laughter-moving humour, and in clever nonsense. Much is given us, of various worth—may a healthy mind and a pure heart within us, prevail to draw from all the best service, the sweetest use ; and may we not be niggardly in giving, toward the quickening and refreshing of others.

O God, the Father of men, send us in the darkness such light as we may need to direct us. Lead us in all our confusions, and with Thy leading, bring us through them at length to a clearer understanding, a truer order, a calmer state. Teach us in the way which Thou shalt choose, as nations, as Churches, as families, as individual souls ; and prepare us with a wise and tender spirit, for learning. We wait at Thy feet again ; for the blessing of those whom we love, whether in their sorrow or their joy ; for the comfort and relief of those who suffer, whose bones are full of pain, with whom circumstances are trying, on whom disaster has fallen, whose dear ones the angry sea has swallowed, or the fire devoured. We wait on Thee for all things requisite and necessary for ourselves and for all men, and beseech Thee to direct, sanctify, and govern both our hearts and bodies in the ways of Thy laws and in the works of Thy commandments ; that, through Thy most mighty protection, both here and ever, we may be preserved in body and soul, through our Lord and Saviour Jesus Christ. Amen.

SERMON.

TWO INCITEMENTS TO LOVE.

" If there be therefore any consolation in Christ, if any comfort of love, if any fellowship of the Spirit, if any bowels and mercies."—PHILIPPIANS ii. 1.

ST. PAUL'S avowed delight in the liberalities and the religious zeal of the Philippian Christians, was kept below the highest point of delight, he intimates, by the want of harmony with which they were disfigured—a want of harmony resulting from a want of mutual, kindly, and affectionate consideration. While their generous succourings of many, and their ardent missionary activities afforded him rich satisfaction, this, prevented his being perfectly satisfied with them ; this, was the dead fly in the otherwise delicious pot of ointment; the wick or snuff within the flame of his pleasure that did abate it. And, in writing a letter acknowledging their late, handsome present to himself, he seizes the opportunity of entreating them to make his joy full, to give him gladness without alloy, when remembering them, by cultivating unity among themselves, and the feelings, the dispositions, the sympathies that would surely promote and sustain it. "You have greatly pleased me," says the teacher to his pupils, "with your general diligence and application, but there is one thing in your behaviour that vexes me; let only that be corrected, and my gratification will be complete—nothing will be left me to desire." So says the Apostle to his readers: "Your liberalities and religious zeal fill me with rejoicing; I am charmed with you, I am proud of you on these accounts, on all accounts, indeed, but one; all you need is to grow less contentious and prone to divisions, through acquiring more of the thoughtful, forbearing, self-forgetting love which goes to ensure concord and peace; make full then my joy over you, by seeking to learn and cherish such love."

And in the text, we have him urging them thereto with four distinct appeals, upon the ground of four facts, which he knew they could not dispute, and would be ready to admit. In the two middle ones, you observe, they are reminded by way of inducement, of their common participation in the same spirit, and of the comfort which flows from the exercise and exchange of charity. Asks the writer, in effect, "Are you not knit together as close kindred beneath all your diversities, in possession of the same heaven-bestowed enlightenment, the same heaven-inspired faith and hope, moved from above to worship the same Lord, to throb with the same aspirations? and have you not witnessed and experienced the power of affection to cheer and encourage, to diffuse happiness, to soothe trouble and pain, how contributive it is to the brightening of human hearts and lives? and should you not be influenced, will you not be led by these considerations, to study to abound in love toward each other?

But leaving the second and third of St. Paul's series of incitements without any further comment, let us occupy ourselves with a few minutes' meditation upon the first and the last, taking the last first. "If there be any bowels and mercies"—or, in the language of to-day, any tenderness and compassion — the meaning being, of course, by the tenderness and compassion which does exist in all—which I know, and you know to be yours, whatever harshnesses and animosities you may be displaying—by it, I summon you to act graciously, to be of one accord, of one mind. It was just tenderness and compassion in which he complains that they were deficient, and which he wanted them to practise; and he endeavours to win them to the practice with the recognition and proclamation of the tenderness and compassion that were already theirs. "Listen," he says, "listen, to the love-beatings within you, and be loving. Lo, you carry within you a fund of brotherly sensibility, expend and apply it." He would draw them on to be kinder than they were, by setting before them the kindliness they feel. And this is the best way of helping and persuading men to improve—the best way in which to try and lead them from lower things to higher, from unworthy to worthier conduct, namely, by fastening upon what they are, in the midst of their faultiness, that is good and beautiful—upon what they have of good and beautiful motions in the breast; by touching these, and calling their attention to them, and demanding that they should be cultivated and followed. It is not by showing one, vividly, the ugly, miserable depth to which he has sunk, that you will be most likely to succeed in rousing him to climb, but rather by showing him whatever he enfolds that is *above* the depravity in which he lies; any stray feature, any fluttering inclination, any lurking susceptibility, that is sweeter and nobler than the foul mean thing he has become, and by pressing him to rise and ascend comformably to it; to get up and go forth in the direction in which it points.

When a boy of yours blunders and fails wretchedly in his task, or falls into dire naughtiness, do not, with a view to his recovery, pronounce him incapable and stupid, or mourn over him to his face as a graceless good-for-nothing, but charge him rather with the crime of not being equal to himself; speak to him of the capacity he possesses which he has not exercised, of what he is sufficiently intelligent to accomplish if he will, or remonstrate with him on the truer heart in him, to which he is unfaithful, and which he has only to be loyal to, to become the best of lads; remind him of the ability which he has found in himself, whenever he has *tried* to succeed, or of the finer conduct which he has shown might be his, and for which, amid all his waywardness of nature, he has the requisite finer instincts and impulses. When you encounter one, seemingly devil-possessed, never fear, never hesitate to assume that somewhere within him an angel hides; and if you would be the means of procuring or assisting his emancipation, just call upon that angel, and be intent on moving him to stand up and spread his folded wings. There is always something vastly better in men than the infirmity they are exhibiting, or the evil they are doing. There is always something better in them than that. They are not, inwardly, altogether so bad as they talk or act. Look down into them, and get them to look down into themselves, and see and know the good that is in them—the good germs waiting to be developed, the good elements waiting to be gathered and concentrated. We never go wrong without falling below ourselves, without being worse than we are. Every man is a temple of some holy ghost, however latent or feeble it may be; and what he needs, is to be made to perceive the sacred thing, and entertain it, and let it lead him, and rule. One says, excusing, while half ashamed of his pollution, "I have but followed the natural impulses with which I was cursed;" but was he not *blest* also, with other and higher impulses to which he has failed to resign himself? and suppose they had been followed instead, how different a creature he might have been to-day! We do unworthily, and we grow corrupt, simply through not listening to ourselves, simply through neglecting to launch forth upon such heavenly tides as rise within us. You, living meanly, sensually, peer into your own breast: is there nothing there, of occasional thought and emotion, quite superior to the life you are living? Embrace that; surrender to that, and *be* superior! You, who are pursuing a course of injustice or cruelty toward others—a course by which they are defrauded or afflicted—is there no sentiment of honour, no pulse of kindness in your breast, which, if you paused to hear, and allowed and encouraged to make itself heard, you would be unable to resist?

In the Church of Philippi were two women—Euodias and Syntyche—who had fallen out. We may imagine them, when St. Paul's letter arrived, all on fire with mutual hostility and ill-will, exchanging sharp, malignant words, spitefully annoying and vexing each other, each ready unrelentingly to do the other an evil turn. And was there no tenderness and compassion in the hearts of these women? Oh! to have seen them at home, perhaps, with their children, so full of patient, considerate, self-denying love: or in some neighbour's house, perhaps, weeping with them that wept, ministering like angels to the sick or sad, pouring themselves out to comfort and help—you would hardly have taken them for the same persons who were showing such acidity and animosity in the Church. And yet, further, was there no lingering throb within them, of tenderness and compassion for each other? Were there no moments when they felt a sudden secret yearning to make it up, and be friends again? when the meeting of their eyes, albeit ablaze with wrath, stirred memories of former happier days, in which they took sweet counsel together? when in the very midst of some spiteful speech or ungenerous behaviour, a breath of pity fluttered in both, which, if one had then made a little advance, would have moved the other to respond instantaneously, with a response that might have brought about reconciliation? Well, the Apostle appeals to this—to the good feeling which existed in spite of their hard and fierce alienation—and exhorts them by it, to harmony and love. "If there be any bowels and mercies"—as you know there are—let these be yielded to, let these have sway and prevail."

But glance now, at that to which he first points, by way of inducement, "If there be any consolation in Christ." That there is, is true enough. How many have found, and are daily finding it, in Him! It was not, however, I am persuaded—it was not of his consoling influence, that St. Paul was really thinking here; and I very much regret to see that the Revised Version has retained the idea, merely substituting "comfort" for "consolation." The word occurs a number of times in the New Testament Scriptures, where it has two distinct meanings, occurring sometimes, clearly, in the sense of comfort or encouragement, and sometimes, as clearly, in the sense of exhortation or admonition; which latter, indeed, is its primary significance, the former having only followed— followed, we may suppose, from the fact that exhortation is often intended to impart, and does impart, comfort. While, then, there are many passages in which it is evidently used to express comfort, there are many others in which it is translated, and evidently used to express, exhortation—not in the sense of teaching, but in the sense of entreaty or appeal. For instance, "Ye have forgotten the exhortation which reasons with you as with children;" "My son, despise not thou the chastening of the Lord, nor faint when thou art rebuked of Him"—where, it describes an address, the purpose of which is to brace, to incite, to firm and steadfast endurance. Or again, "He that prophesieth, speaketh to men, to edification, and exhortation and comfort." The second of these, is the word of our text, and denotes plainly, stirring admonition, as distinguished from instruction and consolation. Now although the Revisionists have rendered it in the text, "comfort;" by the late Dean Alford, Conybeare and Howson, De Wette, Van Heugel, and several besides, it is rendered "exhortation," and I cannot but hold theirs to be the true rendering, since, when in enjoining upon the Philippians to cultivate love, the Apostle points them to Christ, it would be surely, not *comfort* which he meant them to find in Him, but *exhortation*—exhortation to the love to which he was anxious to lead them. "If there be in Christ," he must have meant to say, "any exhortation to tender considerateness and affectionate conduct, then, by that grand exhortation, which He is, in His life and cross, I call upon you to be united in reciprocal kindness and charity."

And the figure of Jesus in the midst of the ages, is it not just this; a perpetual exhortation to men to be a little better than they are—to be less worldly, less grovelling, less selfish, to rise from their low levels to higher ways, to a nobler and purer spirit? The figure of Jesus on those Galilean plains, in those Judean streets, occupied from morn to eve with gracious ministries, surrendered to constant labour in the interests of the poor, the miserable, the ignorant and erring, weeping over the disorders and corruptions of the time, burdened and bleeding for the cause of righteousness and truth, reckless of all suffering, resigned to all sacrifice, in consuming zeal for the kingdom of God—is it not always summoning us to more sweetness and more magnanimity, to loftier aiming and worthier living? Can we ever pause in our course, to look back on it, without feeling ourselves summoned thus, as though a trumpet voice were crying, "Do not rest there; be a little greater than that, be a little finer than that." While we encounter continually, things that are tempting and seducing, that pluck at us and pluck at us, to draw astray and drag down, the tendency of which is to deaden or enervate; how much there is around us, in our circumstances and our contacts, to stimulate—to stimulate to industry when we are indolently inclined, or to patient perseverance when in weariness and despondency we are ready to relax effort; to stimulate to renewed faithful resistance, or to further aspiration and endeavour after improvement. With what rousing voices we are spoken to often in the necessities of our condition, in the needs of those who are dependent upon us, in the observation and criticism of spectators, in the opinions and expectations of others concerning us, in the consequences—the painful consequences—of our errors and mistakes; how, by these, we are kept moving when otherwise we might come to a stand, are pricked to do more, and more excellently, than we otherwise should. Thank God for the many dumb yet powerful exhorters that we find from time to time in our path. We owe to them our growth and attainment; but for them, our acquirings and accomplishings would have been poorer than they are. And have we not met with persons, too, who in their silent example, in their beautiful lives, in the spirit that breathed from them, have been full of exhortation to us—in the presence of whose pureness and earnestness, in witnessing whose deeds, we have felt ourselves called to heights above us, have seen with a touch of shame, the comparative poorness of what we were, and with a sigh of wistfulness, the truer thing that we might be? And is not Christ preeminently such a person? Whenever we meet Him in thoughtful pauses by the way, in moments of quiet meditation over the Gospel page, does He not act on us thus, with rufflings of self-discontent, with a sense of being coarser and earthier than we ought to be?

There are, here and there among us, what may be called, exceptional men. I can think of one or two—men of extraordinary moral intensity and consecration, devoured with enthusiasm for great ideas, and sacrificing everything in devotion to them, inculcating and exemplifying a righteousness far beyond the righteousness of the scribes and the Pharisees of the day, having visions of summits in the clouds that must e'en be aimed at, and striven after, at whatever cost. We designate these men impracticable and chimerical; they are counted perchance by the multitude, half-mad. We say, that "at least, it would never do for all to resemble them." Yet we are impelled to admire them, and they serve to keep us higher than we should be without them. We have no thought of ever imitating them, yet they are a check upon our worldliness and selfishness, and tend to mitigate it —to raise us to something a little more elevated and refined. We are somewhat the better for them. And such an one supremely, is Christ. He stands out like an angel in the sun, for ever above us all, yet for ever moving down upon and affecting us all; painted for ever upon the eye of the world, His resplendent image tells, with more or less restraining and constraining influence. None come

P

nigh to His perfection, or dream, perhaps, of attaining to it, yet none are altogether untouched by it. We, who call ourselves by His name, we, look up at Him again and again, in hours of worship, and on Sacrament Sundays, with reverence and adoration; and, again and again, return to our wonted ways, yet not without some renewed aspiration, and endeavour to cleanse them. We cannot help aspiring and endeavouring the more, for the grandeur of His face; it disturbs us in our worldliness and selfishness, and is always exhorting us against them, is always appealing to us, to rise toward rather nobler things.

XIII.

PRAYER.

ETERNAL God, whose kingdom abideth through all time and all vicissitudes ! whose ways—ways always of mercy and truth—are from everlasting to everlasting ! Thou wast with our fathers in the past, their Teacher and Guide, shaping their ends, and showing them light as they were able to bear it ; speaking to them for needed inspiration, in thoughts and ideas, some of which may have been left behind, some of which, in the eyes of their children, are no longer true. Thou wast with our fathers before we were born, ordering their lives, and strengthening and comforting their hearts. And Thou art with us, at this present, in these later and changed days, under many other forms, under many other conceptions than prevailed in bygone days ; still teaching and guiding us with the same infinite wisdom and patience ; still speaking to us at sundry times and in divers manners for our learning ; still working according to Thy immutable plan, without variableness, and fulfilling Thy divine purpose. The generations come and go, but Thy laws continue ; and from above and around us Thy holy love removes not. We too, live in Thy house, as all our fathers did ; and Thou wilt be with those who shall succeed us on this green earth, in this shifting scene, when we shall have vanished hence to return no more, and presently to be remembered no more ; when men of another speech and of other visions shall be toiling, suffering, sinning, aspiring, here in our place. We shall be gone, and the world will have changed ; old things will be forgotten ; behold, new things will spring forth and appear ; but it will be still the same God and Father of all, over all, and through all, and in all ; and some day, because of Thee and Thy mighty abiding, all, both which are in heaven and which are on earth, will be gathered together in one, and the one will be a whole, in which, as in a sea of glass before the throne, Thou shalt be perfectly reflected, and over which the morning stars shall sing for joy, crying, how resplendent and worthy to be magnified is the finished creation of God.

Everlasting gracious Power, of whom the manifold universe is a manifold manifestation ; who art constantly bursting into endless individual life, in plant, in animal, in man ; never suspended, ever welling ; and in us human creatures, ever reaching and striving towards something greater, towards something fuller and higher! we worship Thee in Thy effluences and unfoldings, and we bless Thee. We bless Thee for the beauty of the fair earth, and for the conscious loveliness which it becomes in us, with whom are eyes to see, and appreciate, and admire, what Thou hast made. We bless Thee for that which Thou art, and which we discern and feel of Thee in bud and flower, in mountain and sea and sky, in bird of the air, in beast of the field. We bless Thee for Thy springs within us—Thy ever-renewed springs of love, joy, peace, aspiration, hope, passion for knowledge and truth, and for the nobler sensibilities and the growing capacity which is ours, in Thee. We bless Thee for our sustainment until now in strength, and adequacy for the work, the burden, the trial of life ; in power to enjoy, to understand, and acquire ; for what we have gained, little or much, in vision and wisdom ; for what the years have taught us and disciplined us to be, that is good ; and for the impulse and desire to reach forth to things before, to seek things above, which continues to stir within us and to produce some corresponding struggle and endeavour. We bless Thee for the measure of true progress which Time brings with it in its course—progress among men in taste and various skill, in useful arts and appliances, in acquaintance with nature's laws and secrets, in conflict with disease and other forms of evil, in benevolent sympathy, in moral discernment and conviction, and in religious ideas. The world does move, albeit with faltering steps and slow ; upon much that once was borne, our feet are come to stand. Thou who groanest and travailest in us, and in us art evermore aspiring ; move within us, we beseech Thee, yet more mightily, and help us still to strive according to Thy blessed inworking.

Enter us afresh, with new increase of the spirit from on high, as we enter a fresh period of time, that our overcomings and ascendings may be greater than they have been, and our succumbings to that which resists, fewer ; that for one step forward in the past, ten steps may be taken in the future. Grant us visions ; stream in upon us at the beginning of the year, with thoughts, emotions, impressions that shall be divinely quickening— that shall engender a deeper, stronger impulse, not soon to be spent, but prevailing to carry us far up the height where those who stand, still climb and cry, " Excelsior."

Give us power to be more patient, more loving, more simply faithful, more earnest, more just in judgment, more steadfast in temptation, more useful and helpful in action, more capable of reigning as kings over evil circumstances. During the coming months let some flaws in us be effaced which have long marred our beauty ; let some faults be conquered against which we have long striven in vain ; let life teach us at length the lessons which as yet we have missed learning ; let right principles obtain over us at length the sway they have never yet gained, however we may have recognized and confessed them ; let virtues in which we may have lost some ground be strengthened and revived. May our homes be better ordered, and our daily work better done, our unconscious influence on the circle in which we move, be healthier, and our hearts more open to the touch of whatsoever is good and true. Another year gone ! and how far we have been from that which we might have been, and had often resolved perhaps that we would be ; how many have been our failings ; how small our advance has been ; how much there is to regret of misbehaviour and shortcoming, of thoughtlessness and folly. Our soul has it all in remembrance, and is humbled within us. Another year begun! and how much may be corrected and amended if we will; what opportunities are opening their gates again, and inviting us to enter; what possibilities wait to be realized; how beautiful life may yet be made. How Thou comest to us, O God, amid our tears of remorse, with new risings of hope, of aspiration, of spirit; help us to answer Thy blessed advent with souls deep set on earnest and brave endeavour.

Father of all, re-inspire Thy Church with larger inbreathings of Him who is "a Priest for ever, not after the law of carnal commandment, but after the power of an endless life." Endue our English senators and legislators with the heavenly gift of wisdom. Bless our country, if it may be, this year, with perfect peace and tranquillity within its borders; and out of past confusion bring forth order. Teach Thou and lead the nations along their several paths, to their several destinies. And may the grace of our Lord Jesus Christ, and the love of God, and the fellowship of the Holy Spirit be with us all evermore. Amen.

SERMON.

JOSHUA'S VISION.

A Sermon for the New Year.

"And it came to pass, when Joshua was by Jericho, that he lifted up his eyes and looked, and, behold, there stood a man over against him with his sword drawn in his hand: and Joshua went unto him, and said unto him, Art thou for us, or for our adversaries? And he said, Nay; but as captain of the host of the Lord am I now come. And Joshua fell on his face to the earth, and did worship, and said unto him, What saith my lord unto his servant? And the captain of the Lord's host said unto Joshua, Loose thy shoe from off thy foot; for the place whereon thou standest is holy."—JOSHUA v. 13–15.

SUCH is the story of what befell Joshua at a certain serious and anxious moment in his history; of the vision which he then experienced, while withdrawn, we may assume, from the Hebrew encampment to indulge in lonely musing.

There are moments when we see without seeking, what at other times does not appear to us, and will not appear. An inward eye that had been closed seems to open, and we stand suddenly in the presence of hitherto invisible things. Midnight, solitude, sorrow, a felt crisis in our lives—what secrets these have whispered, which we had not heard before; what revealings they have brought with them; and it was as though a veil had been rent in twain, as though a flash of lightning had illumined the darkness. We all, have our occasional transient visions of something higher, grander, or more solemn than we are ordinarily sensible of; visions which do naught but touch us with a brief awe and elevation of soul, that quickly vanishes, and no mark of it survives upon us; or which, in fading, leave a permanent effect behind them, and we are no longer the same beings that we were.

Joshua, you know, the pupil and chosen assistant of Moses, had at length succeeded the latter in the leadership of the emancipated Israelites. The aged lawgiver, attracted soon after the exodus, by the promise of great capacities and great qualities which he descried in him, took him forthwith into training, with a view to the future, and made him his minister; and when, towards the termination of the forty years' wanderings in the wilderness, and with the goal of Canaan in sight, the old man knew that he was dying—that it could not be his to conduct the people whom he had delivered into the land of their hope and dream, he resigned the command of them to the younger man, whom he had learned to love and trust, and had been gradually exercising and educating for the post. Like many a discoverer, directing and helping others on the way to benefits in which he himself is not to share, Moses, the redeemer, had sunk down in death but three days' journey short of Jordan ; and the charge of the tribes devolving thenceforth upon Joshua, *he* has led them across the river, to the country they are to conquer for an inheritance.

At last, they have entered it. Here they are at last, just over the border. Behind them stretches the desert, the scene of chequered and memorable experiences ; where they had both suffered sharply, and tasted joy; where fiery flying serpents had flamed, and the glory of the Lord had shone. Before them, lies the new and unexplored ; and a little in advance of the halting host, alone, under the walls of Jericho, the first opposing stronghold to be attacked, their warrior-leader is looking round, and pondering. He has accomplished his task thus far. Thus far, the burden has been borne without fainting, and in the teeth of many difficulties progress has been made ; but the end is not yet. Much still remains to be done. He has now to begin afresh, in fresh scenes; another period of toil and endurance is opening before him. So, *we* stand to-day, upon the threshold of another year, waiting, after we have finished, to commence again. And, as *he* waited, gravely meditative, with earnest thoughts stirring in him concerning his duties and responsibilities, there came upon him the vision of the text; for, unless he had been meditative and earnest, he would not have beheld what he beheld, we may be sure. It was the shining answer to what was taking place within him. One sees only that which one is tuned and prepared to see; and, to catch inspiring glimpses, one must be aspiring. All things must be met by us half-way. It is always, as Coleridge said of Nature,—

"O Lady, we receive but what we give;
Ours is her luminous vesture, ours her shroud."

For none but those whose hearts are kindling, does the bush burn with fire. May ours be the inner temper of mind to-day, to which angels of God shall be able to show themselves.

But notice first, the agitation of uncertainty in the breast of the son of Nun. Suddenly, while he brooded, a man stood over against him, with his sword drawn in his hand. He saw a vast armed figure, towering above him, in fighting attitude, and asked, with painful suspense, "Art thou for us, or for our adversaries?" wondering anxiously what the apparition meant—whether splendid aid or terrible hindrance; what it portended—whether success or defeat in the approaching campaign. You see, this was the form in which the future appeared to him; the future in the strange country, of which he had been thinking—a mighty man with a drawn sword in his hand. Yes, of course the future would be filled with the clash of war. Nothing but conflict could be expected; conflict perhaps, severe and prolonged; but what of the issue? with whom would the victory lie? with Israel or the enemy? Ah, if he could but tell. Mystic form of the Future, wilt thou reveal it to me?

And it is with like uncertainty that we front now the new year. We have most of us lived long enough—we most of us know enough of life, to discern, as we lift our eyes, a man with a drawn sword in his hand. That there will be more or less of disagreeable and trying encounter, is sure. We shall have difficulties to grapple with, in the sweat of our face. Temptations will assail us; vexations and annoyances will have to be borne; it will not be all smooth with us at the smoothest,—

> "Into each lot some rain will fall,
> Some days will be dark and dreary."

But will it be upon the whole, one of our happy and prosperous years? Shall we get through it, however threatened or assaulted, unrifled and unharmed, without being sore wounded or overthrown in the way, without any crushing sorrow or devastating calamity; with no serious loss, with no bitter shattering disappointment? The character of past years has varied. Some, notwithstanding many little rufflings and unpleasantnesses experienced in them, we have looked back upon with satisfaction and thankfulness, and have called them good years. Ah, we did well in them. They were marked by much sunshine. Our enterprises prospered; our friendships yielded only sweetness. Our homes remained unstricken by aught of ill; and when in the still midnight, the bells were heard ringing out the old and ringing in the new, we were loth to bid farewell to the old, so happy had we been with it. Other years, perhaps, we were glad to have done with. They are remembered as black years, in which the sun shone only at rare intervals, and for a brief space, between ever-returning clouds; in which disaster followed disaster, and dear hopes were smitten, and the anguish of bereavement laid us low. And when the bells rang out we thought to ourselves, "Ah, toll the funeral of the wretched past, and let a deep grave be dug for it."

> " 'Rock,' I said, 'thy ribs are strong.
> That I bring thee, guard it long!
> Hide the light from buried eyes,—
> Hide it, lest the dead arise.
> Year,' I said, and turned away,
> 'I am free of thee this day;
> All that we two only know,
> I forgive and I forego.
> So thy face no more I meet,
> In the field or in the street.'"

The years have varied with us. In some, if we have had to fight, we have conquered. In others, the tide of battle has rolled against us, leaving us broken and mauled.

And what will be our portion in 1882? What has *it* in store for us, of suffering, of joy? What dovelike days of balm will it contain? What weary nights of weeping? How shall we think of it when it has fled—with quiet smiles of content, or with bowed head and mournful countenance? Behold, we know not anything. We enter it blindly, so blindly; its scenery is hid. "New year coming on apace, what hast thou to give me?" Comest thou promising peace and brightness, or big with thunder and gloom? We ask in vain, as Joshua did when he cried, "Art thou for us, or for our adversaries?" For observe, that question of his was not replied to. "Nay," said the armed angel; "I am no token, no prophecy of that, one way or the other." But what does he say to the wistfully inquiring man? "As the captain of the host of the Lord I am now come."

Here, then, was what Joshua saw, presently, in looking forward to the future. Not what was going to happen—not the victory or the defeat to which he was destined in marching against the Canaanites and struggling to gain possession of the country; but, that it would not be himself *alone* at the head of the Hebrew army; that One would be there, superintending and disposing, ordering and commanding, whom the people beheld not, even the very same angel of Jehovah's presence who had been with Moses and the Israelites in the wilderness during all the vicissitudes of their journey, whether they were in trouble or at rest, whether they prospered or were plunged in adversity and affliction. He saw himself divinely overlooked and attended; planning, manœuvring, fighting to the best of his ability, as the chosen general, *under* the constant eye and control of an unseen Generalissimo, who had His purposes, whose purposes were good and right, and would be always fulfilling themselves in and through all. He saw, to his comfort and relief, that the forces which he led were not *his* host merely, but the host of the Lord, and that they, together with their leader, were in the hands of the Lord.

It was thus that the Future answered his appeal, "What hast thou hidden for us in thy thick darkness?" It answered, "God is here—caring, managing, ruling to the end; the God of Abraham, of Isaac, and of Jacob." An inspiring vision, to have been borne in upon him as he stood alone in the plain, with the grim fortifications of Jericho frowning down on him, and thought of the work to be done, with its difficulties and dangers. Better, surely, than any glimpse or foreshadowing of coming events would have been—better, surely, than finding a sign of what these would be, to feel the conviction of such a Presence. "Lo! a prognostic, an omen," he fancied for a moment, and then, instead, the next moment, a clear, deep sense of Jehovah invisibly near, conducting and governing all. So sometimes, as we wait in sincerity and simplicity of mind, the eye grows purged, the perception clears, and the poorer thing with the seeing of which we had begun, melts, giving place to something finer and more true. And if we be able to receive it, what can be more inspiring for us in our entrance upon the unknown land of a new year, than the vision, not merely of an Existence in the universe over and above all phenomena, and producing and sustaining them; but of a living Being, transcendent in wisdom and goodness, whose purpose is our education and the education of the world, and who is working evermore, in whatever happens, in whatever chances and changes may befall, to forward It; of One who is not only with us in our doings and sufferings, our aspirations and struggles, our mistakes and stumblings, but *in* them with continuous tuitional intent; under whom, we are pursuing our ends, by whom, in all paths, we are led, in whose kingdom we are from morn to eve, let it be with us as it may.

Many earnest souls around us are starting afresh to-day, as they have come through the year that is gone, with no such vision. Joshua's angel does not manifest itself to them. Lifting their eyes, they behold nothing but the walls of Jericho and the encampment of Israel, and over all, an empty sky. Nor are they the less ready for the battle, or the less patient and strong, hopeful and brave, in essaying to conquer. And we may be sure too, that guidance and help from above, is theirs; for the presence and energy of the Captain of the Lord's host does not depend upon men's seeing Him. He is not absent or inoperative because they are unable to discern Him. Nevertheless, happy are they to whom He is visible. *They* are inspired, as none can be without the sight. For as one has said—let me just quote his words, "Blindness to God's existence cannot but entail a large and constant loss upon the blind. Although other and deeper springs of divine influence be not closed; although there may be other and more effectual means of inward guidance still accessible to God's providence than those which any deadness of insight can obstruct; yet, all the tone of the reflective life cannot be otherwise than injured by the exclusion of this great Object from the field of vision. Not to see what exists, modifies of course continually the whole range of thought and action which has a real though unperceived reference to that existence. As our ancestors, who did not know that air had weight, reaped unconsciously most of the benefits of the all-permeating atmospheric pressure, but lost, necessarily, that which depended upon the recognition and conscious use of its weight, so those who know not that God is, while they experience, almost as much as any, the blessing of His existence and His character, cannot have the blessing which arises only from taking into account the fact of Him, and of what He is." Let us be thankful then, if to-day, as we are girding our loins anew for the work of life, and for whatever life may bring—let us be thankful, if we can behold with Joshua the angel of Jehovah's presence, and, in setting out, pause a little to entertain and foster the strengthening vision.

"But what saith my Lord to His servant?" cried the son of Nun when he felt the august Presence about him, and bowed himself to the ground before it. "What saith my Lord to His servant? Ah! now that I have Thee here; now that Thou art revealed to me in the way, speak to me; tell me something. Surely, I shall hear some great thing from Thy lips—surely, some great secret will be whispered to me. With the Invisible Power thus consciously nigh me, I may expect wondrous words, important disclosures." We can understand and sympathize with the expectation, can we not? Have we not at times, imagined to ourselves, among the lonely hills or in the hush of a solemn sunset, Nature bursting into speech; the dumb, majestic sky breaking silence; a Voice issuing from out eternity? and fancied the breathless interest with which we should listen, to be instructed and enlightened *then*, as we had never been before; receiving perchance, some strange, grand news— some solution of life's mystery—or, at least, some precious help and hint towards a solution? What might not God Almighty tell, we are apt to think, if He were once found speaking. So thought Joshua, waiting in awed anticipation with his face to the earth. And from the mystic Presence overshadowing him, what syllables fell? What was it that *he* heard to whom *it* grew vocal? "Loose thy shoe from off thy foot, for the place whereon thou standest is holy." Was that all? That was all. No declaring of things that had been kept hidden, no weighty revealings. Only a plain and familiar admonition, to cherish and preserve within him a right temper of mind, a right spirit—to see to it that he walked reverently, and cultivated purity, as one who dwelt in a temple. That was all the heavens told him, when they leaned toward him with a word. "Take heed to yourself, to your character and conduct; be dutiful, be loyal to the vision that is yours. Recognize and answer the claim on you to be holy." Was the Hebrew leader disappointed, I wonder; as a youth has sometimes been, when, looking eagerly to learn from one who has grandly achieved in life, some special secret of success that should make life, and golden honours, easy, he has got from him nothing but talk about steady application, and patient, plodding toil.

And should we be disappointed, were the silent sky, in sending out a sound, to drop upon our ear no more than such an admonition as Joshua heard? What, however, do we need so much, for all present and future benediction, as to be taught a truer, finer ordering of ourselves? and what better, richer, more brightly fruitful New Year's gift could we have from above, than a deepened sense of duty, and a fresh impulse toward reverent and noble living? Yes, oh yes, "Blessed are the lowly in spirit; theirs is the kingdom of heaven. Blessed are the pure in heart; they shall see God."

XIV.

PRAYER.

O GOD, the lonely, awful height, too high for us to attain unto. Some few, perhaps, look up to us, while we look up to others, whose greater wisdom or greater goodness we feel, and these again look up to others still, who seem to move on levels of thought or character, above them; and, from the lowest to the loftiest, we all look up to Thee, the perfection of beauty, the Lord and the life, too, of the whole universe of souls. "Thine is the goodness, and the power, and the glory, and the victory, and the majesty; Thine is the kingdom; Thou art exalted as Head over all; both riches and honour come of Thee, and in Thy hand it is to make great and to give strength unto all. Wherefore now, our God, we thank Thee and praise Thy glorious Name."

It is good to think of Thee, and to remember that we have a Father who is the Ruler of princes, the Governor of the kings of the earth, whose household we are, both small and great, both rich and poor; beyond whose guiding and controlling hand nothing lies; who, without respect of persons judges according to every man's work; who, with an understanding that is infinite, is seeing evermore to our true interests; upon whom devolves the burden of planning and providing for our education. It is good to think of Thee, and to remember that Thou art appointing our times for us, and the bounds of our habitation, for ends that Thou hast chosen, and towards which all things are working—that we are not fortuitous developments, but Thy offspring, that we are not wandering waifs among the shadows of time, but children at home—that we are not *only* that which doth appear, but are more than we seem, related to an invisible world, spirits, partaking of the Spirit of God.

Great Father, come nigh to us, even into our inner consciousness, and awaken and draw out the filial elements that slumber, and call forth of Thine own within us. Quicken us with Thy hidden touch to increase of love, joy, peace, longsuffering, gentleness, goodness, faith; make the heart of sons to beat and grow strong in us, to the overcoming and governing of the heart of the flesh, to the guiding and sanctifying also, of the desires of the mind. Help us to meditate and wish in the light of Thy countenance, to breathe our gladness and our sadness in Thy presence; so may all sadness be soothed, all gladness refined, our meditation be sweet, and our wishes, —corrected where they are foolish or wrong, where they are worthy, deepened and intensified and made mighty to rule and mould the conduct.

We thank Thee, O Lord, for the pleasures of the summer days, for the world of beauty in the midst of which we walk, for the much which Thou hast given us to admire, and hast taught us to admire, for the love succours, and the love joys that are ours, for work and rest, for rest and work, for kindred and friends, for dawnings of light after anxious groping in the dark, for the recurring bliss of some new idea, some new stimulus to thought, some fresh discerning, for sunny memories and edifying fellowships, and hopes that inspire. We thank Thee, too, for the clouds which are Thy chariots—and gorgeous chariots they are sometimes, in the sunset; for the springs which Thou sendest into the valleys; for the trees that are full of sap, and the birds that sing among the branches; for the watering of the hills from Thy chambers, and for the food which Thou bringest forth out of the earth. May it please Thee "to give and preserve to our use the kindly fruits of the earth, so as in due time we may enjoy them." And bless the husbandmen by whom the fields are tilled; let not their labour fail; make them glad, if it may be, according to the days wherein they have been afflicted, and the years wherein they have seen evil; bringing them at length through straitness and difficulty into a larger place. Bless the humble toilers who toil for us at the plough and in the furrow—the rude, simple folk, whose lives are hard, and their knowledge small. May health and peace be in their cottages, and may their children grow up, through better school instruction, to receive some better inheritance. Those, too, we remember in our prayer, who go down to the sea for us in ships, and are in peril often upon the deep waters, with those who labour in factories and in dark places of danger underground, and those who are paid to fight for us if need be. "Let every man wherein he is called, therein abide with God," and "let us consider one another to provoke unto love and to good works." O Lord, look upon Thy family, and give grace to all Thy sons to feel and behave as *brethren*. Deliver us from envy, hatred, malice, and all uncharitableness. Make us ready and eager to be of use; may we seek the good of men, especially of such as are poor in that in which we happen to be rich, and such as need what we have the means of supplying, whether it be comfort in sorrow, assistance in difficulty, or instruction in ignorance. May the learned recognize that they are debtors to the unlearned, and the strong that they are debtors to the weak.

Inspire and guide with Thy Spirit, the few who are endowed above the many, with high position, with command and influence, with gifts and resources, to the end that they may be ministers to the many. Help any who have a dream that seems to them a vision, to tell it honestly and faithfully; and grant to the sons of wisdom to be ever redeeming the opportunity with timely wise words or deeds. Be with those to whom the voice says, "Write!"—to keep them pure and to teach them counsel; and direct and prosper their consultations who conduct the affairs of our nation, and are occupied with the making and shaping of laws for us. May integrity and a good understanding lead them always to such conceptions and such decisions, as shall truly meet the needs of the time, and tend to the true furtherance of the country's weal. We thank Thee for all noble craft, and all worthy craftsmen, for the service of large-hearted philanthropists, and for the frequent liberal devisings of wealthy merchants, praying that these may be so faithful in the mammon which is sometimes unrighteously used, as to be inheriting thereby, more and more in themselves, of the true riches.

We thank Thee for the faith that Thou art among us in divers gifts and distributions of the Holy Spirit, and that under Thy rule and governance we shall yet see greater things and better than these.

And in wishing blessing for all kindreds and peoples of the earth, we desire to unite to-day with the American nation in hearty thanksgiving for the hope of their President's recovery from the blow of the assassin, sincerely craving that the good hope may be realized, and the sufferer soon restored to the work and duties of his high post.

"Almighty God, who hast given us grace at this time with one accord to make our common supplications unto Thee; and dost promise that when two or three are gathered together in Thy name Thou wilt grant their requests; fulfil now, O Lord, the desires and petitions of Thy servants as may be most expedient for them, granting us in this world knowledge of Thy truth, and in the world to come life everlasting. And may the grace of our Lord Jesus Christ, and the love of God, and the fellowship of the Holy Ghost be with us all evermore."

SERMON.

GOODNESS AND MERCY BEHIND US.

"Surely goodness and mercy shall follow me."—PSALM xxiii. 6.
"The God of Israel will be your rearward."—ISAIAH lii. 12.

THESE two passages are the expression by different men, in different ages, of the same religious confidence—namely, confidence in an Unseen Presence shielding from harm, and ensuring blessing—in an Unseen Presence, encompassing the weak during their exposure to danger, and that might be depended upon for protection and support, whatever threatened, from whatever quarter, in an Unseen Presence, covering unguarded points, and accompanying unguarded moments.

In the Psalm, King David speaks, uttering there, probably, toward the close of his life, though under images borrowed, for the most part, from the scenes and occupations of his earlier days, the trust which a long experience had taught him—trust in the great Jehovah's watchful care and providence. He sings of Him first, as his

Shepherd ; and, remembering what he himself had been when a youth to his father's flocks upon the Bethlehem hills, the figure had a world of sweet meaning for him ; he, too, like those sheep of Jesse's that were once his charge, and which he tended and cherished so devotedly,—he, too, was in the hands of One who looked after the supply of his wants and the guiding of his steps ; who knew well how to restore him when he wandered from the right path ; who would not fail to be with him for comfort and strength in the dark valley—the valley of the shadow of death to which he was drawing nigh. Then, beginning afresh, he sings of Jehovah again as a royal Host, entertaining him with a feast, at which the wine-cup overflowed, and rich unguents were lavished, even while difficulties and troubles lay thick around him, and perils frowned. In the midst of these, in spite of these, the Lord gave him inward peace and happiness. He was a traveller through a toilsome, foe-infested desert, finding a banquet spread for him by the way, and able, notwithstanding the terrors of the desert, to sit down and enjoy. The Lord made him glad with His countenance, though the outward scene was gloomy and severe ; and then he winds up his song by representing Jehovah as a solid column of defence between him and pursuing enemies and evils. *They* might be following him fast and fiercely, but *He* was following him too, and much more closely. There were evils and enemies advancing upon him, perhaps, that he did not perceive, that he could not detect, whose secret, subtle tread was inaudible to him; but he rested in the assurance that with them, and ahead of them, always, was the Lord—the Lord mighty to save—the pledge, at least, of never-failing goodness and mercy for him in all that might betide; so that, however untoward or portentous the situation, he was living really, and would be living in a sanctuary all his days.

King David, who had sung thus, was no more. He had long since fallen on sleep, and been gathered to his fathers. But while, one after another, believing souls take their departure, faith survives and abides, their spirit remains; and now, far down the centuries, it is Isaiah, the seer, who in the book of his prophecy, repeats the same strain of holy confidence. Looking forward to a time of bitter adversity for his nation, during which they would be suffering bondage and oppression in exile from their land—he yet anticipates for them, as being the chosen people, still, notwithstanding their sin and its punishment, an ultimate glorious return. He sees, beyond the vision of lamentation and woe, beautiful upon the mountains, the feet of the messengers carrying glad tidings of deliverance; he sees the multitude of captives, their chains broken, pouring along the homeward road; going forth, not in haste nor by flight, as of old from the brickfields of Egypt, but at their leisure, and boldly; and he sees the safe progress and the successful issue of the march, secured by the attendance of an invisible escort, the Lord Himself, moving before them, and the God of Israel forming their rearward—a sure guard against aught of mischief creeping from behind, against aught of mischief that might come upon them unawares.

But these words of Isaiah and David have suggested to me certain reflections, which, if you listen and be still a little, I will endeavour to give you. And first, the ugly things that are lying in wait for us, sometimes, when we are wholly at rest and quiet, like ambuscades towards which all blindly, gay troopers ride, carolling love ditties or exchanging jests, and are suddenly cut down. How, sometimes, ugly things have lurked in our path, big with sorrow for us, that could so easily have been avoided, and would have been *had we only known*. But we knew not, we suspected not, and were allowed to go forward lightly, as though we were going to receive a boon instead of a crushing blow. Here we are tranquilly taking our way with no thought of danger, apprehending nothing; and calamity or catastrophe is impending, which one whisper of warning, an impulse to halt or turn aside, the starting of a new idea, might suffice to avert for us; but there is no sheltering rearguard. We are left to be fallen upon, and ravaged. If a hint could have been granted us, if something could have happened just to retard our steps or alter our movements, just to *incline* us even to caution and watchfulness,—the least thing might have been enough to procure a great redemption.

If, for instance, the President of the United States had but been haunted yesterday week by a strong presentiment of disaster; if, between him and the purpose of the would-be assassin, a mental impression or an obstructing circumstance had but been set up in arrest of the act which has caused such wide-spread alarm and anxiety—that might have issued so fatally for the sufferer, so lamentably for a great country; the feared fatal and lamentable consequences of which, however, we all rejoice to hope are now not likely to be realized! Often have men said, "Oh, why were we not led to hesitate *then*, to shrink back from proceeding, to change our course? Why did no foreboding rise within us? Had only something occurred to detain us a little, to make us lose that train or relinquish that enterprise." Occasionally, indeed, we are visited and disturbed before some tragic misfortune with an unaccountable anticipation of evil to which we refuse to listen, shaking it off determinedly, and thrusting it from us; and it has seemed to us afterwards as if a guardian angel had been striving to save us—as the angels sought to save Lot's relatives from the doom of Sodom—and, striving in vain, had been obliged to leave us to our fate. Now and again, how remarkably presentiments have come to be effectual in snatching from approaching ills! A man has renounced a plan, or withdrawn from a decision, in obedience to an impulse he could not explain, and of which he was half ashamed, while yet unable to resist it; and obedience to the mysterious impulse has proved his happy escape. Or else he has been hindered, to his extreme vexation, and the vexing hindrance has been his salvation. It was as though a presence had been following to shield and redeem him where he saw not the lion crouching in his path. But in the case of each of us, how close we have often been, doubtless, without perceiving it, to calamities which yet were spared us; that drew very nigh while we heard no sound of their footfall beside us, and, all but touching us, passed harmlessly by! Were the woeful things which since our birth have *almost* befallen us, and which unknown to ourselves we have just evaded by a hair's-breadth—were these displayed before us, what a grim and ghastly host we might be found confronting! We little dream of the number of instances in which we have run carelessly along the edge of dark pits, within an ace of engulfment; of the terrible pursuers that have been at times at our heels, and on the point of seizing us. Not seldom, would our heart be strangely agitated with wonder and awe and gratitude, at night, could we but see all the misery that has been barely missed by us, all the blessed restrainings and avertings during the hours.

And, again, may we not say that goodness and mercy are frequently following us to our salvation from threatening mischief,—in the truer thoughts, the better feelings, that start up behind our frequent false inclinings, and prevail against them; in the wiser mind that presently wakes to arrest and scatter the foolish; in the wholesomer heart that rises to check the unhealthy? If all the inward, evil promptings we have had, had been carried out; if we had been abandoned to *do* all the wrongness or the folly that we have been transiently disposed to do! From what degradations we have been snatched once and again, upon the brink of which we were tottering; as we lingered and leaned ready to slide, there was that from within which laid hold on and drew us back.

St. John, of the Apocalypse, beheld a door opened in heaven, and heard a voice inviting him to ascend; have we not on occasions beheld in our own breast, a door opened *in hell*, and then, suddenly shut to as by an angel's hand? We have been sorely tempted, and have seen then, the doleful depth to which we might have sunk; and were capable of sinking—have seen then, possibilities of evil in us that made us shudder; but goodness and mercy followed preventingly, and we were saved. Or suppose that in certain moods of ours, in certain moments of passion or soul-relaxation, opportunity had concurred—as with some in like moods and moments it has concurred to their undoing, to their headlong plunge into baseness, or crime—how different matters might have been with us to-day? The opportunity that might have been our ruin, did *not* concur, and in its absence we were delivered from the evil that lay waiting to be developed by it. How much of what would be termed our virtue, seems to us, when we reflect, to have been but a providential hindering of our inclination towards, and our ripeness for, what would have been the very opposite of virtue! We have been guarded and hedged in, to preservation from ourselves. Elements of the tiger and the beast have been caught sight of again and again, out of which, we feel that, under duly exciting circumstances, something dire and dreadful might easily have been produced. Is it not so with the best of us? Can we not say, on looking back, that here and there, in this and that crisis, it was as though God had been our rearward, warding off from us devastation and havoc that threatened? How near we were to it! Had the environment of the hour been other than it was, who can tell what our conduct would have been? Are there not those of us, moreover, who may be able, and are moved, in reviewing their lives, to give thanks for sorrows or misfortunes that came just in time to be the means of rightening and restoring them when they were beginning to go wrong, when they were sinking into deadness or worldliness of soul? Do they not recall with gratitude, how, in some directions in which they were fondly eager or feverishly ambitious, a disappointment met them—a disappointment that contributed, painful and bitter though it was, to stay the spiritual decline that had begun within them—to turn them from the low flats on which it found them, back to the higher levels, the clear, sweet uplands from which they had drifted? Oh, the rescue there was for them in that sore disappointment—the salvation of which it was the instrument! It is to them as though they had been visited by an angel of the Lord, sent to save them.

In much prosperity, perhaps, you were gradually deteriorating—fine a man as you seemed, and enviable to others—you were gradually deteriorating inwardly, gradually losing your former fineness of heart, and who shall say to what it might not have grown, had the prosperity continued uninterrupted; but there came sharp reverses, trouble and grief poured in, and in the bath of deep waters you recovered tone ; it helped to brace and establish you anew.

And now once more ; true as it is that every day bears upon it the fruit of yesterday's sowing, that we are constantly inheriting, whether for good or evil, what we have been, and have been doing— true as this is, yet are we not often conscious that we are spared reaping the full harvest of a foolish or unworthy past—that there is a withholding in part of what we might have suffered from it, of what it might have inflicted upon us? Have we not felt, when enduring the judgment of some previous mistake or misdeed, that the judgment was tempered with mercy—that it was not so severe as it might have been expected to be ; that while pursued certainly, by the mistake or misdeed, the pursuit was less fierce than we could have hoped? We indulged, say yesterday, in feelings —we gave way to passions, that should have made us weaker before temptation to-day than we are— that were calculated to leave us more distempered, more badly susceptible than we are. They were succeeded by pangs of repentance, by a flood of deep contrition that has stopped and turned the effect of them, and swept us above their evil working. We have been delivered thus from a good deal of the scourge they had prepared for us It must have seemed to us all, at times, that goodness and mercy were following our transgressions, to some mitigation of their consequences, that we were not receiving from them all the stripes that we might have looked to receive And has it not surprised us at times, to note the ultimate shaping and expression of one whose early habits and doings we had known and lamented—whose ultimate shaping and expression, on *account* of these, we had always foreboded would be far otherwise—to note how much more comely he has grown to be than these had ever led us to anticipate? As Tennyson says,—

> " How many a father have I seen,
> A sober man, among his boys,
> Whose youth was full of foolish noise,
> Who wears his manhood hale and green."

Oh, yes, while the iniquities and inequities of the past *are* laid upon us, we are constrained to acknowledge often that they might well have burdened us more heavily than they do. They are not upon us to the uttermost, there are withholdings — there are abatements, as though a gracious Power were keeping them back from us in part. Yet with Tennyson may we add,—

"Who would preach it as a truth
To those that eddy round and round."

For no wayward or erring motion is ever without its resilience, a resilience not to be escaped; and in what grievous and terrible forms such motions are constantly returning! Oh! the severe flagellations, frequently, of an unwise or faulty past! When, however, they are most severe; when we appear to be spared nothing; when the strokes fall pitilessly, are we not still to believe and shall we not,—that if goodness and mercy have not followed to moderate and soften them; goodness and mercy are surely following, *in* them; that the cruellest onset of the furies, which our wrongdoings have evoked, is *itself* the rearward of the God of Israel, to give us deliverance, and to bring us home through their blows: for, "to Thee, O Lord, belongeth mercy, *because* Thou renderest to every man according to his works"?

XV.

PRAYER.

LORD and Father of our spirits, who art in secret, let us not be at this time too outward and abroad to find Thee ; let us not miss Thee through being insufficiently retired in soul. Give to us that still inwardness which is needful if we would see God—that withdrawal of heart into the heart's own sanctuary, not made with hands, where Thou hidest, waiting to shine forth. Help us to turn aside and uncover our head, and take the shoes from off our feet, as Moses did in the Midian desert, that, like him, we may hear the mystic voice and know in ourselves, though without being able to prove, that there is One above who bears the people's burdens, and rules for its ultimate redemption a world made subject to vanity, and groaning and travailing in pain until now. Comfort of God, which we need by the way, bring us into the hush of silenced earthly passion and silenced self-will, and into the seclusion of spirit where Thou mayest be able to visit us and to build us up with power from on high. As Christ took from the crowd, and drew out of the town, the blind man of Bethsaida, that his eyes might be opened, so lead us to the inner quiet in which some divine vision may be granted us.

We thank Thee, O Lord, for the use and benefit of the multitude, for the busy streets, for the goodly exercise and discipline of work, for the books that interest us, and the questions that engage and agitate us, for the education of life's toil and battle, for the noise of controversy and inquiry. And how near art Thou to us in all these continually ; in all these how near are we to Thee, as we seek to be dutiful and true? But to-day, for a while, we would come apart, like the disciples with the Saviour, that He who has been with us, and with whom we have been, may show Himself anew to our hearts.

God, our Father, under whose teaching we all are, whose is every day of our life for some instruction of us, for the working within us of something toward our further culture; let Thy will be done upon us; make us pliant and ductile under Thy hand; may we not fail to learn the thing which Thou meanest. Behold, we know not what Thou meanest in the situations that befall us, in the often strange medley of circumstance to which we are subjected, and we do not need to know. Enough for us to be accepting reverently and striving daily, according to our lights, amid all; so surely will Thy purpose be fulfilled in us, and Thou wilt see and be satisfied, though we discern not. And we thank Thee for the thought that that may not be the all of good which we are *sensible* of deriving from the experiences and the discipline of life; that under it we may be acquiring much which we do not perceive, of which we are unconscious, like our own children at school. Yes; there is more being wrought in us, doubtless, with Thy hand than we know, and we must wait, doubtless, for our removal hence to know *all* that Thou hast taught, and art teaching us here within these shadows of time. Then, perhaps, in another place, in the future world, gains of the present will appear, to fill us with surprised delight—the conscious gainer of five talents discovering that in gaining them, he has gained something besides and greater, even a store of secret quality fitting him for rule over five cities.

Lord, when we look back, now and again, as we pursue our course, and call to remembrance what we have done, what our works and actions have been—some praiseworthy and some blameworthy, some pleasant to recollect and some painful and humiliating—at such times, give us to feel that it is not so much what we have *done* which is important, as what we have *become* through the doing—the effect it has left behind in us, the inward man it has fashioned and made —that the great thing, the eternal thing, is the *being* which the doing has gone to form ; and that there may be more good fruit in us from some mistakes and sins over which we have sorrowed to repentance, though the memory of them be covering us with shame, than from some brave and comely deeds, on which we can reflect with satisfaction. Give us to feel this, we pray Thee.

And we thank Thee, O God, for all helpful thoughts ; for all that have come to us in solitude, when " as we mused the fire burned," for all that has been ministered to us toward our edifying in intercourse with men, for all inspiring ideas or suggestions and impressions that we have got from books. We thank Thee for the wisdom of the ancients with which we have been instructed, and for the good which, unconsciously, wise children have sometimes done us ; for quickening words of sacred Scripture, and cheerings and stirrings of noble song. And, while we are being helped thus from divers quarters, and in divers manners, grant that we ourselves may be found helpful, and more—the older we grow— more healthy and happy in our personal influence, more richly soothing where sooth is needed, more apt and discreet in counsel where counsel is needed, more capable, too, as being no longer children, of entering into the pains and pleasures of others with lively, succouring sympathy ; and, however the years may fail to bring us the worldly success and prosperity which they bring to some, or the social elevation and power, may they bring us increasingly the more blessed wealth of inward peace and content, and the nobler strength and command of self-control ; and yet, again, as life goes on, may our temptations to evil become fewer and fewer, not through dimness of eye and dulness and decay, but through our own finer sensibilities and holier affections, and the growth within us of a pure heart.

Give might to those, O God, who, while desiring earnestly high things, and wistfully pursuing after them, are sorely beset and retarded, as yet, by rampant lower impulses, against which they have to struggle hard, and which do often drag them down into the mire, when they fain would climb. Let Thy mercy help such with strength to persevere, and with the comfort of the hope that some day that which hinders shall wax weak beneath their constant resistance, and die away, and they shall be glad because they are quiet.

To Thee, O Father of the world, we commit the keeping of all souls ; desiring, at Thy feet, counsel for the perplexed, consolation for the afflicted, with the grace of patient endurance, corrective influences for the erring and the disobedient, deliverance from deterioration of heart for the outwardly busy and the men of numerous cares, good influences and sound training for the young, unexpected friends for the dernful and desolate, a spirit of meekness, with ambition to serve, for the possessors of brilliant gifts, guidance for those who are called to guide, and wisdom for those who rule. Thou, who hast made and lovest all ; in Thy hands we leave all, trusting and worshipping Thee in the faith of Thy Son Jesus Christ, both now and for ever, world without end. Amen.

SERMON.
EDIFICATION BY PLEASING.

"Let every one of us please his neighbour for his good to edification."—ROMANS xv. 2.

HUMAN follies, mistakes, and confusions, are continually expiating themselves, it may be said, in the instruction that flows from them, in the warnings and lessons of wisdom which they furnish toward the education and progress of mankind. There must needs be heresies among us, and faults and infirmities also, that through them we may be taught a knowledge and receive impressions not otherwise acquirable, perhaps. These things are instrumental to life and growth—fadings, failings, from off the great tree of humanity that contribute in their measure to feed and nourish its roots. Only consider, for instance, how profitable have been to us the errors, ignorances, and strifes of the Primitive Church—the manifold valuable teaching they have been the means of providing for us! We owe to them nearly all the New Testament

Epistles. It was in Apostolic conflict with them that ideas of duty were expressed, and divine principles of conduct disengaged, which are serving still for counsel and guidance.

Now, the exhortation of the text was given in relation to a matter then disturbing somewhat the little Christian community in Rome, namely, the vexed question concerning the eating of meat that had been sacrificed to idols. Such meat—the part of the offering apportioned to the officiating priest and the worshipper—was often used afterwards in social entertainments, or found its way into the market for sale; and not a few of the brethren,— most probably the Jewish converts, who had been brought up from their childhood to look with horror on everything connected with idolatry,—were conscientiously unable to touch it. They deemed it unclean and polluting; and, while refusing it themselves, felt strongly that it ought to be shunned by all the members of the body. To see any of the body partake of it, revolted and pained them. But others had no scruples of the kind, holding that nothing in the shape of bodily food could morally defile a man; and these, claiming the right to enjoy the liberty of what they thought, correctly enough, their clearer, larger views, were wont to indulge freely in the so-called accursed flesh, to the distress of those who shrank from it—rather too proud, perhaps, of showing how superior they were to the superstitious notions by which some were fettered; rather too regardless, perhaps, of the wounding and offence they caused. And why should they not gratify themselves in doing what their more enlightened consciences allowed them to do? To which St. Paul replies: "Because it afflicts so, the weaker souls among you, whom you, as the stronger, are bound to consider, and to avoid troubling when it can be done without contravening or surrendering principle. In their presence, then, instead of following your own wishes by eating what you feel quite justified in eating, and what I quite hold with you may lawfully be eaten, and need not be recoiled from—in their presence, forego your own wishes, and seek to make things agreeable to them, by abstaining—they must not be unnecessarily grieved by you;" and he urges such gracious giving up to them, not for their mere comforts' sake, but for the *edification* of them to which it would be likely to conduce, whose edification, they being admittedly weak in the faith, the strong in the faith ought certainly to be willing to promote, and anxious to promote in any way that might

Edification by pleasing. 253

seem fitted. "You would acknowledge," he says, "that in comparison with yourselves they are poor, crude, unformed creatures, wanting sadly building up; help, then, to build them up, by *pleasing* them with your abstinence from the idol meat when you happen to be at table together." And can we not perceive how that would be calculated to assist in edifying them? Would not the calmer, happier frame of mind produced, be more favourable to sound thinking and healthy growth than a mind ruffled and fretted? Our best, whether in judgment or action, is not so easily reached when we are suffering discomposure and worry, as when the heart within us is tranquil and at peace. Again, would not the generous self-abridgment submitted to on their account have a beneficial effect on them in calling forth their admiration and affection? Could they observe it and not be stimulated by it to respond with something of a better spirit than before; and not be moved by it to behave more worthily or more sweetly than they had done? Ah, the power which there *is* often, in a little magnanimity shown to another, of starting finer motions in *his* breast!

Yet, further, would not the kindly attention paid to their scruples—the kindly respect evinced for them by those who did not share them—would it not tend to soften their prejudice against the views of the other side, to make them more ready to weigh arguments from thence, and more open to conviction; winning them, perhaps, to re-examine the subject with a care and a candour they had never previously given it, with a care and a candour that might end in their ultimate conversion to truer ideas? The mistaken, are too frequently averted from the truer ideas with which we would possess them, and driven to hug more tenaciously their own, by the contemptuous or derisive treatment which these receive. With a lack of due tenderness, and due reverence on our part, for what they honestly think, we help to keep them where they are, and prevent the requisite listening to and entertainment on their part, of what might otherwise gradually commend itself to them. The Apostle was right in his suggestion that for the strong ones to please the weak, by refraining from the particular food, out of regard to their sentiments respecting it, would be for the good of the latter, to their probable edification.

And now, for a few minutes, concerning *pleasing* people, as a means of edifying them. It is often more highly useful than we imagine. Simply to give pleasure to another ; to set him pulsing inwardly with new happiness, may involve for him a whole train of blessings. Many and great benefits may issue from it. If you have done nothing else, you have made the outward scene, and all life, look fairer to him. You have rendered his work easier, and lightened the weight of the burdens he is carrying. You have engendered a state of mind more open to miscellaneous sources of gratification, and more capable of extracting enjoyment from a multiplicity of things. Any envy that may have been rankling in his breast—any animosity or ill-will—will be for the time arrested and suspended, for the happy are never envious. He will throb more generously, judge more generously ; will be more able to rise above small vexations, and more ready to act forbearingly or kindly to others. And is not this much ? We never know how much further and higher good we are ensuring or providing for, in simply causing a human heart to sing for joy. Have we not seen a new suavity, a new tenderness, a new largeness appear in men, or glimpses of a better nature that had been slumbering, under a sudden cheering of their spirits, or a sudden glow of gratified feeling ? —and have they not shown then, a wholesomer susceptibility than they had done? Have we not been encouraged then, to counsel or appeal to them with regard to duty, as before, perhaps, though wishing much, we had not ventured to do? Why, only look at the illuminated, beautified face of him to whom you have given delight, and do not think meanly of your work; believe that with the delight you have given him something more, even a touch, however transient, of healthier soul.

Some persons seem to entertain the idea that pleasing and edifying are opposed to each other—that the latter is not to be effected in conjunction with the former—that to edify, in fact, we must always more or less *dis*please. Edifying, with them, is probably, for the most part, to be exposing and rebuking faults; but that may not be to edification at all. The mere girding at faults frequently does more harm than good. The great thing is to try and foster a spirit, a condition, that may tend to wither or disperse the faults; and many faults there are which have their root in some unhappiness or misery, with the healing of which they would presently slough off and disappear. Let none of us imagine that we cannot edify without displeasing, or that there is no real edification to be wrought in mere pleasing. It is a mistake with us, by the way, that we are prone to show ourselves pursuing the two things apart, as when, for example, in discoursing to children we first tell a charming story obviously to amuse them, and then, growing grave and dropping into a more serious tone, proceed, with the obvious aim of doing them good, to append the moral—in the words of Charles Lamb, "tagging it to the end, like a 'God send the ship into harbour,' at the conclusion of our bills of lading." Now, in doing this, we mostly miss our mark; for with the termination of the story, and the commencement of the moral, the attention relaxes, and the children, saying to themselves, "Ah, he has finished amusing us, and is now going to do us good," learn to think of pleasure and edification as excluding each other.

Be satisfied then, often if you can but soothe or gladden; you may be contributing thereby to more redemption and purifying than you wot of. As the late Lord Lytton once wrote,—"To send a little child to bed happier, with a heartier thanksgiving, he knows not why, to the Author of all mercies, and a livelier fondness in his prayer for his parents; to cheer the moody veteran, who deems the young have forgotten him, with a few words that show remembrance of what he has done in

S

his generation; to comfort the dispirited struggler for fame or independence, in the moment of fall or failure, with a just commendation of the strength and the courage which, if displayed in the defeat of to-day, are fair auguries of success on the morrow. All this may not be so good as a sermon; but it is not every one who has the capacity to preach sermons, and any one is able to do this." Nor need we hesitate to add that the worth of it in its moral effect, may often equal or transcend the worth of many an excellent sermon. Be assured that help of the very best kind is sometimes ministered in giving pleasure; that to brighten with a ray of happiness a mourning or an aching heart, is sometimes to aid not a little in forwarding the salvation of a soul.

And why is it that in some homes we are conscious of such a charming and wholesome atmosphere, and find the members, one and all, so attractive and exemplary in their several characters? Were you to look into it, had you the opportunity of examining it closely, you would discover, probably, that they were all in the habit of considering much, each other; each thinking less of what would please himself, or herself, than of what would please the rest, or another. In a family where each does *that*, you will always have a beautiful atmosphere, and a set of refined people, too, with plenty of admirable quality; for they who are greatly given to study and consult the happiness of others, do become themselves greatly edified, are built up into more and more nobleness of nature, and will exert continually, without purposing, or aiming at it, an edifying influence. It is not alone that we often edify those whom we please, in pleasing them, but that, in forgetting ourselves to please, we so promote our own edification as to render our very breath edifying.

But now, will this do? Is it enough to say, "Let us go forth to please"? Much depends on the sort of person you are, on your fundamental motive and inspiration. One must start with a sincere interest in men, and a pure affection for them. Observe how St. Paul puts it, "not to please yourself, but your neighbour." He implies a love for others which loses sight of self, and is prepared to deny self for their happiness. There is a pleasing of others, you know, for our own comfort, as when a man relieves a beggar to get rid of him and be left at ease. I may wish and endeavour to gratify you, not from care for you, but for myself, in order that I may be gratified.

It is thus especially with the sultry flatterer. It pleases *him*, and gains your favour toward *him*, to soothe you with his blandishments,—for flattery is often sweet even when we are conscious that it is but flattery,—and not seldom, he will be seeking for himself the malicious enjoyment of seeing how far you can be fooled, how much you are capable of absorbing, what amount of extravagant stroking you can take, and be content to purr under; after which, he departs to enjoy the further pleasure of despising you, and, perhaps, to exemplify the truth of the asseveration, that "the greatest flatterers are frequently the greatest slanderers." One may be as mean and selfish and mischievous in laying himself out to please, as another in seeking to torment or irritate. But what is it that would lead you to try and minister gratification? Is it a pure love? Then you may follow your impulse safely. You will never then, be led to minister thus, by pandering to unworthy passion, by encouraging and aiding men in evil, by speaking or acting in any way in which the pleasure given would involve their moral distempering or tend to work them harm. "Only love"—as St. Augustine has said, in his often-quoted sentence—"only love, and do what you like."

But will the true good of others always admit

of our pleasing them? Alas, no! Unless we be heedless of edification, and hostile to it rather than auxiliary, we must sometimes displease and render unhappy. I have read of somebody, with whom it was a maxim to "make no one angry or sad;" but the love "which seeketh not her own," would surely find it very difficult indeed, now and again, and scarcely possible, to carry out that maxim. It could only be done by consenting now and again to let things go wrong, by neglecting to attempt any bettering of them. We must e'en discompose and vex occasionally if we would help and heal. How disturbing and distressing Christ could be! How often He pained or ruffled people, sending them from Him like the rich young scribe, grieved by His saying and very sorrowful, or like the Pharisees, mortified and stung! What trouble of dissatisfaction—self-dissatisfaction—He often stirred; yet was there ever a heart more tender and philanthropic than His? He was full of the richest good-will to men, and loved not to have to wound, nay, was Himself wounded in wounding. And the question is, what you are centrally meaning and pursuing in displeasing, and whether you displease with reluctance and regret; for there are those, it seems to me, who rather like doing what they should only be able to do strenuously against their inclination. In rebuking or condemning, you hear them remark, perhaps, with an air of stern resignation, " We must not always care to please; we must not shrink from uttering what is right, and needful to be uttered in the interests of truth and progress, however afflicting it may be "—which is quite true—but all the while, they secretly enjoy rebuking and condemning, when it ought to be unpalatable to them, and a bitter task.

Beware of learning to grow fond of any censurings, opposings, or protestings to which duty may call you, which, for the sake of edification, it may be incumbent upon you to engage in. Herein lies the real Philistinism, not in opposing or protesting, but in becoming fond of it. Beware of this, as much as of yielding to the weakness which would shirk the opposing and protesting that are required for good, from a dislike to cause unpleasant tumult or vexation. Be able freely and unhesitatingly to create discomfort and misery, out of earnest concern for the peace of righteousness, while at the same time inwardly crucified with the work, and bewailing the harsh necessity; yet withal, let Love teach you how much is to be done in aid of edification, simply by aiding happiness and giving pleasure.

XVI.

PRAYER.

O THOU, of whom Christ spake with joy as revealing hid things to babes,—lead us, we beseech Thee, into the true child-spirit; educate it within us; help us to be purifying and refining ourselves toward it more and more, that we may see into Thy heavens and behold the golden streets that appear not; that clouds and skies, winds and calms, truth and life and duty may take us into their confidence and tell us secrets that are not told to *any* soul—that whatsoever good and divine thing, pride or worldliness, irreverence or distrust, hardness of heart or an unalert unquestioning mind may tend to keep concealed, we may have disclosed to us and enjoy possession of. Let us not be silly babes, who are answered according to their folly, whose frivolousness finds nothing serious, whose littleness finds nothing great; nor tough and stunted babes whose growth is arrested, who only *seem* to kneel and bow the head, because they are dwarfs; but let us be the brisk, fresh, nimble, earnest babes, whom Christ contemplated, and of whom He Himself was supreme Example, who was always, through all his years, from Bethlehem to Calvary, the holy Child, Jesus. Convert us to His simplicity, His healthy awe, His sensitiveness and liberty of spirit, on whom the heavens opened, and the angels of God ascended and descended. May we be not only humble, but in faith bold and daring, not only submissive, but full of energy and passion, not only meek to receive instruction, but forward to inquire. Give us, like children, to be ever speculating and asking and thirsting to know, and to be ever at rest and courageous as those who dwell in their Father's house and beneath the shadow of His wings. So may we be richly taught of Thee, and have Thy hid things revealed to us; so may we be plastic to Thy moulding hand, and open to hear in all that speaks, its very divinest message, its very finest sound.

O Lord, our souls have their seasons as Nature hath; it is not always May with them, nor always December; they know summer and winter, seed-time and harvest; they sow and reap and gather into barns: now, it is gloom with them, "the white mist clings like a face-cloth to the face, and the land is still;" and now, joy clothes them with garments of praise, and they lie bright and warm in the sun. Be Thou with us in all our inward seasons, that we may not fail to realize the promise of any, nor suffer loss and injury beneath the threatening of any; that none may leave us harmed by the experience, however for the time we may seem to be disordered or endangered, and that none may visit us with their grace in vain. Be Thou with us in all, that in each there may be some contribution to us, some ministry for us; in our changing moods let Thy unchanging love be ever ruling and overruling them for good. When the pulse is low, and the spirits droop, then, guard us from disease; when the heart is filled with rejoicing, then, sanctify the joy, and guide and control its utterance. We thank Thee for all true and beautiful doing that is found in us, for works and deeds of which we need not be ashamed, for the worthy way in which we have been able to conduct ourselves under trial and temptation, and in different situations of life. May we wait with patient hope for the true and beautiful *being* which is not yet, but towards which we are thus gradually advancing, and which every right-doing goes to help in forming. We think sometimes how much better we have done than we are: may it be our thought and our comfort then, that we have been sowing the seed of something better that we shall be hereafter, that no action is lost, but is to be found again in ultimate character, when "every one shall receive the things done in the body according to that he hath done, whether it be good or bad." Forgive us, O God, that we have so often failed to do well, have so often been weak and wayward, and acted below the highest we saw, to subsequent reproach of heart, missing the opportunity afforded us of adding to our moral strength and stature, and adding instead, to the strength of the evil or the defect in us that will yet have to be conquered. We mourn over the many wrong-doings of which we hear and read, over the daily record of vice and crime in our midst. What iniquities, what manifold iniquities are wrought every day beneath the sun! But we thank Thee for the many right things and noble that are done among us, for the abundant salt of the earth, for the multitude of just, upright, gracious lives on which the heavens look down, and we thank Thee for the faith that Thou art against them that do wickedly, and with them that yearn and labour for needed healings and redemptions.

We thank Thee for the faith that there is no lost piece of silver—bent, tarnished, disfigured—that does not bear upon it, under whatever dark coating, Thy image and superscription—that there is no sinner, no vilest transgressor of mankind who is not Thy child, after whose recovery and education Thou wilt have to see. We are sad often for the sufferings of which we hear and read, sufferings that we can do nothing to relieve or soothe, which we have no power to minister to. The story of them comes to us, and we can only sigh, and pass on. Alas! for the multitude of sick beds on which men writhe in pain; for the multitude of hearts stricken and torn with anguish; for the multitude of them that eat and drink in misery. But we thank Thee for the sympathy and the succour which suffering is ever calling forth; that in every place where it groans some pity is shown, some hands are stretched out to aid. Let us not be sad for what we cannot remedy or mitigate, while we are failing toward those around us to whom we might give comfort or render service, whose burdens we might assist to lighten; or while, through our negligence, our thoughtlessness, our want of love, some near to us, are being troubled and made less happy than they might be. Let us cease from useless tears, to be and do whatever we are able to be and do, however little that may be, in the way of kindly helpfulness. Be Thou, merciful Father, in the house of mourning, where loved ones lost, are wept for, or loved ones in pain, are anxiously watched and nursed ; where the shadow of affliction is dark and heavy, or the cross of disappointment is borne. Be Thou in such houses to sustain and sanctify, to draw forth the bruised heart in resignation and trust toward Thyself, and out of weakness to make strong. Be with those with whom friends are few, whose feet walk in lonely places, where there are none like-minded, whom the winter of adversity, or the breath of misrepresentation and slanderous tongues may have left forlorn and desolate, like a tree stripped of its leaves by autumn winds. Be with such, we pray Thee, and so inwardly and so intimately that it shall be enough for them that Thou art with them, the Father in secret, who seeth and understandeth all. Accept these our prayers and meditations, which we make in the faith of Thy Son Jesus Christ, our Saviour, who for His revelation of Thee to the soul, is worthy to receive thanksgiving and honour and blessing, both now and for ever. Amen.

SERMON.
RESPECT OF PERSONS.

"My brethren, have not the faith of our Lord Jesus Christ, the Lord of glory, with respect of persons."—JAMES ii. 1.

"THE Just One"—such, we are told, was the name by which the writer of this Epistle was known in Jerusalem, where, resembling the ancient saints of the nation even in outward aspect, "with the austere features, the linen ephod, the bare feet, the long locks and unshorn beard of the Nazarite," his severe righteousness commanded universal reverence; the people, it is said, vying with each other to touch the hem of his garment. Here was a bishop to whom men bowed low, not in awe of his official dignity, but in homage to the sanctity of his life; and his great anxiety seems to have been that they who bowed to him might be taught and constrained to copy the holiness they admired. Tradition relates that his knees grew dry and thin from his continual kneeling in prayer for the turning of the disobedient to the wisdom of the just. His

Epistle, at all events, declares most unmistakably, the earnestness with which he desired and sought the improvement of morality. It is nothing but a series of impassioned exhortations to good conduct, mingled with stern rebukings of the vices and infirmities to which he saw his countrymen prone; such as religious formalism, fanaticism, fatalism, blind partisanship, bitter-speaking, falsehood, boasting, impatience, oppression of the poor, and mean truckling to the rich.

Some have insinuated concerning St. James that he was behind the other Apostles considerably, in acquaintance or in sympathy with the essential principles and peculiarities of Christianity, that he was not possessed and penetrated, equally with them, by the distinctive truths of the Gospel, because from his pen no Gospel doctrine flows. What, however, are the moral admonitions and appeals which he is wholly occupied in uttering, but the expression of his fervent longing to see its accepted truths conformed to, and carried out in the details of daily practice? May we not assume that he had learned them so perfectly, and had so deeply drunk them in, as to perceive intensely, the behaviours they ought to produce in the various relations and conjunctures of life, until moved by the vision, and by his knowledge of how these behaviours were wanting on the part of the Christianized Jews scattered abroad, he felt it his special mission, in addressing them, not to expatiate at all upon the Gospel they had embraced, but to devote himself entirely to the task of showing them what manner of men their reception of it required them to be? Yes, his abstinence from enlarging on doctrine, meant, doubtless, his absorbing solicitude to inculcate, and procure action, corresponding with the doctrine held. The "just one" yearned for consistency, and instead of writing about the faith of our Lord Jesus Christ, the Lord of Glory, his own profound surrender to its influence, and vivid sense of the duties and obligations it involved, led him to write, for the present at least, simply about them. It must be his business to remind his readers how, believing as they did, they should be found conducting themselves on different occasions, and in different situations; and, against a particular grave inconsistency which he had witnessed among his fellow-believers, or into which he feared they were apt to fall, they are solemnly warned by him in the text, "My brethren, have not the faith of our Lord Jesus Christ, the Lord of Glory, with respect of persons." The two things, he implies,—faith in Him, and respect of persons,—should never be met together, so utterly incongruous were they, and opposed.

Now, "respect of persons," is a phrase which we all understand well enough. We use it to represent any bias of the opinion, the judgment, or the attitude, to the prejudice of right and equity, from a regard to the mere outward circumstances of individuals; any unfair slighting or disparagement of some, and undue courting or preference of others, on account of their belongings, of what they have or have not, irrespective of what they are. But as Archbishop Trench points out in his "Select Glossary of English Words," "We have forfeited the full force of the phrase, from the fact that 'person' does not mean for us now, all that it once meant. From *persona*, the mask constantly worn by the actors of antiquity, it once signified, by natural transfer, the part or rôle in the play which each sustains; as when an old English author writes, 'Certain it is that no one can long put on a *person* and act a part;' or as when Milton writes, 'If it be at all an honour to the *person* which he bore.'" "In the great tragi-comedy of life," comments the Archbishop, "each sustains a *person*

—one that of a king, another that of a hind; one must play Lazarus, another Dives; and this is the *person* which God—for whom the question is not, what person we are bearing, but how we are bearing it—does not respect." So, to respect persons is to allow our valuation and our treatment of men to be determined by the part allotted them, without reference to the way in which they fill it, or to that which they are in themselves; esteeming them according to their place and their possessions, rather than according to the spirit which they breathe in their place, whether it be high or low, and the life they live with their possessions, whether these be large or small.

St. James, you observe, proceeds to explain his dehortation with a hypothetical example. He supposes his readers to be convened in religious assembly, or in some assembly, when two strangers enter, the one, a man with gold rings and fine clothing, the other, a poor man in vile raiment; and looking, fastening, upon the signs of wealth in the former, they at once invite him to a good seat, while the latter, they direct to stand behind, or point him indifferently to some mean place. "Here," says the Apostle, "is an illustration of what I mean.' And what he would blame here, was not that two men of different social rank, and coming from different personal and domestic surroundings, should be found differently placed in public—the one higher up than the other—but the disposition the readiness shown, to pay honour and to offer indignity purely upon the ground of the individual's circumstances, in ignorance or in heedlessness of what his intrinsic quality might be.

Now, there are outward positions, and conditions, which we may assume to betoken worth or the want of it, which it may be taken for granted, have been gained or sunk into in consequence of something demanding and deserving homage, or reprobation and contempt. Finding the men in these positions and conditions, we may be warranted in bowing to them, or in flouting them, on that account. And there are lofty posts and offices, the holders of which we may assume to be worthy of special attention or deference *because* they are holding them ; that they have acquired them, that they have been chosen, elected to them, may well lead us to infer that it is so ; and even when we are in doubt concerning the men, when we have reason to believe that they are far less noble than their posts and offices might suggest, and are aware, perhaps, of that in them which, were they not thus placed, would leave them with no claim whatever to distinguishing consideration or observance; yet, so long as they are thus placed, we may still give them such consideration or observance out of regard for the dignity of the post or office, and from a becoming a laudable desire still to magnify it. St. Paul, you will remember, immediately apologized for his rough and passionate rejoinder to the man who had ordered him, during his defence, to be smitten upon the mouth, when he learned that the unfair malignant magistrate was none other than the Hebrew High Priest; anxious not to fail in reverence for the sacred office which Ananias held, however little he might be able to revere Ananias himself.

Then again, there may be considerable variations of behaviour to people of different circumstances, in which we are not at all to be charged with respecting persons. While equally courteous to all, according to their several conditions or their several relations with myself, I cannot possibly salute, entertain, or conduct my intercourse with all in the same manner. Altogether apart from the question of character, of worth, things are often involved in connection with rank and riches on the one hand, and with poverty and low station on the other, which must needs occasion, as they demand also, difference of behaviour; "and to exhibit," as one writes, "an uniformity of carriage to all, with no distinction, would argue a want of penetration or a want of sensibility." But the vice to be deprecated, and which under more than a single form, may be encountered among us, is the vice of sacrificing or subordinating, in our social regards, regard for the moral to regard for the material—of allowing the *person* of men, in the ancient sense of the word, to influence unduly our feelings and our attitudes towards them—to make us indifferent or unjust to the men themselves, ready to condone their badness, or to ignore their goodness. The author of "Ecclesiasticus" wrote: "It is not meet to despise a poor man that hath understanding, neither is it convenient to magnify a sinful man." But there are those, in opposition to his judgment, who think it both meet and convenient; who, while unattracted by aught of sterling worth in the garb of poverty, and capable of treating it with contempt, will fawn and fawn upon brainless, hydrocephalous noodles, laden with ample means, and kiss and kiss in their drawing-rooms, the feet of moneyed lepers, who, were it not for the money, they would scarcely care to touch by the hand. Men are courted by them, welcomed to their homes, introduced to their families, and made much of, in spite of their known moral gracelessness or shabbiness, because of the handsome property, or the fine position, which would be suffered to cover a still greater multitude of sins: and men are studiously held aloof from, are left out, discarded, discountenanced by them, in spite of their known excellence and refinement, because they are without the accidents of property and position, or because, perhaps, while sufficiently well-to-do, they happen to be engaged in some traffic, in some form of honest industry, which is not considered to be quite the thing. "Wisdom," said Solomon, "is good with an inheritance." And how it is enhanced in our eyes often, when allied with an inheritance! How the inheritance sets it off, as a gold frame a picture; increases its weight and authority; secures it readier recognition and deeper admiration, or louder applause. How brightly then, only a little of it shines; and how much more commanding and impressive it is, how much more meekly listened to, than the same wisdom upon the lips of one who is but wise and poor. And virtues, which in lofty station receive exuberant homage, can frequently be witnessed in lowly station with comparative indifference.

Then, there is the worship which many are always prepared and in haste to offer to success, without caring to ask how it has been won. If you have but succeeded they rush to crown you, heedless altogether of what you may be the while, or of the means by which the consummation has been reached; ready at all events, to accept it presently as a full atonement for all which they may have perceived and felt to be ugly, and which, but for it, might have led them to spit upon and renounce you; which, had you miserably failed, would have provoked infallibly their utter condemnation and scorn. Have we not heard it declared concerning some foolish and reckless, or disingenuous and unprincipled proceeding, that "nothing could have justified such a proceeding but success," as though to succeed, carried with it, in the esteem of the speaker, the absolution of all trespasses, and in failure only lay disgrace and shame? And how apt we are to suspect the latter—to look down upon it with disdain, to shrink away and pass by on the other side, with no disposition to inquire what beauty of faithful effort or noble integrity it may hide, and when we know perchance, that there is nought but what is worthy behind it, and should be able to say out, heartily, "The man's a man for a'. that!" "How much more pleasant," writes one, "do the qualities and actions even of a friend appear, when his path is marked with success, than when it is attended with disappointment, and how much more favourably do we think of ourselves in prosperity than in adversity." Yes, there is a tendency with us all to smile upon success, and to let it blind us a little to what may be deserving of frowns, which is one form of the vice protested against by St. James.

Now he protests against it to his readers, upon the ground of its entire inconsistency with their faith in the Lord Jesus. This faith of theirs, he maintained, ought to keep them perfectly free from it. "How can you be guilty of it," he asks, "while you are believing in Him as the Lord of Glory? Inconsistency—it is not always indicative of dishonesty, hypocrisy, or unreality. It may proceed from mere ignorance that does but require to be instructed—from lack of discernment. Men sometimes hold certain beliefs in all sincerity, and with a measure of earnestness, which yet in certain of their actions they are unconsciously contradicting. They do not see what is involved in them. They do not see what follows from them.

There are bearings and applications of them to which they are not alive; they need to be shown these; and *that* may be all that is needed to set them conforming at once, more truly, to what they hold. So with the Apostle's people. The incongruity of respect of persons with the faith which they cherished and confessed, may hardly have been perceived by them until they read in the church his word, "Jesus the Lord of Glory;" and then, perhaps, they saw and felt it, as they were reminded, how a poor low-born outcast Hebrew peasant was to them the incarnation of divinest grace and truth, of divinest dignity and beauty—how, in a poor low-born outcast Hebrew peasant, they acknowledged and worshipped the supreme Son of the Highest. To whom were they looking up daily with such profound reverence? who was their ideal of excellence, their chief among ten thousand, their splendid Prince and King? A man of no worldly wealth or station—a mean-clad Jewish carpenter. Should *they* then, be found affected and biassed in their social intercourses by mere outward appearance, and disposed to appraise men according to their circumstances? Should *they* be seen acting as if rank and riches must needs be associated with worth, and poverty or failure must needs be wanting in it? and shall *we*, while kneeling so meekly at the feet of the rude Galilean, and acknowledging Him in Sunday song and prayer to be the Lord of Glory? Of all inconsistencies there is none greater or more disgraceful, than to have the faith of Him with respect of persons.

XVII.

PRAYER.

LORD of all power and might, we rejoice in Thy works,—in what we see of divine beauty and order, in the means and ends, the processes and issues that command our admiration ; in the good and perfect gifts which we are gratefully sensible of receiving under Thy disposings ; of what are felt to be the mercies and blessings of life. We rejoice in Thy works, as the summer sun shines, and the summer-robed trees cast their shade, as flowers and fruits abound, and in the fields the corn swells and yellows towards harvest. When the land is at peace, when progress is manifest and truth exalted ; when worthy effort is crowned with success, and with seekings and searchings, knowledge grows ; when the ministry of dark things is visible, and good is found accruing from evil, *then* we rejoice in Thy works. Yet we would feel that there is more, much more in them to rejoice at than we perceive, that it is not only when we can sing, that glory is, but when also we are sorrowful and perplexed ; that could our eyes be opened to invisible secrets, as were the eyes of the prophet's servant on the Syrian hill, our weeping and complaining might often change to praise, and cause for joy be discerned in what now troubles and dismays. Lord, accept such songs as we are able and constrained to offer, and pity us when we can offer none,—however Thy work may be deserving of them,—but only sighs and lamentations instead, because that which would set us rejoicing is hidden from our sight. Thou knowest well that we cannot always admire and be thankful when there may be much ground for it, in consequence of our inability to see—to see what Thou art really doing in what is being done. Pity, then, the fears and tears of Thy children that are due to lack of vision, and when by reason of it we cannot be glad, though wisdom and goodness rule no less than when we are, help us at least to be trustful, and in the patience of faith and hope to possess our souls.

O God, how foolish, doubtless, we often are, not only in our mourning but also in our mirth, in our satisfactions as well as in our grumblings and discontents! If we are foolishly afflicted at times, how foolishly sometimes are we pleased! "Shouldest thou find comfort in these?" might well be asked of us now and again when we smile serenely or proudly strut. Could we but see ourselves as we are seen by larger, other eyes than ours! Yet Thou whose face is against them that do wickedly—Thou dost not scorn the mere foolishness of human ignorance or human weakness. It is not with Thee as it was with the fabled divinities of old, who amused themselves by laughing at the follies of men! Thou considerest our frame and makest allowance for all, and art graciously patient with us in the hope of our growing wiser, as Thou seest that we shall in due time. In the mean while let this be our prayer, that, however foolishly often we may both laugh and weep, we may never laugh or weep out of any baseness, out of any meanness. The Lord save us from all sadness that comes of wrong-heartedness and from being happy through defect of righteousness! Give us power to rejoice in sympathy with those holy angels of Thine, in whose presence there is joy when truth triumphs, when the fallen are raised, when one sinner repents; and make us capable of some participation in the distresses of Him whom zeal for Thy house ate up, and who was troubled for the multitude, because they fainted and were scattered abroad as sheep having no shepherd.

O God, great God, to whom are known the anxieties of us all, pity and forgive those—and there are many such—who have made a world of coarse care for themselves by their own wrong courses and choices, by their vain ambitions and foolish lusts, by their unwillingness to be content with moderate things. Comfort those—for there are such—who, in the midst of their days, with much work calling them, and little ones dependent on them for education and support, are painfully sensible of failing strength, or apprehensive that they are doomed to the hindrance of ill health, perhaps to the interruption of early death, and who look forward to the future with concern, not for themselves but for others that are dear to them. Merciful Father, Thou seest the inward pain of such, and their thoughts often upon their bed, in the nightwatches, and as we think of such we must need cast them upon Thee. Be Thou the Counsellor of those who are anxious to do well and wisely in difficult circumstances, under heavy responsibilities—in relations that require careful acting and the exercise of much sound judgment; and the Counsellor especially of all earnest-hearted parents in their domestic solicitudes, in their desire to order their households aright, in their endeavours to study the best for their children. Lord, Thou knowest how sincerely wisdom for duty is sometimes sought. Thou hearest the secret cry from the ends of the earth of them that seek it. Let the eyes of the blind see out of obscurity, and let the meek be satisfied with teaching. Purify the aims and anxieties of those who are set in high places, who are called to govern and rule, and bring to understanding those who err in spirit.

Be with us, we pray Thee, in all our thoughts and in all our occupations, to guide and sanctify. Make us wise in dealing with ourselves, that nothing of service which we might render may be lost to the world through any self-losing of ours, or self-vitiating, whether in body, mind, or soul. May we not fail to yield what we might yield and are meant to yield, from any neglect of self-attention, or from any untruthfulness, insincerity, or affectation.

Help us to be both profitable and pleasant in our circle, as the smell of a field which the Lord has blest. Teach us to be at once careful and careless of how we appear: for mere appearance is nothing, and on appearance much may depend;

and give to us for the happiness and refreshing of others, increase of those sweet manners that blossom from self-forgetfulness and love and an honest and good heart. Thou receivest these prayers of ours. Return them to us, we beseech Thee, in some quickening and strengthening of the spirit to seek more earnestly the good of our brethren, and for ourselves, the things that are at present above us, even the things that were fulfilled to perfection in Mary's Divine Son. "And unto him who is able to do exceeding abundantly above what we ask or think, according to the power that worketh in us, to Him be glory in the Church by Christ Jesus throughout all ages, world without end. Amen."

SERMON.

CHRIST'S PROMISE TO HIS APOSTLES.

PART I.

"And when He is come, He will reprove the world of sin, and of righteousness, and of judgment : of sin, because they believe not on Me ; of righteousness, because I go to My Father, and ye see Me no more ; of judgment, because the prince of this world is judged."—JOHN xvi. 8–11.

SUCH, according to the record, was Christ's prophetic announcement to His apostles of what would be effected by them after His own disappearance from the scene, through the energy of the new and higher spirit with which they would then be inspired. He has been warning them gravely, that they must expect no smooth and peaceful time for themselves when He should have taken His departure—that they must reckon, indeed, on encountering much trouble and storm. He and they had been standing comparatively alone among men. The world of their day was not particularly in love with them, did not regard them with particular favour; the Master had rather disappointed and offended it; there were signs, ominous signs, that it was growing tired of Him, and waiting its opportunity to arrest and crush Him. It would not be long, He has told them, before they would be left, without His supporting presence, to the tender mercies of this world, and would find its tender mercies cruel. It would hate them, as it had hated Him; would thrust them out of the synagogues; yea, and whosoever slew them would think that he did God service. His talk seemed to imply that they were going forth to be victims; only to be struck down and trampled on. And no wonder that, in His own words, sorrow "filled their hearts," because of the things which He foreboded.

But now, all at once, His tone changes, and He begins to paint another prospect—to describe their coming achievements and triumphs. Though outwardly assailed and ill used, they were to be inwardly comforted and strengthened. In the midst of their sufferings, a great sustaining, animating spirit would descend upon and burn within them; and, thus endowed from above, it would be theirs to influence gradually and profoundly the mind and heart of the hostile world. They should prevail, in fact, to work a complete revolution in many of its sentiments and feelings, to rouse in it the agitation of new moral ideas and sensibilities. While it raged against and persecuted them, *they* would be victoriously convicting and convincing it in respect of sin, righteousness, and judgment.

And, if Christ anticipated such a state of things, and confidently predicted it, it was no more than what has often happened—that men whom the world of their day has fiercely opposed and reviled, have yet been quietly acting on it with the very thoughts and views which excited its animosity, on account of which it opposed and reviled them. The world has ridiculed them as impracticable visionaries or wild monomaniacs; has pointed at them the finger of scorn as an eccentric minority, utterly insignificant and powerless; has poured contempt upon them in the pages of its magazines and reviews;—the principles they avowed and advocated were principles which no sane person could hold; they were pestilent troublers of Israel, with their vain dreams and absurd notions, and ought not to be listened to; to follow their counsel would be ruinous to the best interests of the country. Yet, all the while, the persistent utterance of these men has been surely undermining the old ways of thinking, and slowly conducing to create a new public opinion in harmony with what they inculcated. They have been impressing themselves, little by little, on the world that inveighed against them, and penetrating its stony ground with seeds destined to produce a harvest of change in the direction of their own anathematized thoughts and views. Before they died, perhaps, their effect has begun to be evident in the diffusion of quite a different tone, in the altered stir and movement of the mass; and after their death, they have been honoured far and wide as benefactors and seers.

It has been thus once and again, and thus, Christ foresaw that it would be in the case of His apostles. The world will assail and vilify and rend you, He said; nevertheless, by you, in the power of the Spirit possessing you, the world will be swayed and turned.

And now, let us look at the work which He promised they should accomplish. It would be threefold: first, conviction in respect of sin, and conviction in respect of sin, because of the people's non-belief in Him.

His actual meaning here, appears to me to have been generally missed. He is generally supposed to have meant that the people would become convicted of having committed sin in rejecting Him; but I do not understand Him so. The sin of which they were to be convicted did not consist, surely, in their rejection of Him, any more than the righteousness of which they were to be convinced, consisted in His going to the Father and being no longer visible to His disciples, or the judgment, in the judging by Him of the reigning spirit of the age; but as with His judging of the reigning spirit of the age, and His departure to be with the Father, so with their rejection of Him, these were the things, which to His mind, would contribute to bring about the convictions prophesied. Their rejection of Me, He says, will be instrumental toward convincing them of sin; *that*, under your Spirit-inspired ministry, will be the means of flashing upon them all their wrongness and deformity, of opening their eyes to the evil in themselves of which they are at present unconscious. Christ descried His approaching fate; knew that the nation were dissatisfied with Him, were preparing to renounce Him; that in a little while they would finally abjure and cast Him from them; and His late repeated intimations of what awaited Him were sorely troubling His followers. But let us be resigned, He cries, in the assurance of the beneficial result to the nation from this crowning iniquity of theirs. Their rising at last, in a storm of blind passion, to sweep Me hence, full of truth and grace, will issue in an awakening from their long self-ignorance; through it, they will come to discern what manner of persons they are and have been, how miserably faulty and astray; through it, the hitherto hidden corruption of their spirit will be revealed to them.

One of Christ's chief objects in His ministry would seem to have been, to disquiet and disturb men concerning themselves; to pierce their dull self-content with a sense of defect, with a sense of being below the mark, and far off from the kingdom of God; to kindle within them new moral perceptions that should make visible to them the ugliness or the poorness of what they were, and of what they were doing, and leave them sighing for some better attainment. But His efforts had not been attended with much success. If a few here and there had begun to labour and be heavy laden under a consciousness of imperfection and disorder; the multitude remained tolerably at ease, dreaming that there was little amiss with them, and that they were not unworthy to be called the Lord's people.

Well, says Christ, let us wait; their wrongness

and depravity are about to break forth in open rejection of Me, of My grace and truth, and then, they will behold themselves, and tremble with shame at the spectacle; in that culminating ebullition they will be shaken out of their insensibility. We remember how the prediction was fulfilled; how the crowd are said to have returned from Calvary "smiting their breasts;" and in what numbers they were pricked to the heart when once the apostles commenced preaching after the Crucifixion.

Now is it not often thus; that a more than usually gross act in the midst of a long course of reckless misconduct or unfelt degradation, seems to have something of a convicting and converting force. A man, for example, has been living basely or meanly, going on from year to year with no pang of compunction or remorse, with no discomposing vision or ruffling glimpse of his wretched figure. At length, in a moment of great evil excitement, he does a deed of surpassing baseness or meanness, nothing within him protesting, nothing within him interfering to make him shrink or hesitate; but directly it is done, a revulsion against it starts in his breast, and in the revulsion he straightway sees vividly all the odiousness of his past life, and of the character it has formed; straightway sees vividly the ill-shapen, foul-grown creature that he is, and begins to abhor himself, and repent in dust and ashes. It is as if a new moral sense had been suddenly, quickened in him by the shock of this last greatest outburst of his unwholesomeness; as if this had suddenly overcome the deep slumber of his better nature, and compelled it to rise and assert itself. Sin, arrested and cured by its own extremeness, withered and burnt up in the flame of its own fiery crisis! Sin at its worst, sufficing to provoke the soul against it, and slain through its superabounding! It has been thus sometimes with men; they have gone the downward road step by step, without the least shudder at the road they were travelling or the least inward demur, never thinking of themselves as deserving condemnation; and then, in making a sudden rush, in taking a sudden, big plunge, the imprisoned divine element within them has been disengaged, and they have stood, not merely aghast at what they have just done, but looking back in humiliation and disgust at the way along which they had come so tranquilly; seeing not merely the loathsomeness of this last act, but the error and the wandering of their whole life, the blameworthiness of the years that had been spent with such content. It has sometimes been a great mercy to men whose eyes were closed to their failings and stains, that they have been suffered to fall into a great sin, that the bad element in them has been allowed to gather some day to a terrible outward head; thereby, at length, have their eyes been opened, and they have learnt to know themselves with redeeming grief and pain.

My countrymen's rejection of Me, says Christ, will be fraught with blessing for them; because of it, they will be brought to conviction in respect of sin.

But look now, at the second thing which He reckoned on His apostles accomplishing among them with their Spirit-inspired ministry. You shall convince also in respect of righteousness, and in respect of righteousness, because I go to the Father, and ye see Me no more; because, going to the Father, I shall cease to be present as I have been with you.

By convincing others in respect of righteousness, He must have meant convincing them *toward* righteousness; bringing them to see an ideal of being and behaviour loftier than had hitherto shone before them, to feel stirringly its authority and claim, and to yearn and reach after it; arresting them with an exhibition of higher aims and attainments than they had been in the habit of contemplating, and inflaming them with desire and earnest purpose to pursue these.

The apostles had already been sent out on a mission to attempt this. "Go and preach, saying, Repent ye; for the kingdom of heaven is at hand." And they had gone preaching this, but as yet had not effected much; they had not succeeded in producing any wide and deep conviction with regard to righteousness. The Master promises, however, that the time was coming when they should succeed mightily; that later on, a spirit would burn in them and their words which should set the people dreaming of truer and heavenlier things, and aspiring to rise to the height of them.

And what was it that would tend to their investment with such new power? Their subjection to new circumstances; their loss of the visible Christ—the withdrawal from their midst of the Jesus who was daily walking and talking with them—because ye shall see Me no more. "It is expedient for you," He had said, "that I go away: for if I go not away, the Comforter will not come unto you; but if I depart, I will send Him to you." He saw that, so long as they had Him living and acting among them, they were never likely to be emancipated from their carnal notions and ambitions, from their false ideas of the nature of His kingdom; were never likely to escape altogether from the bondage of their earthy hopes and thoughts concerning the Messianic redemption into the freedom of a larger, purer view; but would be always comparatively worldly and sensual, detained from reaching nobler conceptions and becoming possessed with nobler aspirations by more or less entanglement with Jewish prejudices. His continued presence with them was preventing their growth beyond *these*, from the seeds which He had sown in them; was preventing their due development along the line on which He had started them. They needed to be bereaved of Him for their elevation. He confidently anticipated that, when once He was gone, the seeds which they had got hidden in them from Him, would spring up and unfold, to the scattering of the low notions and ambitions that clung to them, and they would see things in a new light, would understand and appreciate His moral aims, and be surrendered wholly to the spiritual reality. And we know that such was the result of His disappearance; that, after His departure, they shot up far above what they had previously been, and became men "full of the Holy Ghost," discerning and worshipping a Redeemer of *souls*, enthusiastic about salvation from wrongness and sin. Christ foresaw that it would be so, and the power with which it would clothe them; that, thus purified and raised in tone, they would be the means of awakening and inciting to righteousness, as with all their preachings of repentance they had never yet been.

What, many a worker has gained often in might to do, through losing—through losing, to his grief, what he had prized as valuable, and fancied he could scarcely do without! There were things most dear to him that he has lost, and it has been the making of him. Leaning on them he was weak, and knew not how much they were contributing to keep him weak; deprived of them, to his dismay, he has straightway grown strong and stronger. When was it that he began to be so increasingly enterprising and energetic, to take a higher range, to produce his best, to be so wonderfully useful? When, perhaps, the outward support, the soothing praise, the popularity he had enjoyed, ceased to be his; when this and that pleasant prop upon which he had rested were removed. How it set free and drew out the forces latent in him, and made him thenceforth the braver, better, more efficient workman that he was capable of being! Many are the instances—more than we know, doubtless—in which greater and higher achieving, or beautiful developments of character and gift, have been largely due to some painful loss. Not seldom has such loss helped to promote superior performance, to give us noble labours and famous accomplishings with which otherwise the world might never have been blessed. And all that we want often, in order to our becoming more useful or more successful, in order to our attaining the heights that remain afar off, and which we vainly wish we could reach —all that we want often, is not that something should be added to us which we have not, but that we should just *lose* something. While we are crying fretfully, "Oh that such and such things were mine of which others are possessed! then would I conquer and do grandly;" the hindrance is not in what is withheld from us, but in what *cleaves* to us— in some little indulged weakness, in some infirmity or false habit of ours, simply to get rid of which would be our transformation into new creatures; would leave us armed and equipped for speedy triumph. Have we not known men concerning whom we have thought, What might they not be and do, if only they could lose a little, here and there?

The apostles of Jesus were to be greatened through loss—through the loss of His precious bodily presence, and of their comfortable repose thereon. This kept them from full spiritual perception and consecration: with the vanishing of this they would become filled with the Spirit, and so be mighty to convince in respect of righteousness.

Yes, *so* be mighty; for it is according to the measure in which we ourselves are earnest, that we are found capable of kindling earnestness. It is as we ourselves learn to aspire after and love the highest, that we are found influential in moving others to aspire and love. You cannot communicate more than you are, say and do what you will. We wonder, sometimes, at the ineffectiveness of apparently suitable and adequate means; and the secret lies in the *absence* of the Spirit. We wonder again, sometimes, at the effect produced with poor and unpromising means; and the secret lies in the Pentecostal strength and richness of the Spirit.

XVIII.

PRAYER.

Great love of God! the light of which has shone into our hearts; leave us not to darkness; let not Thy blessed shining be withdrawn from us, but may it remain with us and be in us to the end, a power of life and a power of comfort, such as we have found it often in bygone hours, when it has soothed our sorrowfulness, or strengthened us under some sharp temptation, to be better and braver than our lower part was inclining us to be. Praise to God for the inward consciousness of His love. Were it ever to be wholly taken from us—to die away like a beautiful dream, leaving us orphans—we trust that we should not be less steadfast in duty, less patient in trouble, or less constrained to flow with all kindness and charity towards our fellows. We hope we should still be ready and able to follow strenuously after righteousness, and to fight a good fight; and, indeed, we think we should, thanks to the training received, to the dispositions and habits formed, under the influence of Thy felt love. But sore loss would it be, nevertheless, to lose this. Life would be so much harder, the burden so much heavier to bear, if only that we should be left without the help and the inspiration of that joy in the Lord which is creaturely strength, of that brighter and happier heart, which singing at work makes the work easier, and not seldom a better and more perfect thing; which, shedding its own light around it, makes "the desert and solitary place," if not glad for it, yet less drear and sad.

So we praise God for the persuasion of His holy love, and pray to be kept in the persuasion until our labour is done, and we lie down to sleep our last sleep in hope of the morning. May this world be a great place to us, a holy and splendid, not merely as a place stored with manifold wonders, but as the house of the Father and the home of the Father's family, where the things seen, of beauty and marvel are the works of His hands, and the laws that rule are of His ordaining; where He is secretly fulfilling Himself through and in all happenings, and His children are being educated for immortality, according to a wisdom that cannot err and a goodness that fails not; so shall a greater spirit be nourished in us, and we be enabled to do more valiantly.

It matters something to us always in relation to our culture where we dwell, in what sort of habitation, amidst what scenes and surroundings; and they who dwell in the house of the Lord all the days of their life, wherever they rest or wander, and on whatever their eyes look, must needs be helped thereby to finer growth. It was good for Jacob the patriarch, when, after his divers journeyings and sojournings, he went at length to reside in Bethel, where of old he had seen that the heavens were open upon the earth, and that in the desert Jehovah's angels were busy. Then, when he went to reside there, he and his company cleansed themselves and changed their garments. And it is good for us, inspiring, purifying, when we can feel that the world is Thine, that our feet stand always within Thy sanctuary, that the place in which we eat and drink is holy ground. O God, it is hard, very hard, for some, Thou knowest, to believe that they are in Thy house. There is nothing round about them to hint or to suggest it, but almost everything to hide and belie it. They see and suffer so much misery and disorder, so much injustice and wrong, perhaps. What wretched homes and conditions are theirs! What do they find of love or gracious care? We cannot wonder if they cry, "Where is now your God?" as we, indeed, ourselves are sometimes tempted to cry when we think of them. Lord, have mercy upon such, remembering how, in the darkness of sin's crisis, and out of the depths of His anguish, Thy most perfect Son once cried, "God, why hast Thou forsaken Me?" Did not the cross during a moment, make it hard even for Him to believe? was not He, even He, in His extremity, a momentary sceptic concerning Thy presence? Let His weakness—the weakness of the most perfect Son—plead for those to whom, under black clouds of confusion and evil, the heavens seem empty; and for us, also, when as at times the night hides Thee from our sight. Help us to remind ourselves that the Father's house must always have its mysteries, at least until the children are grown up. Nor let us fail to do what we can toward helping others, by endeavouring, as we may be able, to soften and brighten their lot for them, and, with goodness and love of ours, aid them in entertaining the thought of a God whose goodness and love are over all. Let the goodness and the love that are in us of Thee assist to give some glimpse of Thee. We thank Thee for the stubborn and flourishing evils of the world that are being threatened, although at present it may be but faintly and afar off, in the grief and moaning of the few because of them, in the sorrow, the disgust, the indignation they awaken here and there, and more and more as their ugliness appears; and we pray for the growth and deepening of Thy Spirit—for this is Thy Spirit—in the breast of the few until it shall overflow, and spread abroad; and, for their instruction by it, unto all wisdom as well as all zeal. We bless Thee for the Spirit that came of old, and still comes, from Him who was so filled with the Father, and so expressive of the Father's glory—the Spirit of holy inspiration, the Spirit of light and truth, the Spirit of comfort and love, the Spirit, not of bondage and fear, but of liberty and sonship. Open our hearts, we beseech Thee, to receive and foster it within us; may it work in us freely to the working out of our salvation; may it guide our motions, and command and consecrate our passions; may we recognize its presence in diversities of gifts and diversities of operations, and confess and feel with joy that it is with us and among us.

Help us to be daily putting on the Lord Jesus, that we may be clothed with grace and power, and walk in white raiment before men; that He, descending into us even to our innermost depths, may ascend through and spread forth over us, a growing robe of beauty and a growing equipment for useful and merciful ministry.

O God, we would fain be taught in the way that Thou shalt choose, taught to see more clearly, to think more truly, to feel more nobly, to live more purely and more serviceably; and, through these prayers of ours, in faith and trust, with sincere filial desire that Thy will should be done, may we be prepared and purified to learn of Thee, and to be blest in that which Thou appointest for us, unto whom, our only wise God and Saviour, be thanksgiving and worship and praise both now and for ever.

SERMON.
CHRIST'S PROMISE TO HIS APOSTLES.
PART II.

"And when He is come, He will reprove the world of sin, and of righteousness, and of judgment: of sin, because they believe not on Me; of righteousness, because I go to My Father, and ye see Me no more; of judgment, because the prince of this world is judged."—JOHN xvi. 8-11.

THIS, as we have seen, was the threefold effect which, according to the expectation and promise of Christ, His apostles would be hereafter producing upon the world of their day through the power of the Spirit within them, while they were being assailed and persecuted by the world. There was to be, He intimated, an action of society upon them—a most troublesome and discomforting action, driving them often to sore straits, plunging them in much pain and affliction. They would be scoffed at, ostracized, ill used, and some of them would probably be slain; but in the mean time, and notwithstanding, they would be acting on the mind of society, influencing multitudes to think and feel as they had not done in relation to certain great subjects, working a change in the moral sentiments and sympathies of many; and thus, whatever became of them, however they might be bruised and torn and down-trodden, the victory would be theirs. For they are the real kings and rulers among men who, though uncrowned, except, perhaps, with a crown of thorns, prevail to quicken and mould in the realm of thought; who, though poor and reviled, maybe, are silently swaying and shaping there. If you should kill me in your superior strength, with your overpowering sword, and I should have left you pierced and kindled to some inward revolution, with winged words of mine, it is I who shall have conquered, not you.

What can be wrought that has such immortality as an impression for good or evil upon a human soul? Which is the greater, to have wrought finely in stone, in sculptured marble, in the province of scientific research and discovery, or to have wrought finely on a number of living souls?'

You shall be accounted fools for My sake, said Jesus to His apostles; you shall be buffeted and tortured and defamed; but you shall exert, withal, an illumining, purifying force in the region of mind. And to whom but to them belonged the dominion and the triumph?

Now, of the threefold work which it was prophesied they should accomplish when the Master was gone, under the inspiration of the Spirit that should then possess them; the third part remains for our consideration. While, as we have already seen, they were to convict in respect of sin because of the nation's rejection of Him whom Heaven had sent, and in respect of righteousness because of His departure to the Father, to the disciples' bereavement of His bodily presence, they were also to convince in respect of judgment, and in respect of judgment, because the world's prince had been judged. That is, it seems to me,—as they were to be the means of awakening in their countrymen a sense of sin, of defect and culpability, which the latter had not experienced before, and of bringing them to perceive what true righteousness was, and to aspire and reach after it earnestly; so, should they be the means of revolutionizing, more or less, their judgments; of leading them to form new and different estimates—to see many things in a new and different light. As though it had been said: "Under your teaching, they shall learn to appraise more correctly, to recognize the comparative emptiness or insignificance of what they have been accustomed to think much of, and to reverence or rate highly what they have hitherto despised or failed to appreciate at its due value. You shall move them, you shall constrain them to relinquish one and another of their cherished axioms with regard to men and life; to use other weights and measures; to withdraw homage where they have meekly rendered it, and, where they have withheld, to give it. They will stand inwardly convicted of the falseness, the unsoundness of some of their practical views and conclusions, and will be made to reverse some of their established verdicts."

Such changes would follow, of course, if not at once, yet by degrees, from the new consciousness of fault, and the new conceptions of duty that were to be roused in them. Let me acquire fresh moral sensibility, and have my eyes opened to, and my heart captured by, a higher moral ideal, and it must needs affect me in my judgments, in my judgments of people and events. Not a few familiar objects and subjects will begin to present themselves to me in an altered aspect; there will be an alteration for me in the relative worth and importance of things; some that bulked largely will

X

contract and shrivel, and some that were lightly regarded will command attention and interest.

The apostles could not convince in respect of sin and righteousness without convincing at the same time in respect of judgment: but as there, in each case, they were to be aided towards success by a particular circumstance, by something that had occurred, namely, by the rejection of Christ of which the nation had been guilty, and by their own loss in His departure to the Father; so *here*, by a particular circumstance, by something that had occurred, they were to be assisted in convincing with respect to judgment, namely, by the fact that the prince of the world had been judged. That would contribute to bring about the conviction.

Now, the *prince* of the world of their day must stand for whatever ruled its movements, for whatever mainly swayed and directed its life. It would be the Speaker's personification of the ideas and feelings, the notions and prejudices, by which Jewish society was governed—His personification of what we should term the reigning public sentiment, or spirit of the age; as when St. Paul wrote congratulating those who had been liberated from walking "according to the course of their age, according to the prince of the power of the air, the spirit that wrought in the children of disobedience." And what was it to which the world of Christ's day may be said to have been in subjection?

There was first, surely, religious custom, the traditions of the elders, the doctrine of the scribes. These were the supreme authority to which all bowed, and from which no appeal was attempted. Every question must be decided by these; these settled the things to be believed, and the conduct to be observed. It was enough to follow where they pointed, to take as right and true what they enjoined. Thought slept, and moved not, no spirit of inquiry breathed abroad. Few dreamt of doubting the order which they found existing, or the creed in which they were educated. The people lived in drowsy, slavish submission to what everybody held and practised, to what had been spoken by them of old time, to the voice of those who sat in Moses' seat. Accept the general custom; obey the traditions of the elders; rest in the doctrine of the scribes—that was their rule; and upon the face of the mental waters scarce a ripple stirred.

Then, again, there was the worship of outward prosperity and success. They had learnt to consider these as the blessings with which Heaven rewarded the good—as marks of worth; and the opposite as betokening Heaven's displeasure or aloofness—as signs of inferior desert. The great thing was to prosper and succeed, for then Jehovah was smiling and all must be well; but to fail and be defeated, to lie broken and crushed, what else could it mean than to be God-forsaken? The favour of the Almighty could not be theirs who were out at elbows, to whom honour and sympathy were denied, who were left to be stricken and smitten without deliverance; neither could the truth be with them. Men were to be estimated according to the measure in which they got on and flourished.

Such were some of the ideas and feelings which may be said to have governed the world of Christ's day, to which it was more or less in bondage. And now, by the time the apostles were engaged in preaching, after He had finished His course and vanished from the scene, what had happened? Had there not been a tremendous manifest judging of these regnant ideas and feelings, as mistaken and false? Had they not been exposed and exploded in Him? By Him—by what He had become and done, were they not being shown up and sentenced and condemned? He, the lonely Heretic who had gone, contrary to custom, and set at nought the tradition of the elders, and called in question and contradicted the doctrine of the scribes, to His own discomfiture and disgrace, until He was hunted down and crucified for it—had He not made evident, at length, that these authorities were not inviolable or immaculate; that they might be resisted, to triumph over them in the end, and be proved to have been in the wrong; that it was possible for the impugner of them, though apparently for a while crushed by their wrath, to survive and win the day; that the truth was not always with them, but might be found in opposition to them? See, the inspiring, exalting influence which the gibbeted Heretic had grown to be in the hearts of His bereaved apostles ; and the captures He was making, the new life of new faith, and new peace and blessedness, which, through them, He was diffusing. Here was mental independence exemplified and vindicated against the principle of subjection to outward authority.

He, again, the low-born Son of Mary, the vagrant Galilean Peasant, whom the elders despised and persecuted, who suffered and perished miserably—had He not refuted the idea that poverty was shame, and demonstrated how full of grace and truth *they* might be, who had not where to lay their head, whose path was hard and stony, and to whom the waters of a bitter cup were wrung out? Was He not revealed as having been great, and the chosen of Heaven, after all? Had He not established that the successful were not always in the right; that behind weakness and failure, majesty and glory might lie hid; that to be baffled and beaten might be the secret promise of God, and the cross the lot of one whom God waited to crown? See, how Jesus of Nazareth was beginning to commend Himself, and to prevail and conquer. By Him, the prince of the world, its ruling notions, and prejudices, had been openly judged. And this, beheld by the people, and impressed upon their minds as they listened to the apostles' preaching, was to assist materially toward their conviction in respect of judgment; toward leading them to form and act on new and truer judgments in relation to men and life. By the time you are dispersed among them after My departure, said Christ, the prince of their world—its ruling notions and prejudices—will have been visibly judged by Me; and it will conduce to their conversion in respect of judgment.

You observe how confidently He counts upon this event having such effect. His words, hitherto, had not had much effect in loosening the adherence to the false thoughts and axioms to which the many were in bondage. He had taught and exhorted comparatively in vain. The dominion of the false thoughts and axioms remained unbroken; but when at length, they saw these so strikingly contravened, so utterly overthrown and demolished in Himself—in His person and work—then, their deliverance would be accomplished. Then they would begin to cast them off, and learn to think differently, to entertain different views; then, the spell of authority—the authority of custom and tradition, under which they had lain dumb and dead—would be broken, and they would rise in freedom to examine and inquire for themselves; then, prosperity and success would cease to be relied on as indicating worth; and the poor and afflicted would no longer be condemned or suspected.

And, what one man can do often, and has often done, toward altering completely the sentiments of many on some points, in regard to some matters; not by what he says or proves in argument, which may issue in nothing and be wholly ineffectual, but just by what he himself exemplifies, by his own witnessed course, by his own boldness, and the fruit of it, by the work which he shows! What sudden release is sometimes given to many, thus, from superstitious notions, from doubts, fancies, or fears that had long held them bound; as when the brave, impetuous boy, defying the strong bully of whom all stood in awe, and beating him, creates a revolution in the general judgment, and emancipates the school. How often it is that people's ideas and feelings about certain things, the way in which they look at them, the estimate they take of them, have been determined or largely affected by their acquaintance with some one man; not with his theories and views, but with him; by their observation and experience of him! They have lived with him and seen what he was, have beheld his action, or marked his career, and it has influenced their judgings in certain directions. That is why they have come to trust or mistrust so, to reverence or sneer as they do, as they did not before knowing him. It is not reasoning or persuasive speech which has changed their mental attitude, but his conduct, the character which he has expressed in their intercourse with him.

Look at this sardonic, cynical creature, with his railings against the world, and his contempt for the race; to whom human life is a poor, mean comedy, with no dignity or reality in it, and men at their best, are wizened and grotesque; who holds that none are so good or so sweet as they seem that each has his price at which he may be bought; that nothing is genuine; who smiles incredulously when you talk of honour and love and unselfish devotion, and considers that professions should always be suspected, that friendship is little more than a name;—look at him, listen to his weary bitterness;—how came he to be judging thus? Not thus, but far otherwise, was he wont to judge in days gone by;—what has preverted him to such views as these? Was it not, are there not instances of the kind in which it has been, just one man's revealed shallowness and faithlessness—perhaps, alas! one woman's? And as by the manifested qualities and doings of one, people are sometimes driven to judge unworthily and wrongly, so are they sometimes led, on the contrary, to sounder and healthier judgings, to appraise here and there more fitly, to be governed here and there by truer thoughts. Stand in your lot to the end, acting uprightly, acting nobly; only be loyal always, and brave, sincere, and pure, and you cannot tell whom you may not help to convince in respect of judgment.

You observe the calm assurance of Christ that what He was and did would be fruitful; that however little He might have effected hitherto with His teachings, and however He might be rejected of the nation, He Himself, in His whole expression, would be found telling ultimately upon the minds of men with quickening, converting power. I shall not have been what I have been, I shall not have done what I have done, in vain: it will leave an impression behind it, will come to work stirringly and redeemingly in the mental realm. This, on the eve of dying, was his quiet assurance; and what he expected came to pass. After Him, the waters ceased to be stagnant, and began to flow and rock; thought shook itself free, and set out in quest of truth. After Him, a new spirit of humanity awoke, and the dignity of man grew to be discerned and acknowledged as it had not been before. The judging of the prince of the world in and by Him was not in vain. And we may be equally certain that none of us can live honestly and dutifully, and not be powers on the earth, forwarding and elevating powers. To live thus, is to be of a certainty, beneficially operative, however untraceable our individual effect may be.

Life is never barren or impotent; words, theories,

controversies may be, but not life—whatever its character or quality. The meanest, vilest, most erring life does something, and not merely in an evil and harmful way; it goes also to serve for something in connection with the great divine purpose of human education and development. It is used up without observation, and secretly, in aid thereof. But an honest and dutiful life, though ever so dumb, and ever so lowly—*that*, is sure to be beautifully productive; and the grace of it will be surviving among us, and contributing to the growing health and soundness of the world, long after it has passed away.

XIX.

PRAYER.

FATHER of men, who hast made us for Thyself, and wilt give us rest at length, when *Thou* shalt have found rest in gaining us to be wholly Thine. We must not expect to enter into peace until Thou art satisfied, nor would we. The cross must needs be in our lot whilst Thou art crucified for us, as Thou art and wilt be till evil is purged away, and all things that offend are gathered out, and the righteous shine forth as the sun in the kingdom of the Father. Then, then, will come Thy Sabbath and ours, and Thou shalt make us glad with Thy countenance. Help us, in the mean while, to trust Thee, believing that Thou carest for us, that we are paternally governed, and therefore often to our wounding and perplexity, that Thy gracious purpose is in all our pains, and is slowly fulfilling itself through them. Help us to be receiving daily, with our daily bread, the power to be sons of God in fellowship with Jesus Christ, power to rest in the faith of Thy love, and to cast our burdens upon Thee, to hope and quietly wait for Thy salvation, to look through the seen to the unseen, through the temporary to the eternal, saying, "For which cause we faint not;" power to reign as kings over circumstances, to lift ourselves above the motions of the flesh, and the influences that tend to weaken or defile; to follow after righteousness; to be sympathetic helpers one of another; to seek the things that make for peace through edifying, and to extract the moral uses of dark things. Let none of *us* be beggars and slaves in the world, who are sons, who are called to overcome the world, and to whom the world belongs;

but may we take up and maintain our birthright, and enjoy and achieve, as children of our Father who is in heaven. Give us to feel how we are valued by Him who made and owns us, who has built us such a house to dwell in, and has provided us with such means of education; who has taught us so many things in divers manners, and has borne with us so long and patiently; who pursues us so persistently with pains and penalties, with inward remonstrances and upbraidings, when we attempt to fly from Him, as fled the old prophet from the voice of the Lord; who has sent us Jesus Christ, and has raised up for us, again and again, other masters. Give us to feel the value that we are to Him, even when we are least worthy in our own eyes, and of least worth in the esteem of our fellows; so save us from sinking into self-contempt, and set us aspiring afresh to be more and better than we are. "What does it matter," men have sometimes said—"what does it matter if *we* continue to go wrong who have already strayed so far and fallen so low, if we be further defiled till we perish in corruption, *we* who have lost name and place, of whom none but bad things are expected?" Grant such to know, O Lord, that they are Thine, and that *Thou* wouldst care if they should make shipwreck of themselves. When any are weary of trying, and inclined to let circumstances drag them at their pleasure, to be reckless with the recklessness of self-despondency and self-despair, put Thou new strength into them, rouse them with a sense of sonship and dignity to

> "Be not like dumb, driven cattle,
> To be a hero in the strife."

O God, keep us in good heart for duty, full of animation and energy for it; constrained continually in all departments and relations to seek to do our very best. Since "he who aimeth at the sky, shoots higher much than he who means a tree," may we be always aiming loftily, however we may miss always hitting the mark desired; and may we feel the importance of our doing well, and becoming perfect, in the interests of mankind, and for the sake of the family to which we belong; that, being members of that body which is the Lord's, we must needs labour to be our bravest and noblest, because of the body, and cannot fail, cannot grow misshapen, or act unworthily without injuring, or defrauding it, for "one sinner destroyeth much good," and no man perishes alone in his iniquity. Help each of us to be a tree of life in the midst of the garden, whatever our girth and the spread of our branch may be; though our shadow be not large, let it be always a wholesome, healing shadow, and may such as sit beneath it be not withered or weakened, but revived. Thou to whom we offer the fruit of our lips, giving thanks to thy name, to whom we come again and again with our prayers and praises; teach and strengthen us to do good, and to communicate, for with these sacrifices Thou art well pleased; thus will Thy purpose be fulfilled in ourselves and in the world. Fountain of love! discipline and meeten us for use, and give us in all our endeavours the deftness of love; preserve us from being awkward and clumsy, through coldness of heart, for what so awkward and clumsy as cold fingers? and when our benevolent attempts are ineffectual, when we err in method, and blunder to the hindrance of those we assume to help, is it not often because we are not sufficiently warm with real affection and sympathy? In undertaking to counsel, persuade, or comfort, make us wise with the wisdom of love. We thank Thee, the Source of good, for all true work that has been done by us in our lot, and for all faithfulness and worthiness in effort; we thank Thee for all gift enjoyed, and all skill acquired, praying that both gift and skill may be exercised in righteousness, and that Thou mayest receive from them according to Thy will. We thank Thee for grace bestowed on many men to serve in different ways, and commend them to Thee for Thy guidance, their labours to Thee for Thy blessing. Pity, O Lord, the purposeless, the indolent, the frivolous, the self-centred, and those who toil from day to day in the sweat of their face, to amuse and gratify themselves; begetting within them, if it may be, some higher impulse, and showing them a more excellent way. Thy pity, too, in our present peace and quietness, we crave for all who are care-harried and trouble-tossed; for all in whose houses there is sorrow and woe; for the broken beneath blows of adversity; for them that groan in secret behind a smiling mask; for the transgressor whom his own deeds at length are bitterly scourging; for the poor, hunted, hiding criminal, loathed and raged against by all. Oh, pity of God! oh, pity of God! Are not Thine arms about us all? Let them be about us still and evermore, even until the last lost sheep of the wilderness be brought home with rejoicing, and we be able to offer worship and praise, in which there shall be no note of sadness, as, joining in the universal song, we say, "Blessing, and honour, and glory, and power be unto Him that sitteth upon the throne, and unto the Lamb for ever." Amen.

SERMON.

THE VISION OF THE DYING CHRIST.

"And when He is come, He will reprove the world of sin, and of righteousness, and of judgment : of sin, because they believe not on Me; of righteousness, because I go to My Father, and ye see Me no more ; of judgment, because the prince of this world is judged."—JOHN xvi. 8-11.

SUCH was the vision which Christ had toward the close of His life, of what was about to take place among men in the world of moral mind ; His *dying* vision, of the beautiful stir and transformation that would soon be occurring there. This, was what He beheld approaching as He stood, Himself consciously marked for removal—on the eve, as He believed, of His own departure from the scene ; this, was what He saw preparing to come to pass. While knowing that His time was short, that in a few hours, probably, He would be snatched away, it was borne in upon Him that glorious things were impending—events, according to His estimate, of the deepest interest and importance ; and must it not have been all the harder for Him to be resigned to His fate?

There are moods in which we may experience something of a passion for death; when a kind of impatience seizes us to get out into the thick darkness and discover for ourselves what it really hides. A familiar friend has lately vanished within it; or we have been reading, perhaps, a paper like Mrs. Oliphant's "Little Pilgrim in the Unseen;" and it has set us dreaming, wondering concerning the state beyond, until we felt as though death in any shape would be welcome for the sake of the revelation it would bring. We were so curious; we yearned so for a glimpse behind the veil. In such moments, however, it is well to remember, and try to echo, the sentiment expressed by Thoreau in his last illness, when a visitor wanted to speak with him of the other world. "One world at a time," replied the sick man—"one world at a time." And the true philosophy, surely, is to be content with one world at a time. We can scarcely afford, indeed, to give much thought to the next, while we have this to occupy us.

But if now and then for a brief space death looks inviting, and is wished for as a means of solving inscrutable problems; there are circumstances that

Y

tend to make the prospect of it especially repugnant, in which the ordinary shrinking from it is increased and intensified, when it is with deep reluctance that we find our path steepening towards it. As when, for example, we have some dear, engrossing work in hand that we crave to finish, and which, were but a little longer respite granted us, we should be able to finish satisfactorily, instead of leaving it, after years of labour, a comparatively lost and useless thing, because incomplete; or as when we are in the midst of investigations promising grand results, we think results, which, after much devoted toil and many a disappointment, are just beginning to show themselves near, like green blades above the clods. Ah! then, the pain of hearing death's footfall on the road! What would we not give to have him delayed for a while, only for a while! And to one who is profoundly interested in human progress, in the march and growth of ideas, how hard it must be to find himself slipping away, with indications all around him of coming great developments, with multiplying signs in the air of winter melting into spring, with a sense of slumbering seeds at length stirring and flushing the ground, prophetic of bright harvest days not very far off! He would fain tarry where he

The Vision of the Dying Christ. 323

is, to witness and enjoy the unfolding. In such a time as the present, for instance—a time of tumultuous transition, of mental movement big with births of change; when so many old things are ceasing to satisfy, and so many new conceptions are struggling into form; when discovery is making ever fresh strides, and inquiry is pushing ever further afield, and the thoughts of men are widening;—in such a time as the present, it is difficult for him to reconcile himself to dying. He deprecates missing the outcome of all this; the improved conditions, the finer methods, the more excellent ways in which it may issue, the stronger, clearer, healthier mind that may be diffused abroad, the loftier heights on which, ere long, the world may be resting, the Christ that is to be. He is ready to cry, "O age! creep not on too fast with thy decaying touch. Would that I were younger, that I might hope to behold the advances and the gains of the next fifty years!" He looks, at times, upon the children who climb his knee, and the babes in their perambulators, with a mixture of envy and awe, thinking, "What other and greater things will their eyes be seeing, when mine are closed!"

And when Christ foresaw what He did—the

blessed convictions that were going to be wrought among the people in respect of sin, righteousness, and judgment, the moral awakening with which dead souls, on whom little or no effect had been produced, were about to be disturbed—would it not be calculated to leave Him with a hankering to remain; would it not be with an added sigh that He turned to meet the death awaiting Him? Alas, that He must needs be taken with such a time at hand—He who was so consumed with zeal for the quickening of diviner life in human hearts!

Again, the general rousing to truer sentiments and aspirations which He died anticipating, would be largely owing, He knew and felt, to what he had done. He, with His poorly achieving, meagrely successful ministry, had laid in silence the secret foundation for it; He would be hidden at the bottom of it all. It would be the harvest which He had sown with tears. As John the Baptist had prepared the way for Him, He had prepared the way for the apostles' future doings. The fruit which they were to gather in such abundance, He had dug and planted for; the soil, soon to yield so richly to their labours, He had fertilized: they, while He was away, would be realizing the results of His germinal work. We remember His words outside Sychar after the interview with the Samaritan woman, when He remarked how the fields around them were already whitening for the sickle, and added—we can imagine with something of a plaintive tone in His voice—" One soweth, and another reapeth. I send you to reap that whereon ye have bestowed no labour: others have laboured, and ye are entering into their labours." He saw the hopeful signs of productiveness in the fields where He had toiled; saw the promise which here and there they were beginning to show; but knew that the reaping would not be His, that *that* must be left for those who should succeed Him; that by their hands the sheaves would be bound, when His were folded in death.

So has it frequently been, that one has seen afar off, his performings or his discoveries opening out into splendours of inheritance in which he would have no share. He has penetrated the wilderness and caught sight of the goodly mountains beyond; but it will be for others to go forward and take possession along the path he has carved; not for him.

Moreover, the agents in accomplishing the great things of Christ's pre-vision, and of His preparing

—how inferior they were to Him! When He was gone, there were to be convictions in respect of sin, righteousness, and judgment. The world was to be impressed and shaken as it had never been before. Effects were to be produced transcending any that He had ever produced; and the instruments, the honoured instruments, would be these disciples of His, whose weaknesses and ignorances He had been wont to pity; upon whom He looked down from a height of vision and consecration far above theirs. They, in the power of the Spirit that would be given them, would do more, much more, than He had done, to whom the Spirit had been given without measure. It was they, His inferiors, who were to be the means of convincing so mightily in respect of sin, righteousness, and judgment; not He, their superior. He was not discontented that it should be thus—the satisfaction of a true soul being always, that a true work has been wrought or is to be wrought, by whatever hands; but He had to be content with this.

And it is so, constantly. The man who carries out and perfects and applies usefully the invention of another, is generally a good deal less of a genius than the inventor, and possibly could not hold a candle to him; although the latter, perhaps, is to be less widely known and recognized. The expounder and interpreter of a great thinker's ideas, by whom they are disseminated, and made impressive and operative to some conspicuous effect in society, is but an intellectual pigmy, maybe, in comparison with the thinker whom he interprets and expounds to such quickening results. And they are not the more profound and comprehensive minds who do the most outward and striking work in the world —whatever they may do of supreme importance behind the scenes and in secret;—but rather, the narrower and more one-sided, who, wanting in princely breadth, are capable perhaps of more intenseness. The former move the springs and feed the fountains of action, the others do the work which shows; as when, according to the Gospel story, St. John, with the discernment of the deeper love, perceived the Lord in the dim figure on the strand, and whispering the news to St. Peter, St. Peter, the shallower, but the more fiery and impetuous, dashed into the surf to go to Him.

· But now, again, Christ, predicting what would be accomplished after His departure, had within Him the firm persuasion, not merely that he was fated to be put to death by the nation, but that this was necessary to bring about the triumph of His truth in the ministry of His apostles; that he must needs be rejected and cast out, before he could become through them a convincing and converting power. He seems to have felt this all along from the beginning, and in no way does He appear to me more sagacious and acute, more divine in understanding. No sooner had he begun to grow somewhat popular, and to be looked up to by numbers as a heaven-sent Teacher, than He began to see and prophesy, not simply that the chief priests and elders in their animosity would sooner or later devise and procure His destruction, but that He would have to be destroyed in order to rise; that not until the Son of man had been lifted up upon the cross would He draw all to Him. Never was He led, by any apparent progress made, by any increase of followers, or other token of success, to indulge the thought that His kingdom in human souls might possibly be established without that. Nay; it was just when His popularity with the people was at its highest, when He had been listening to the voice of a great multitude hailing Him Lord and King, and when, in addition, certain strangers of the Gentiles were begging permission to come and sit at His feet,—it was then that, while unable to repress an exclamation of joy at the cheering signs, He paused to say, "Verily, verily, except a corn of wheat fall into the ground and die, it abideth alone: only if it die, does it bring forth much fruit." However promising the aspect of things, He did not expect to convince really and thoroughly, yet. Really and thoroughly to convince, He must first suffer and be slain. It was not merely of the rulers' purpose to kill Him that He thought, but of the necessity for it, to give Him the dominion He desired. He grasped and accepted the principle that "except a corn of wheat fall into the ground and die, it abideth alone;" that no new ideas, no new truths, can be victorious and prevail until they have been scouted and crucified.

And it is so always. There are always three stages in their history. First, they are allowed to steal abroad quietly, winning here and there without observation: here and there, in odd out-of-the-way places, in obscure corners and lower parts of the earth, finding easy reception; being the while, by the majority, ignored, or regarded with indifference, and perchance with pitying smiles. Then, as they make way, little by little, and seem to be moving in a straight line, however slowly, toward ultimate universal acceptance; gradually, a storm of opposition gathers and bursts, and they are fiercely assaulted, held up to opprobrium, denounced and impaled; society rises against them and thrusts them out. The apostles, perhaps, go mourning for a while, saying, "We trusted that it had been He who should have redeemed Israel;" and then, comes the resurrection, then begins the final stage, the stage of triumph. This is the law of a new truth's progress. It proceeds, not by a succession of onward steps from its introduction to its eventual settled reign, but by temporary advance, followed by rout and scattering and through rout and scattering, as with rebound, to the heights of calm establishment. It goes forward for a season, to be at length violently attacked and driven back, perhaps almost out of the field; and presently, as if resilient from thence, it rushes in, often, with wonderful force and swiftness, to the winning-post.

There is something analogous to this in trying to break a habit. At first, it seems to be meekly yielding to your effort; afterwards, it turns upon you with well-nigh overpowering fury; and, struggling with it then, in the sweat of your face, you have broken it.

So, also, in seeking to learn a science or a language. At first it seems easy: you move along readily and smoothly, until you have learnt enough to see the long steep road before you, to see how much there is to learn. And then, you are assailed by weariness, disappointment, despair, and the inclination to give up; to contend resolutely against which, is to be carried on with increasing interest, and with more and more of facility to summits of attainment.

But let us always remember the law of a new truth's progress, and whenever Christ is crucified, understand with cheerful resignation that it is only a stage in what has been called "the spiral process of growth." The Lord Jesus understood that well, nor did He merely console Himself with the thought when the cross had befallen Him. He perceived beforehand the inevitableness and necessity of the cross—that it would behove Him to suffer ere He could enter into His glory. I shall not rise to power, He perceived, until I have been thrust down and rejected.

Notice, in conclusion, one other thing. While describing what His apostles would effect under the inspiration of the Spirit; how, when once the new and greater Spirit took possession of them, they would be found convincing irresistibly in respect of sin, righteousness, and judgment, He yet saw clearly that it would not be the Spirit alone, but the Spirit, and circumstances concurring with and aiding it: *its* coming upon them, in conjunction with the people having lately done Him to death; with His being no longer a bodily presence among them; and with the open and striking judgment by Him of the prince of the world. These things would all combine with the descent of the Spirit upon them to give them the success predicted.

We are not generally so clear-sighted as this. We often make the mistake, for example, of attributing a religious teacher's remarkable success to one thing only, or to one or two things in himself. We note his tremendous earnestness, or his wonderful eloquence, and say, "There lies the whole secret of it;" whereas, while his eloquence and earnestness are important factors, there will be several factors, doubtless, outside him, largely assisting, which, in other cases of equal earnestness and eloquence, where there has been comparative failure, have been wanting It is never the man's special gift and quality which by itself produces the impression witnessed; circumstances are present, coinciding, and contributing; something special in the time, in the composition of the mental and moral atmosphere around him; in external condi-

The Vision of the Dying Christ. 333

tions and events—as Christ recognized that it would be when His apostles went forth to preach filled with the Holy Ghost. There would be the nation in a state of reaction from the deed of blood to which blind passion had driven them—the nation subdued, softened, half regretful; there would be His own absence; Himself, no longer visible or audible. And the person is sometimes a hindrance to the full appreciation and reception of the truth which the person exhibits; his removal is sometimes conducive to the truth's freer operation.

And then, there would be the manifest judging of the Judæan world's ruling ideas and prejudices that had taken place. All this He saw would help. If the Spirit were essential—and without it there would be no power—it would not be the Spirit alone, but with all this aiding. So many things, He saw, would be working together to bring about the one thing which He anticipated—the conviction of the multitude in respect of sin, righteousness, and judgment.

And how many things are always at work in producing any revolution of public sentiment, or any quickening or conversion of a single soul! We point to this or that as the agent; but how much has gone toward promoting it that we descry not! Numberless little influences, perhaps, of which we have no suspicion. We see the result and say, "This or that did it;" but this or that which we see has been only a link—the last link, maybe—in a long chain of cause. Infinitely complex is the process of every great change wrought in a human mind.

XX.
PRAYER.

EVERLASTING patience of God, which has borne and carried us all the days of old, under which our fathers and forefathers lived as under a sheltering panoply, and which still covers us, their children! The ages have not wearied it; how it has waited and has not fainted, when the progress of thought has halted, and lessons that seemed to have been learnt have been manifestly forgotten, and the angel of experience has whispered and pointed in vain, and good seeds sown, have been long, very long, bringing forth their fruit, and we have needed to be led into wilderness after wilderness of error, and to be kept wandering there, up and down and to and fro, ere we could be brought to possess the destined inheritance of truth. Everlasting patience of God, that does not strive nor cry, neither is its voice heard in the streets; still bear with us, still wait for us, for our ears are dull of hearing, and again and again we miss or mistake the word of the Lord before we can truly catch and understand it, and our eyes are holden often that we discern not, until too late, the presence of the Lord, because, forsooth, the form of the presence has been unfamiliar and strange. Still bear with us, still wait for us, for we are slow to learn, and precept must be upon precept, line upon line, and so much has to be worked out of us that the better thing prepared for us may be wrought in, and so much has to be broken up within us that the better thing may be built and established. Help us, O God, to be patient together with Thee, while yet at the same time earnest with Thee, who slumberest not nor sleepest, and whose hands are stretched forth all the day long. How we cry! but Thou art not wearied with our cries; Thou knowest well that we need to entreat of Thee, to complain to Thee, to wonder, and groan, and hope, and pour out our souls before Thee; it does not weary Thee—and not because Thou payest no attention to our cries, for Thou hearest from the heaven of Thy wisdom and goodness. And when we pray we are not as those who beat the air; Thine ear is open toward us continually, Thy holy love receives our burdens, and into something of blessing for us Thou turnest every true-hearted cry—something of good Thou workest for us, even with the cry which, while sincere, is foolish and blind For are we not children of a Father who is wise, and able to minister above our thoughts? We only weary Him when we cry out of feigned lips, or when the cry is for some heavenly gift and good at which the life aims not and strives not after, when the yearning cry is evermore contradicted by the unearnest, negligent, slothful life: then may we think of Him as saying, in the words of Israel's prophet, "To what purpose is the multitude of your sacrifices unto me? Bring no more vain oblations. When ye spread forth your hands I will hide my eyes. Ye are a trouble to me; I am weary to hear you. Wash you, make you clean, put away the evil of your doings; cease to do evil, learn to do well; then come and let us reason together."

O God, let us not pray too beautifully—too beautifully for what we are—for what we are in our daily seekings and cultivatings and endeavours. Help us to walk worthy of our prayers. What are we that we should take upon ourselves to speak to Thee, to tell Thee our thoughts and feelings; to beseech good of Thee, the Infinite Charity, the Eternal Mercy; to show Thee, the All-Seeing, that which is in our heart? We are Thy children and Thou art our Father, and to lay down a burden of trouble, rejoicing, or desire, at Thy feet, is to take up always something that we laid not down. So we speak freely to Thee our longings for more virtue and elevation; for more strength to be faithful and brave and patient; for a little more light, a little more truth; for "increase of grace to hear meekly Thy Word, and to receive it with pure affection, and to bring forth the fruits of the Spirit;" for the speedy fulfilment of Thy kingdom in the world, crying, "Lord, hasten it," though, indeed, there can be no haste with Thee.

So we speak freely to Thee our sorrowful regret for frailties and failings of which we are conscious; our discontent with present attainments; our weariness often by reason of difficulties; our grief often by reason of the disappointments of the way; our anxious interest in the welfare of others, in the progress of good works, in the success of noble and beneficent enterprise, in the true prosperity of our nation; our tender concern for some who are afflicted and distressed, whom sickness has laid low, whom adversity has overtaken, whom death has bereaved; our sympathizing joy with those who are rejoicing in the sunshine of happy days, to whom blessed deliverance has been granted, to whom good fortune and enlargement have come after straitness and pain; in whose house there is gladness because the hour of the woman's travail is past and a child is born; whose hearts are bright with hope; who have won for themselves, worthily, in the course of the years, place and honour and troops of friends.

And freely we speak to Thee, the sorrow we have to-day for the removal from among us of one who, while great in special gifts which we all admired and valued, was great also in the spirit that endeared him to all—at least, to all who can appreciate the beauty of that charity of which St. Paul wrote; one whose lips were full of instruction and good counsel, who was always ready in his high public place with timely words of wisdom and exhortation, and who knew well how to look discriminatingly and sympathetically upon the things of others. We speak to Thee, God and Father, freely, our painful sense of loss in his departure, our disappointment that he should not have been suffered to continue, our wish that he could have lived a while longer—yet at the same time, our faith that he is not, because Thou hast taken him, and that when by a good man's death the value of earth is

Z

diminished, the value of some other part of Thy universe is increased. So we thank Thee for the good, the great, the wise with whom we have been blest, and who have gone from us to shine and serve other where; resigning them meekly, as meekly as we can, to Thy holy will, and committing them, together with all who remain, and with ourselves, to the keeping of Him of whom the whole family in heaven and earth is named, even the Father of our Lord Jesus Christ, in whom we surely trust for the safety both of the dead and of the living. And unto Him be worship and praise, now and evermore, world without end.

SERMON.

THE WHEAT AND THE TARES.

"But while men slept, his enemy came and sowed tares among the wheat, and went his way. But when the blade was sprung up, and brought forth fruit, then appeared the tares also."—MATTHEW xiii. 25, 26.

THE thirteenth of St. Matthew is, on the whole, rather melancholy reading if you understand it aright, and can sympathize with Christ. These parables of His, recorded here, are of the most part sad in tone. The first four, at all events, express a somewhat dolorous, desponding mind, and show Him clouded with gloomy presentiments. Led by the multitudes attracted to His ministry, and by the apparent impression produced, to reflect upon the value of the work that was being done and its probable issues, He pours out to the people under a veil of figure the thoughts that fill His breast; tells them in figures, how He estimates, and what He expects or forebodes. We may wonder, perhaps, that He should have unbosomed Himself thus, that He should have made such a subject the theme of public discourse ; but the utterance would be a relief to Him, was possibly a necessity for Him, whether the audience were to be edified or not. And while He sometimes refrained from speaking because it might not be useful or intelligible, He often spoke freely the thing that occupied and weighed upon His soul, without much regard to the capacity of the hearers, or to what they would be able to find in it for themselves ;—just stating what at the moment He saw and felt, as it pressed for deliverance ; just allowing it to break forth unchecked in its own way. And the Spirit of the Lord should have liberty. The seer with a vision possessing and burdening Him, must not be pausing always to ask if it will be likely to be understood and appreciated, if it will be calculated to profit or enlighten any. Let him not trouble about this, let him be content to declare his vision. It should be enough for him that he has something to say which craves to be said, and says it. He need not consider always, the use when he has the burning or the motion within him.

And what are the thoughts concerning the value of His work and its probable issues, which in a succession of parables Christ pours out to the people? He reckons, that of the seed which He is busily scattering, and which seemed to be finding lodgment in the minds of many, but a small portion would bear real and permanent fruit. Three parts, say, would either fail to take root and be utterly wasted, utterly lost; or, rooting, and giving fair promise for a while, would yet fall short of yielding. The incipient growth, soon withering, or gradually choked. Not more than a fourth part, say, would germinate and spring up to productiveness; so little would truly fructify, so much would come to nothing. He sees, moreover, the meal of His pure doctrine, His simple religion, destined to suffer great and grievous adulteration— to be subjected, in the progress of time, to a permeating leaven of corrupt influences; and the new Church, the new society, which He was forming, insignificant at present, as a grain of mustard seed, destined, with its approaching rapid increase and ultimate wide extension, to be infected from the world with unclean and devouring elements; the fowls of the air flocking to build in its foliage and feed upon its branches. He foresees, further, that while He was infusing among men, beautiful beliefs, divine principles and inspirations, from which corresponding graces and virtues would assuredly arise, yet, alongside and in connection with them many peculiar infirmities and uglinesses would be developed; that through a mysterious evil working, a seemingly malicious something, threatening and tending ever to mar or impair whatever of good is born, the very infusion of these beautiful beliefs, these divine principles and inspirations, would carry with it its own crop of unhappy maladies and mischiefs; that out of the midst of the wheat which He was sowing, tares would appear in close proximity, as if from an adversary's sowing. Such were some of the forebodings that troubled the heart of Christ, and which He indulged aloud.

But now, in the text, three things are hinted by Him—so at least I read—with respect to the presence of evil amidst the good. Here, first, is the secrecy, the undiscernibleness of its beginnings—"while men slept;" words which could hardly have been meant to indicate negligence or inattention on the part of those who should have been alert and watchful, and whose vigilance might have prevented the hostile sowing, since the servants, who later on, ejaculate their astonishment and disappointment at what is found among the corn, are in no wise charged with having contributed to it by omission of duty. The words were intended, doubtless, as an equivalent for, during the night, during the interval when men are naturally wrapt in slumber, and cannot perceive what is done. The Speaker would be suggesting thus, with a passing touch, how hidden and unobserved are the beginnings of evil; how, in regard to its first startings and earlier motions, we are like them that sleep.

What impressions of all sorts on mind and moral nature are constantly taking place around us of which there is not the slightest sign, which nobody descries or suspects! Every moment, a vast multitude of souls are receiving from without, from some impact of circumstance or experience of life, to some more or less pregnant effect upon their character or thought, and nothing of it is beheld by any. All in the dark, formative influences are for ever falling, formative processes for ever going on. The seed of a lovely conversion is being sown here, the seed of a lamentable perversion, there. Here, the seed of a mischievous prejudice or weakness; there, the seed of a fine susceptibility or sympathy. And no eye catches sight of it, no ear hears the sound thereof. The winds blow, the birds fly; and while we walk abroad unconscious, little seeds are dropping and rooting on all hands, that will be manifested ere long in weed or flower.

Oh, the germinal impressions wrought daily upon our children of which we dream not! What a busy scene it is within them, of reception and assimilation toward future becoming; what concealed engenderings are occurring there from morn to eve! Something out of your home talk or behaviour, or from the atmosphere of your spirit, has just now sunk down into your child, to be healthily or unwholesomely operative in him, to tell detrimentally or beneficially upon the making of the man that shall be. Just now, something has been sown in him while you slept, which is destined to emerge in his growth, disfiguringly or otherwise. Mental movements and events are so silent, so invisible. In these, were the beginnings of the individual conduct that has surprised us, of the great outward changes, the great outward revolutions and convulsions, by which society has been shaken. But we neither saw nor heard; in secret were they sown and prepared for. What moral grandeurs and catastrophies are having their foundations laid to-day, without observation!

With respect to the beginnings of evil—if we could but detect and recognize them, to take the little ones and dash them against the stones. If we could but mark at a glance, when and where *that* steals in and is allowed to nestle which threatens serious mischief to the soul : when and where *that* happens within us from which, unless presently remedied and rectified, miserable degenerations or pollutions are to ensue! If we could but have known of what such an indulged mood or such a weak moment was the seed. The serpent's eggs that are nursed often unawares! So unconscious were we of the *turn* that conducted into the road which has brought us to the plight lamented; so unconscious were we as we took a certain step, harboured a certain feeling, or came under certain influences, that we had started then, the long train of error and wrong-doing which afterwards followed. You wake up some day to find yourself, to your surprise and shame, the slave of a particular habit. You had not noted how, little by little, the habit had been slowly forming and gathering power; how from day to day the silent repetition of acts had been silently forging a chain with ever-added and ever-stronger links; until at length, seeking to move, you found yourself a slave, a Laocoon, helpless in the coils. The births of evil, how still they are! We do not hear their whimpering, we are not present to witness them, and be warned that a monster is born.

But here, again, is the facility with which it grows, its independence of fostering care or aid. " He went his way." Was not that a stroke of the Artist, with which He meant to intimate the little that is needed to insure the progress and spread of evil? The enemy just sowed and went his way. There was no necessity for him to come back and look after what he had sown; no necessity for him to visit and watch for the purpose of helping, or to feel anxiety about due sunshine and shower. What *he* had sown was safe to grow. The Christ had to work hard and long to quicken as He sought, to secure the least of such fruit as He desired. Much of what He scattered abroad would perish and produce naught. Many an impression made by Him upon the minds of men would be made only to be destroyed; would be met, and choked or withered by adverse influences. Any good which He might awaken or implant would encounter manifold resistance, and required diligent tendence lest it should succumb and fail; required to be waited on and ministered to in order to its furtherance. But the sower of the tares, when he had once dropped what he carried, was free to go his way without more ado, and without the smallest solicitude. Noxious weeds want no watering. Oh, the pains you have bestowed upon some precious plant, or some fair young fruit tree ; and while, in spite of all your pains, it has faded and died, perhaps ; the neglected weeds around you, how they have waxed and flourished ! Do but be negligent, indeed, do but refrain from effort and fold your hands, and evil is sure to spring up—as the dust gathers and accumulates in the closed, forsaken chamber. You do but need to go your way lightly, and things are sure to go wrong ; so quickly behind you will disorder begin to show its ugly head, or deterioration set in. Good habits have to be formed with stern endeavour, and in the sweat of your brow ; bad habits form themselves as we stand idly by.

Or, whisper a generous, charitable sentiment, and breathe a scandal. If you would have the one to take root and extend, you must e'en repeat it again and again with earnest persistence. It lodges for a while, and slips, lays hold, and loses hold ; it halts and falters and does not readily propagate ; it is apt to fall dead by the way, and is not likely to be diffused unless it be urged and re-urged. But see the other! How it is caught up and carried onward from lip to lip ; how it runs swiftly and spreads widely, like a tongue of flame over the dry heather! You have but breathed it once and gone your way, and presently, it is here, there, everywhere, greatening as it flies. And truth and virtue, we must toil hard to promote and keep alive; error and vice rise unsolicited, and sustain and disseminate themselves without support.

"Ah, what a proof of human depravity!" some have sighed; "how indicative of our radical badness!" But I look at it in another light. To my mind it is rather a bright and cheering fact, for it seems to me that the evil which breaks out upon us so easily, and grows so freely with no effort on our part, is never so really ours, and can never be so enduring, as the good to which we attain only by dint of labour and struggle, which is brought forth with pangs of yearning desire and stress of conflict. That, is more vitally and deeply mine than the evil which comes of itself—spontaneously eruptive—and will surely survive it, having immortality, when it has died away. The latter is at superficial thing comparatively, and comparatively weak. It is not the living, virile, and compact product of ardent aspiration, of strong wrestling and pain. It has not I myself—my heart and forces —poured into it, as the good has, and in the course of time will fall off from me, exhausted and dispersed. The strenuously wrought out good is eternal—and it alone. The tares that spring up while we go our way, and while we go our way, creep defilingly over the field, are destined to destruction, when the wheat that has been striven for with diligent tillage shall be gathered into barns as food for man and God.

And now, again, here is the inevitable following of evil in the wake of good; the inevitableness of its accompaniment and concurrence for a season, wherever good is sown. "The enemy came and sowed tares among the wheat." This is what Christ prognosticated would happen; that His sowing of wheat would involve a sowing of tares. Such was His acute and profound discernment. He understood that the new life, of divine faith and hope and love, which He should be the means of awakening, must needs conduce temporarily to some special failings and frailties; that there must needs emerge from it and attend upon it, temporarily, some special unfortunate distempers; that He would not be able to raise and enlarge men without their becoming thereby, in some respects, twisted and bent, at all events for a time. And has it not been so? With all the devotion and consecration, with the splendid courages, zeals, and self-sacrifices which He has inspired, what bitterness and uncharitableness, what dissensions and animosities, what sourness and meanness, have mingled; nay, of what sad passions His inspiration has been the occasion, what unsightly features of character, and false feelings and ways, it may be said to have precipitated! I am not thinking of the corruptions of primitive Christianity, nor was Jesus foreboding these in the text; these are foreboded by Him, apparently, in the parables of the mustard seed and the leaven. What He forebodes here, apparently, and I am intending, are the evils incident to the very spirit of Christianity.

For example, there is the evil which *has* arisen from it, of undue self-regard. The spirit of Christianity is aspiration—aspiration to be better and purer, to enter in at the strait gate, to conquer the flesh and subdue the devil within us, to reach the true eternal life and be redeemed from sin. This is good and beautiful; but it has tended to create more or less of unhealthy self-attention and self-inspection. In seeking salvation and righteousness, and in learning to cleanse themselves, men have learnt to be too much engrossed with themselves, with their own spiritual welfare and prospects; and thus, their finest development has been hindered; their worthy anxiety and striving has led to their becoming somewhat contracted and warped; the vessel has been flawed in the polishing. Moreover, the moral earnestness which is the spirit of Christianity, has tended to beget often undue severity toward those who are not what they should be, and inconsiderate hastiness and harshness in judging them. Its very depth and intensity have had the effect of making men rather cruel at times, rather wanting in just allowance for, and humane sympathy with, ignorance and weakness; rather inclined to censoriousness. *Because* they have been so nobly impatient of the wrong, and so rightly imbued with a sense of the guilt and ugliness of sin, they have been a little hard upon the transgressors, and have been able calmly to contemplate for them, as not in excess of their desert, the punishment of an eternal hell. These things, however, begin to cure themselves after a while. In the progress of moral growth, the unwholesome self-intentness comes to be remedied by increasing altruistic regards; and increasing love teaches forbearance and mercy, and casts off at last with a shudder, the dogma of everlasting torment. As the wheat unfolds from blade to ear, the tares are manifested, to be complained of and exclaimed against, until eventually they consume away.

The spirit of Christianity, again, is burning zeal for truth—the truth to be prized and cherished before all. A noble spirit! yet how often it has brought forth with it, and does bring forth, something of bigotry and uncharitableness; an unwillingness to recognize those who cannot see the truth where we see it; an inability to appreciate *their* labours who are not seeking it with us and in our way, or to give *them* credit for having found aught of it who have not found precisely what we have. How often the noble zeal has brought forth with it, and does bring forth, an ignoble fear for the truth, leading to angry and inhuman persecutions on its behalf, to endeavours to guard and protect it by unworthy means, to attempts even, to discourage and repress inquiry after it, lest such inquiry should prove prejudicial to its interests! As when a writer in the *Pall Mall Gazette*, deprecates seriously the investigations of a society recently formed for psychical research, lest they should imperil our acquired enlightened *un*belief in the supernatural; for scientific zeal is no less prone than theological and religious zeal, to evolve a measure of bigotry and prejudice. Great earnestness, in whatever relation, tends always to some unseemly dogmatism, or detracting narrowness; it is temporarily unavoidable, it belongs to the imperfection of human nature. But let us be patient; it is only for a time. As the wheat grows, the tares manifest themselves, as tares, and are lamented and condemned; and when at length the wheat is fully ripe, the tares shall vanish as rubbish in the fire.

PRAYER.

Thou the ever-living One, the ever-present One, who never ceasest from among us, who never leavest us, though we may have left Thee in turning from the voice and vision of the soul, in quitting the path of fidelity, to the higher law of the mind: restore us to ourselves and Thee with some reclaiming thought, some reinstating impression. Bring us home from our wanderings to the purer self, to that filial temper which knows the Father, to the love which Thou art, to the Spiritual, which we are, in the midst of the flesh. Bring us from our rufflings into the sanctuary of Divine calm that awaits us in the depths of our own breasts where Thou hidest, who art our root and ground. Give us retreat from our surface, which misrepresents and belies us, to our centre, which is the truth and reality of us. Raise us from the lower parts to the height of our nature, from those lower parts upon which we are prone to decline to that height which we are prone to forsake, and from which we often remain needlessly self-exiled. May the quiet of the Sunday hours be to us a means of healing. May meditation and reflection come to purify us, to chasten and exalt our tone. In the atmosphere and order of the House of Prayer may we learn to breathe more deeply, more truly; to recover dimmed sight, to find our right mind, the humility which is wiser than conceit, the simplicity to which understanding enters, the holy sensibility to which secrets of beauty are revealed, the deeper reverence which sanctifies knowledge, the aspiration which enriches the soul. Through good words heard or read let some word of the Lord be conveyed to us for our upbuilding. Through the song in our mouth, as we sing together in concert, let some song of worship and praise be kindled in our heart.

SERMON XXI.

"*WHOSOEVER HEARETH THESE SAYINGS OF MINE, AND DOETH THEM.*"

"Therefore whosoever heareth these sayings of Mine, and doeth them, I will liken him unto a wise man, which built his house upon a rock."—MATTHEW vii. 24.

ONE or two books have fallen into my hands of late, notably one by Count Tolstoï, entitled "The Kingdom of God is Within You," in which the Christian Church is charged with neglecting and contravening certain teachings of Christ; in which the practice of the great body of its members is asserted to be sadly at variance with ethical precepts of His contained in the Gospels; and in a late number of an English Magazine, *The New Review*, the Russian Count wrote, pleading for some reply to his indictment.

Having read with attention and interest what he had advanced, both in this article and in the volume mentioned, I waited, curious to see what reply would be made, and by whom.

Very shortly—in the next issue of the same review—several answers appeared from different ecclesiastical dignitaries, Anglican, Romanist, and Nonconformist, to which I turned eagerly, but the reading of which, I must confess, dissatisfied and disappointed me. For the most part—to my view—they revolved volubly round the point without really grappling with or touching it. In place of meeting the indictment with direct denial and an exposure of its falseness, its groundlessness; or admitting it with an array, if not of reasons, of justifying excuses for the conceded disobedience; they enlarged on the accuser's extravagant enthusiasm and somewhat censorious spirit, and on the unlikelihood that he should be right when the general sentiment of Christendom was against him; sought refuge in quoted expositions of the ancient fathers, in the opinions that had prevailed and the course that had been pursued through the generations and ages, or intimated the impossibility of acting as it was insisted the followers of Jesus ought to act, and the disordering, destructive consequences that would ensue if they did. So unsatisfactory to me, indeed, and disappointing on the whole were the answers, that I have felt unable to refrain from adding, just here at all events, to the handful of people I am in the habit of addressing on religious subjects, the answer *I* have to give.

Some of you will have read doubtless the utterances referred to and the rejoinders elicited, and may be feeling rather perplexed and bewildered between them ; a little disturbed, perhaps, by the former, and not quite quieted by the latter : but, whether or no, it is laid upon me to say my say on the matter for a few minutes this morning.

The charges of inconsistency with, and violation of, Christ's explicit instructions on the part of those who call Him Master and Lord, are principally two,—relating to *resistance of evil* and *the holding of property*, to which two, at all events, I confine myself for the present, and meet them straightly with the countercharge that the accuser —whom one cannot but love and honour for his conscientious earnestness and his courageous fidelity to conviction—has yet, in regard to these particulars, misconceived and misrepresented the instructions of Christ, and demands of us what the latter never enjoined nor meant to inculcate. God knows that the best of us are far from exemplifying His ethics as they should be exemplified ; that there is enough unfaithfulness among us which we must e'en acknowledge, and deserve to be reproached with. And for much that Count Tolstoï has written we may be thankful; much of it we may well ponder gravely and lay to heart: but, just here, I maintain, his requisitions are not the requisitions of Jesus; and this, you will please observe, is my one simple contention, without any purpose of dealing with the morality of war, or discussing at all social and economic problems. The only question which now engages me is the question—What, on such and such points, was *the actual teaching of Jesus?*

First, then, concerning *resistance of evil*. We are told that He instilled absolute non-resistance; that, according to Him, no force is ever to be used by us for protection or defence against assault; no punishment or prosecution of offenders attempted; that it should not be ours, under any circumstances, to repel invasion, to refuse to tolerate injustice, to strive with one who would injure, oppress, unfairly exact from us, or to share in consigning malefactors to gaol: but ours always to accept meekly whatever ill may be done, or violence offered. In proof of which, the passage is adduced from the Sermon on the Mount: "*I say unto you resist not evil; but whosoever smiteth* thee on one cheek, turn to him the other also; and if any man take away thy coat, let him have thy cloak also; and whosoever shall compel thee to go a mile, go with him twain."

"You read that in your churches Sunday after Sunday," it is said, "avowing belief the while in the Divine authority of Him who uttered the words, and habitually ignore what they command—are constantly behaving in contradiction of them; you decline to suffer wrong quietly; you reject the idea of allowing the aggressor on your rights, the enemy of your peace, or the filcher of your goods, to have his way. Instead of enduring in silence, you proceed to contest, to beat back, to bind and incarcerate when you can. How can you thus coolly ignore and contradict your Master's directions?" And when I reply—as I do—that the real sense of His words is not that which they *seem* to bear, it is retorted of course that I am presuming to explain them away; that they must be taken as they stand, without gloss or curtailment. Here is His plain unqualified enactment: "Resist not evil"—submit in everything; and what business have I to qualify it? to insinuate that it means other or less than absolute non-resistance?

Yet none will deny that He did not always

intend to be taken literally; that He spoke often in bold tropes and figures; was much addicted to paradoxical expressions, as when He said, for instance, in His enthusiasm about Faith, that "the smallest grain of it would suffice to remove yonder mountain from its base and bury it in the sea"; or forbade all thought for the morrow, yet sent His disciples to a distance to prepare and arrange for the next day's passover; or counselled that we give to every one that asks aught of us, yet Himself again and again refused to give when asked, refusing the Pharisee's request for a sign, to respond with a syllable to Herod's repeated questions, or to grant the prayer of the man who besought His aid toward the settlement of a family dispute: His injunction to give always to those who ask could not imply, as St. Augustine once sagely remarked, that we are to give always *what* they ask, since such giving might often be prejudicial rather than beneficial to the recipient, and St. Augustine felt therefore, as he further remarked, that, so far from breaking the injunction, he was only carrying out the very spirit of it when he withheld from a worthless tramp the alms he supplicated and gave him instead a serious lecture on idleness.

Jesus often meant something quite other than the letter of His words conveyed, and to the extreme puzzling of His hearers at the time, as when He stood and cried: "Except ye eat My flesh and drink My blood ye have no life in you." He often exaggerated somewhat that He might the better pierce and penetrate the crust of dull mind or worldly heart; would often clothe a truth in an exaggerated form, that it might arrest attention and lead, through roused thought and inquiry, to an ultimate discernment within the exaggerated form of the truth that would not be otherwise discerned.

Never, perhaps, was there a teacher in regard to many of whose sayings we need more to wait on them patiently for a right understanding of them, or to be careful lest, in interpreting them according to the letter, we miss entirely their meaning and spirit. And let me ask those who demand that we accept the precept under consideration without any limiting or qualifying, whether they fulfil their own demand? Is there with them no resistance of evil? What are they doing, pray, in combatting so strenuously doctrines and practices of the Church which they conceive to be erroneous and fraught with mischief; in lifting up their voice so loudly against what they deem false and wrong, or in dealing with faults and unbecoming habits of their children, in endeavouring to cure these with applications of corrective discipline? And are they not most actively at one with St. Paul, in his exhortation to the Ephesians, to "resist the Devil"? Do they not agree fully with the Scripture portrayal of the life of the good as a struggle, a fight, a warfare; and that as Jesus is said to have come to destroy the works of the Devil, to be followers of Him, we must be ever contending in various ways with evil? What are we here for, indeed, but to contend with it. "Yes," they answer, "of course every one knows and acknowledges that, but it was not of this that Jesus was speaking, only of resisting evil done to ourselves or others with force or violence." Ah, then, they too—as I wanted to show—are obliged to limit and qualify. They too must give their explanation, which is, that He meant to condemn, not *all* resistance of evil, but simply resisting with force and violence. I, therefore, without suspicion of explaining away, may be allowed to give *my* explanation, which is somewhat different, and, as it seems to me, truer than theirs, being grounded on the antithetical relation of the precept to an old Jewish maxim which He had just quoted: "Ye have heard it was said *an eye for an eye and a tooth for a tooth*," but (in contrast, in opposition thereto) "I say unto you resist not evil."

Here, then, we have surely an elucidation of His precise meaning, as a condemnation of the *lex talionis*, of all resistance of evil *with evil*—with its own weapons—with a reply of its own ugly spirit; as though He had said: "It shall not be yours to retaliate wrong with wrong, malice with malice, injustice with injustice. You are not, when assailed with spite and animosity, to assail with returning spite and animosity; or, when suffering in some way from another's unholy greed and lust, to withstand or chastise out of any similarly unholy passion. Let there be in your resistance no echo, no answer of his evil mind, of the evil thought or impulse which actuated him; in your defensive or opposing stroke, none of his bad animus, his unworthy rage or revenge: in grappling with, and seeking to baffle or protect yourself against him who would pluck out your eye, no like desire and aim to gouge out his."

When, then, I punish a transgressor, not for the sake of punishing him, with no vengeful wrath towards him, but that the law which he has broken may be guarded, and he be taught perchance to respect it; or put an ill-doer in chains with no ill-will towards him, but in the interests and for the safety of society, and lest he should grow worse, to his own and others' misery, through being permitted to sin with impunity; or help to repel an invasion of my country without aught of the maliciousness or the wanton grasping at dominion which instigated the invasion; I am not resisting evil in the sense which Christ deprecated. It was resisting evil with *itself* which He deprecated. Sometimes, indeed, His great law of love, of which the precept is an expression, may require us to suffer quietly; if, for instance, there is likelihood of winning and reclaiming the offender thereby, better by enduring meekly than by withstanding or chastising. But sometimes the same law may require us to do the very contrary; if we honestly feel, for instance, that to thwart his movements, to stop with violence the outcomings of his wrongness, is necessary for his good, to save him from strengthening himself in his iniquity, to school him toward repentance and improvement; gentleness and severity, appearing thus at different times as identical—as love, in fact—manifesting itself now at its one pole, and now at the other. Times there are, indeed, when *not* to resist evil with drastic measures—with measures inflicting distress and pain—would be an infraction of the law of love, would mean—as it too often does—not love at all, but only indolence, cowardice, or mean self-indulgence. The far easier thing, perhaps the far more pleasant and comfortable for ourselves, would be to yield or forbear; but the right thing, the benevolent thing, and withal the hardest, would be to refuse, even at the cost of causing temporary wounds and bruises. As a writer on the subject of "The Revolt of Daughters" has said: "It is often easier for an amiable sister to sacrifice herself to her selfish brother in giving way to his selfishness, than it would be to sacrifice herself *for* him by withstanding it, and, in choosing the easier course, she selfishly contributes to increase his selfishness, to the utter destruction in him, maybe, of respect and affection."

Yes, I am not at all softening down the precept of Christ and making it easier for us with my interpretation, which is one reason for believing that my interpretation is the right one; that it sets us something specially hard to do—something specially lofty to attain to; for the greater difficulty often is not to refrain from opposing wrong—to restrain ourselves from battling with it—but to battle with and oppose it without the least breath in us of evil temper or passion, in accordance with the apostolic direction, " Be angry and sin not."

The greater difficulty often is not to yield weakly, but to fight fiercely in *love*, with no desire in dealing sharply and severely with another but to deal with him for his good. Jesus *does* lay down the rule that we render good for our brother's evil, but the form in which it should be rendered— love, which is not merely tenderness or reluctance to vex and scourge—must be left to prescribe; "only, whatever you do," He taught, "in the way of resistance, never resist evil with itself—with its own weapons—in its own spirit; rather than that submit to anything. Rather than that, if a man will take away thy coat, *let him have thy cloak also*, or if he strike thee on one cheek, *turn to him the other*; rather than that, do thus."

And now, briefly, with regard to the holding of property,—Jesus, we are told, plainly discountenanced it, called on all who would be His disciples to relinquish their possessions, to strip themselves of any wealth they might have and disperse it amongst the poor. Did He not say, once and again, " Sell that ye have and give alms, provide yourselves bags which wax not old, a treasure in the heavens that faileth not"? Did He not declare that unless a man forsook all that he had, he could be no follower of His? What was His demand of the rich young ruler, who came asking what he should do to inherit eternal life, but that he should renounce his riches, devoting them to the relief of the needy and destitute? There, we are told, are His recorded words, which he who runs may read; and who that professes to be a Christian can, in the face of them, justify to himself the retention of private property? Who that professes allegiance to Him can be satisfied to retain his abundance, instead of distributing it abroad or sharing it freely with those worse off, especially in these times of huge incomes and large estates, side by side with ghastliest want and penury?

Yes, there are His recorded words; but the mistake is to assume that they were intended for *all* who would sit at His feet and accept His spiritual guidance. They do not state a general essential condition of discipleship—were not for the many, but a counsel of perfection for the few.

He wanted *some* to be thus surrendered, but only on *some* laid the cross of such sacrifice. While preaching to the multitude a higher morality than prevailed, and exhorting them to practise it, to exceed the righteousness of the Scribes and Pharisees, He went seeking from the first to collect around Him a small band of special devotees—of men who should partake with Himself in His entire consecration to the work of promoting the Kingdom, able and willing to give up everything for it, to live with Him on His lonely height of all-renouncing enthusiasm; now one and now another in whom He descried, as He thought, signs of the requisite susceptibility were drawn by Him from out the crowd to come and do this, disencumbering themselves of all ties, denuding themselves of all goods and chattels to yearn and labour with Him; but He never required or expected it of others. He would fain find some capable of making themselves eunuchs for the Kingdom of Heaven's sake. "Whosoever is able to receive it," He said, "let him receive it." If any could, He was glad, and gladly welcomed them to the elect inner circle; but, if they could not, the hard saying, the counsel of perfection, was not for them, and he did not ask them to obey it. The rich young ruler, with his singular moral sensibility and earnestness, seemed to Him one who might be attracted to His side, of whom an all-forsaking apostle might be made, and, struck by his promising expression, He sought to bring him in, trying him with the words: "Be perfect, sell whatsoever thou hast, and take up the cross and follow Me." But the attempt failed. The man, though so good and lovable, was not equal to that. He had fancied, had hoped, that he might have been, or He would not have proposed it. He did not propose it to others who came to Him—did not to His night visitor, the inquiring Nicodemus, nor to the centurion whose faith He admired and extolled; and some who offered to abandon all and be wholly with Him He discouraged. To one who begged that he might be allowed, He replied, "No; go home to thy house, and thy friends, and dwell there as my disciple."

So, were Jesus here to-day, He would assuredly rejoice in any instance of voluntary renunciation and self-stripping for the service of God and man; but He would not exact it of all who call themselves by His name.

Were He among us to-day, He would be found doubtless lamenting the unequal distribution of wealth, the existing frightful extremes of abundance and destitution, and exhorting loudly to more effort and more sacrifices than are made with a view to the remedying of these. But there were no such frightful extremes in His land and time; no such miserable poor as we have in our midst to rouse His remonstrance, and wring His heart; then and there He could say—as He could not now, standing in our city slums—" *Happy are ye poor,*" for the poor of Palestine needed little pity, and, living their simple, healthy lives, free from the burdens and cares and sensual temptations of the rich, might well be congratulated by Him.

Hence, not facing our social problems, our monstrous social contrasts, He did not go about, as He might otherwise have done, inveighing against gross inequalities of condition, and pleading for remedial effort and sacrifice, but was intent on endeavouring to raise and refine the moral tone, the moral life of all, on inculcating certain virtues for all classes. It was His absorbing aim to act quickeningly and redeemingly on individual souls; to work a purifying, elevating work on the souls of men, to stir all round to more love and righteousness. And, with respect to riches, He simply taught that we should not be *covetous* of them— should not toil and strain to amass them to the neglect of spiritual treasure, should not encumber ourselves with needless and heart-disordering worries and anxieties in seeking them, but be at once wholesomer and happier in limiting our outward wants and moderating our desires for material things, in cultivating simpler habits, and not risking loss of the life in thought for the meat, or impairment of the body in thought for clothes. Not the possession of riches, then, but the greed of them, is inconsistent with Christian discipleship. His main teaching for His disciples generally, as distinguished from His apostles, we have embodied, it may be said, in the beatitudes of the Sermon on the Mount, in which He portrayed the qualities and characteristics of the children of the Kingdom, namely humility; meekness, in opposition to impatience, self-assertion, or agressiveness of temper; mourning for what is corrupt and false, aspiration after goodness, inward purity, compassion, and peace-making behaviours and ways. Thus, to constitute us Christ's there must be, in addition to humility and meekness, aspiration and inward purity; trouble of soul over evils beheld around us, mercifulness, and behaviours and ways that are peace-making. He, therefore, is not Christ's to whom witnessed disorders of society are no burden, who can be content that iniquities should prevail and injustice be done, who can live undisturbed in the midst of abuses and wrongs that cry for redress; who, so long as *he* is enlightened, cares not much for the thousands who are sunk in ignorance, so long as *he* is raised and refined, cares not much that thousands are left in helpless coarseness and degradation. Such an one, whatever his Christian creed or profession, the Master would pronounce indubitably still an unbeliever.

Neither is he Christ's who has no pity on suffering or necessity which he might assist to relieve; who is harsh and unforgiving to the erring; who is slow to sympathise and lacking in considerateness; who recklessly grinds the face of the poor, and denies them a living wage that he may wax rich and richer; who buys eagerly and with delight cheap things, heedless of the wretchedly paid toil and sweat through which they are alone obtainable; who, while writing large cheques, maybe, for missionary and philanthropic societies, bears hardly on his clerks and employés, and remunerates them meanly: for all this is the very opposite of "*mercy*."

Nor, again, is he Christ's whose spirit and action tend to foment needless discords and disputes; whose tongue is quick to breathe abroad a slander or insinuate a suspicion, producing estrangement between neighbours and friends ; who is careless of wounding the feelings of others or causing offence ; who has the devilish knack of dropping irritating words, of striking roughly a raw, sore place, to the infliction of secret distress and pain ; who, by his temper at home, provokes wrangling rather than promotes reconciliation, or, by his want of amiable sensibility, renders those uncomfortable whom he should put at their ease; by his unfair dealing, his selfish exactingness, his thoughtless injustice, creates again and again a tumult of distempering resentment in the breasts of others; for all this is the opposite of "*peace-making.*"

Jesus, I find, then, has nothing to say to us on the question of property and pauperism, except indeed as there are principles embodied or embedded in His teaching that may be applied for some guidance in relation to the question—such principles, namely, as have just been indicated. I find Him nowhere denouncing the possession of wealth or enjoining its relinquishment when possessed by all who sat at His feet. What He says is, saying it to rich and poor alike, "Strive not to accumulate material possessions; labour not for the meat that perisheth, to the neglect of the meat that endureth unto eternal life; beware of covetousness in whatever state you are; be not content, be troubled and stirred to mourning when aught of evil is done, when there are disorders around you that should be rectified or corruptions that should be purged. Be not just, merely, but merciful—merciful at the cost, if necessary, of some self-abnegation and sacrifice. Study to be peace-making in your behaviours and ways; to be for binding together where you can, rather than for dividing; for healing rather than for rending or discomposing; and peace-making not only through gentleness or non-resistance, but when, for true peace, it may be requisite to flash an intermediate sword." For He who did not strive nor cry, who would not break the bruised reed or quench the smoking flax, made a whip with which to drive out the traffickers from the Temple, and sent them flying before Him; while He who said "Put up thy sword into its sheath," deprecating the kind of resistance about to be offered, said also, "He that hath no sword, let him sell his garment and buy one," intimating, whatever He may have meant by the "sword," that *now*, at length, the time for some kind of resistance had come; and our Christianity lies in seeking to exemplify—as the hour and the circumstances may demand—both these injunctions of the Son of Man, of Him who came preaching goodwill and peace, and, in His deep yearning to make peace, sent "not peace on the earth, but a sword."

PRAYER.

Thou, the Eternal Light of Light, of whom is all brightness, all clear shining and beauty that makes us glad,—the night also is Thine wherein Thou dwellest and workest Thy work unseen, while men sigh because of the gloom and know not what it hides. And the night, though we sleep or lie awake and wail, is a busy and beneficent time. In the kingdom of nature things go on in it beneath the surface, down at the roots of the trees and the grass, which we perceive not and which have their fruit and sweet issues in the things of the morning. So in the darkness of what we call evil Thou aboundest, and we walk in the shadow of God. The mystery weighs upon and chafes us often, yet the world is the greater for it and we are greatened by it, and the mystery in its depth and inscrutibleness breathes Thee as, without it, Thou wouldst not be breathed; nay, is it not our travail out of which Thou, who art and wast, art born to us? is it not the thick cloud out of which a voice has spoken to us that would not else have spoken? Through the sense of mystery it is that Thou comest into our thought, and we awake with the Hebrew patriarch to feel that the place where we stand is holy ground. Through the sense of mystery it is that Thou hast made us religious and hast taught us to worship, and often when in the agreeable and pleasant clearness Thou hast been absent or remote, the gathering murk and mist have seemed to bring Thee nigh. We see with all our eyes, and Thou fadest; we cannot see, and Thou appearest. We understand perfectly, and Thou art not; we wonder and are perplexed, and Thou beginnest to be murmured in the soul as when inland are heard from afar the murmurs of the infinite sea. So blessed be God for the burden of mystery.

But, O Divine Wisdom, Wisdom out of whose fulness we receive when we discern our defect and error, when we know how to be strong for duty, or patient in trial, when we are alive and responsive to the claims and obligations which our daily situation, our daily relations, involve—Wisdom out of whose fulness the wandering step is guided and the wayward spirit ruled, and the heart kept sound and calm, and heavenly discipline is gained from life's labour and vicissitude: O wisdom, make us wise and wiser with Thy inflowing. We would have our needed portion from Thy plenitude, our needed replenishing from Thy fountain. Thou visitest the earth and enrichest it, and again and again right thoughts, fine thoughts, govern the mind, and souls here and there are swept by noble impulse and passion, and beautiful things and great things are done; and again and again the weak become heroic and the simple are filled with understanding, and the erring retrace their way. Thou visiteth the earth and enrichest it, and art not far from every one of us. Pass us not by in Thy continued process and diffusion; leave us not poor, leave us not to fail for lack of Thee. Divine Wisdom, let us have our part in Thee for our due growth and behaviour, as each little flower of the grass, each bud of the field, has its part for due nourishment in the great universal sun of whose beams we all partake. Pity our follies, break up our dulness and slowness, be the corrector of our faults, the teacher of our ignorance.

God, the Spirit, the Light, we thank Thee for the light which we have searched after and found, like the happy merchantman in the parable who found in his search the pearl of great price; and for the light which has come upon us which we had not laboured or looked for, like the treasure hid in the field, suddenly disclosed to the wayfarer. We thank Thee for timely words of counsel, of quickening, of inspiration which we have met by the way, for moving impressions received that have borne good fruit in us and left us more finely inclined and purposeful, for happy thoughts with which we have been visited in the night, until it grew somewhat light about us. And truth—how lovely is truth when we have reached it at length in our earnest pursuit, when after long watching, as those that watch for the morning and cannot sleep, it has dawned upon us and we have felt its sureness! or when we have bought it at some cost and never regretted what we paid for it, and would not sell it, though tempted, for any price! And how lovely is the seeking through the days, with ever renewed quest, and untiring zeal, the rising to fresh inquiry with the sense of regions before us unknown and unexplored, of the ocean towards which our stream flows in long, slow windings, though it be still and always far away; the glimpses caught and lost, the multitude of divers and conflicting thoughts, the dream of finding;— how lovely is the seeking. And in the universal disquietude, the Divine unrest, through all that breathes the breath of life —here is Thy constant, unwearied seeking of us, until Thou shalt overtake and realise Thyself within us.

Thou who art with us while we are far from Thee, endue us with the holy strength of trust, help us to feel that we are heirs, though poor, and that what we have not, and are not at present, to which we would fain attain. Thou art keeping for us against the day of the Lord. Help us to receive more of our own in giving freely of our own, and to find in ministry the larger life of peace and promise. Help us amidst the troubles and confusions of the world to believe bravely in Thy will and governance, and to be co-workers with Thee in seeking to promote according to our power that which is good. The strong, the true, the consecrated, come and go and do not long remain; but Thou abidest. All things are in Thy hand, both life and death: rest us from the strife of tongues, in the pavilion of Thy presence; rest us from the vanishings of time in the sanctuary of the everlasting. Speak to our heart and say, "All the glory of man is as the flower of the grass. The grass withereth and the flower fadeth, but the word of the Lord endureth for ever."

And to Him whose years fail not and whose kingdom is eternal be worship and praise, world without end. Amen.

SERMON XXII.

THE SILENCE OF CHRIST.

"Hereafter I will not talk much with you: for the prince of this world cometh, and hath nothing in Me."—St. John xiv. 30.

HE had talked a great deal with His apostles in the course of the years, the two or three years, they had spent together. The words of wisdom and grace they had heard from His lips as they sat with Him in the house and on the hillside, or rambled with Him through the fields and along the sea-shore! From what we have recorded of His utterances in their company, how one wishes that more had been preserved for us by His biographers. A hundred things He must have said during His intercourse with them, a hundred jewels of thought must have dropped from Him, that have not come down to us. Would that one had been among them taking notes from day to day, who should have left behind a volume of His table talk and His wayside talk: talk with which

He sometimes perplexed, and now gave them new light on truth or duty, now caused their hearts to burn within them. They had listened to Him often, doubtless, with rather unappreciative ears, and may never have duly prized the privilege until warned that events were about to deprive them of it. We can imagine their sadness at the prospect of losing it, their regret at not having treasured and valued it more while they had it; for indeed, they had loved to sit at His feet. But, alas! it is always with the vanishing of the gift that we awake to perceive, as we had not perceived, its sweetness and worth.

"Hereafter I will not talk much with you." He had enjoyed wonderfully talking with them of the things which lay nearest to His heart—of His Father, and righteousness, of the mysteries of the Kingdom of Heaven; had enjoyed wonderfully feeding them with instruction, communicating to them towards their gradual enlightenment line upon line, precept upon precept, out of His fulness—they, the few susceptible souls whom He had picked out among the people, the only persons in Judæa able to sympathise and respond. The exercise had often refreshed His own spirit, we may believe, whatever the effect upon them. But now, the end of all this was at hand. Suddenly, one day, in the midst of discourse, He feels the approach of what must terminate it, and begins, under the sense and vision of the approach, to grow silent. Henceforth under the sense and vision of the impending, He would be unable to talk with them as hitherto. They must excuse Him if His tongue should be somewhat restrained.

Different things operate to render us dumb at times. We are stilled by anxiety, by doubt, now by perplexity, now by dread. There is the stillness of those who hold their peace from shyness, or because the burden within is inexpressible, is too sore and deep to be told, or because none are beside them to understand, none capable of entering into the thoughts and feelings with which they are oppressed, and for the relief of venting which they vainly sigh. It may be just brokenness of heart and despair that closes the mouth, or moody melancholy, shrinking from converse, or the sullenness of secret resentment. There is the strange hush that falls for a while between two friends whom distance has long separated, when, at their first meeting, and after the first warm salutations exchanged, they sit in mutual awkward reserve, and cannot, somehow, flow as of old, though each has so much within him to say and tell. Again, there is the hush that falls between two lovers, which neither cares nor wants to break; when it is enough that heart answers to heart, and soul touches and blends with soul, and no words are needed. But sometimes we are stilled in view of a crisis to be met, the meeting of which will task all our powers; of a business to be prosecuted, for the prosecution of which we must gird our loins and collect our strength; when a call to action is felt which leaves us neither time nor inclination for speech.

And here with Jesus it was beneath the consciousness of a great conflict soon to be entered on that He was growing silent—because the hour drew nigh in which a mighty onset of the power of evil would have to be sustained by Him. With it imminent He could no longer keep up His accustomed colloquies with those about Him. They must be content to have Him quiet and quieter in their midst, a gravely brooding companion too full of anxious forecasting thought to talk; like some warrior on the eve of battle for whom to-morrow's dawn will bring engagement with the legions of the enemy marshalled on the opposite slope—the beginning of a momentous contest in which everything will be lost or won; when, having laid his plans and settled his dispositions, he waits for the morning, not at all socially inclined, but rapt in meditation, thinking, thinking of many things—of his far-away home, and friends, of bygone days and scenes, conjecturing with regard to the future, dreaming of possibilities dark and bright, wondering how it will be with himself and the army and the cause for which they are fighting, when the next sun has set. With a severe ordeal or a great emergency drawing near we tend to be silent. "I cannot talk, I cannot talk," we say to our friends and comrades, "I cannot talk with this before me."

"The prince of this world cometh," says Jesus. Here was the event, the expectation and close looming of which stilled him;—an assault upon Him of the prince of this world. Well we know it was the world of His day, the world of blind prejudice, and false passion, the world of wrong-minded, wrong-hearted men and women in Judea, that was about to strike at Him its last, fiercest blow. They were just the people of the nation who were mustering to fall upon Him in their enmity. What He saw advancing, however, was not so many hostile fellow-creatures, not the multitude of priests and elders and scribes and Pharisees bent on crushing Him, but a power that swayed and drove them like a tyrant lord; the power of *evil*, personified to Him as the prince of the world, for the time possessing and commanding it and making it what it was. These people were not the foe, to His thought; only its instruments and organs. The foe, to His thought, was the power of evil ruling and using them. In receiving their onslaught He would be meeting and grappling with *it*. And may we not say, that here, in His thinking thus, we have intimated the view which He held and cherished concerning men; that they were not in their very nature evil, were not fundamentally evil beings, whatever evil they might be found devising and practising; that the evil they nursed and did was not *of* them, but *upon* them, as a staining, smothering mist, from which they did but need to be cleared—as a temporary invasion that did but need to be rolled off and was destined to be rolled off; as afterwards, in their cruel treatment of Him He prayed, " Father, forgive them, for they know not what they do;" this is not themselves, but the evil in which they are caught, under the dominion of which they are fallen for a while, to their warping and maddening, and from which sooner or later they are to be released. Oh, yes, men were to Him always, and, at their worst, Divine creatures, whom a passing subjection to evil transiently disfigured and disguised—Divine creatures overlaid by it and waiting to be extricated and revealed.

So again, in the attack about to be made upon Him, in the scourge and cross preparing for Him, there were to Him no evil *persons* at all to be sore against or incensed with, for the persons, antagonistic and persecuting, were but the occasion of discipline for Him, the means of His submission to a great disciplinary trial of temptation, but Heaven's method of bringing Him the endurance and struggle needed for His perfecting. He had no feeling of resentment towards them. "I am not," He said to Himself, "about to be set upon by a host of evil persons. I am about to be exercised through them in conflict with evil, over which, though they may beat me down, I may triumph." In which fine way we should learn to regard all disagreeable persons, all annoying persons, all afflicting and injurious persons encountered by us, as simply a moral exercising circumstance for us, an opportunity afforded us of fighting, to bear without being disordered or disarranged by the evil.

Jesus beheld coming against Him, not a people, ill-disposed and angry, with swords and staves, but the prince of this world, the power of evil to try Him. "And it has nothing in Me!" He declared; no lurking element of its own to lay hold of, and gain footing by, through which to capture or shake Me; no answering susceptibility to be appealed to and excited for My downfall.

But why, then, one asks, should the prospect of its coming have silenced Him, have so affected and weighed upon Him that He could no longer talk? *We* may well be silenced on the brink of exposure to some contact with evil, silenced by apprehension, by anxiety, because we are conscious that it *has* something in us, much in us, perhaps, which constitutes the danger for us, which renders our steadfastness and triumph uncertain. We shrink and are afraid, being sensible that it has enough in us to make the issue somewhat doubtful; some slumbering affinity with it, some evil propensity or tendency which is our weakness for the battle, and, amidst all our fortification, lays us just there open to the enemy, liable to be penetrated and taken possession of by him—some little combustible particle upon which the spark from without may fall to our inflaming, some little disloyalty of inclination in the camp that may lead to the letting in of the foe. Ah! who of us would care what came or had to be met of evil, could we feel that it had nothing in us? Then how lightly and carelessly should we be able to front any onset of it. Why, then, should Jesus have been stilled, as though with apprehension and anxiety, before an impending conjunction with the prince of the world, who had nothing in Him? Why should it have checked the quiet flow of His intercourse with His disciples?

Well, purity—would not purity naturally recoil from transacting with evil, from being thrown into collision with it and compelled to touch it in combat? Can you not understand that the loftier and more perfect the purity the greater would be the recoil?—not from a sense of weakness, not from fear of incurring contamination, and inability to maintain itself uncorrupted, but from repulsion. We cannot but shrink when necessity is laid upon us to deal in any way with what our nature loathes, to breathe an air abhorrent to our deepest principles and sentiments. Delicacy suffers great pain in associating with aught of coarseness, pain of which less delicacy has no conception. What more distressing to a loving soul than to be driven into company with the uncharitable, or to a noble mind than to be obliged to consort with meanness? No wonder, then, if the purity of Jesus was discomposed and dismayed at having to meet in close contest the power of evil; if He shuddered in contemplating a grapple with the prince of the world, *because* the latter had nothing in Him.

And yet to me, the words, "Hereafter I will not talk much with you," seem not so much a confession of incapacity for continuing converse with them in contemplating the grapple, as a forecast and prophecy of what would result from the fact that he who was coming had nothing in Him—that therefore, His wonted converse with them was surely drawing to an end; as though He had said, "*That* determines My destruction, makes certain the silencing of My voice, precludes all hope of my remaining with you. In consequence of *that* you will soon have Me speaking with you no more." And so, indeed, it was. Had the evil found something in Him, in the shape of some moral weakness, or cowardice, or taint of worldly tone and disposition, tempting Him beneath the pressure of the people's prejudice and opposition, and the threatened cross, to trim a little, to compromise a little, to modify a little the message given Him to utter, to swerve from or lower a trifle His ideal—*then* after all, He might have escaped and saved Himself. But since it had in Him nothing of the kind, He was doomed to perish. His freedom from aught through which the coming of the devil in the nations' dissatisfaction and hostility could move Him from the path of His soul's vision, was His sentence of death.

And what is it which now and again has been the ruin of men—the ruin of their success in life, or their popularity, the ruin of the prosperity which they would have liked well enough to preserve, or of ends which they would have liked well enough to compass? What is it that has spoiled their business prospects, plunged them in a sea of trouble, prevented their getting on and making way, as they might have done but that the prince of the world had nothing in them constraining them to waver at all in their adhesion to their high ideal, to turn at all for the sake of lower interests from the truth and beauty which their eyes had seen, because they had it not in them to deviate a hairsbreadth from principle or to be unfaithful in the least to their light, happen what might. Others beside them in whom the prince of the world had enough for this, who knew how to palter a little with conviction or decline from thence upon the expedient, have avoided disaster and kept their place and flourished abundantly; but *they* have lost ground and failed to do well for themselves, through *being* better. Nothing is more ruinous often for a man than to be without response to the temptation of the evil. A little response would have saved from ruin. "Yet 'tis perdition to be safe, when for the truth we ought to die."

But there is yet another meaning which we can imagine for the words of Jesus in the text. He may possibly have meant, " From henceforth no more talk with you for your instruction, but instead, action, endurance, victorious prevailing on my part, for your *seeing*." From henceforth exemplification indeed is to take the place of communication by a word; for the prince of this world, whose coming puts an end to words, has nothing in Me; so, in My encounter with and triumph over him you will be beholding what I have spoken concerning loyalty and consecration, livingly illustrated. No longer discoursing to you of trust in God and resignation to His will, of the conquering might of faith, of love for the highest which naught can quench or cool, of losing one's life to gain life, of the sure and steadfast standing of the Kingdom of Heaven against the gates of hell,—no longer discoursing to you of these things, I shall be showing them to you in My conflict and its issues; what hitherto you have heard from Me with your ears you will be seeing in Me with your eyes; with voice silenced I am going to be a supreme instance and expression of the doctrine that My lips have uttered—for the prince of this world cometh, and hath nothing in Me.

And in the last ordeal He suffered on earth, He did display in Himself grandly truth which He had taught and talked of through the days. Men looked upon His cross—upon the moral sublimity of the Victim, upon the Sacrifice and the fruit it bore, and saw there in vivid presentation what, during the days, He had said. It is fine to be able to embody thus what has flowed from us in speech, to be able to image brightly in flesh and blood of action or endurance or victorious prevailing, the excellence that our tongues have commended or described. Would that we could *be*, always, in the sight of our fellows something more of the grace, the fortitude, the faithful devotion we have descanted on, and inculcated, and not lie open to the charge brought by one of his friends against the patriarch Job : " Behold, thou hast instructed many, and thou hast strengthened the weak hands. Thy words have upholden him that was falling, and thou hast strengthened the feeble knees. But now it is come upon thee, and thou faintest : it toucheth thee and thou art troubled." Would that all poets singing nobly, noble sentiments, could live for us equally the songs they sing! Would that all prophets of the Lord to whose strains we listen could but live before us fully the virtue about which they are eloquent! Blessed are they to whom it is given in some noticeable measure so to " set it forth and show it accordingly."

THE END.

H. R. ALLENSON'S CATALOGUE OF BOOKS FOR THEOLOGICAL AND GENERAL READERS

ARRANGED ALPHABETICALLY UNDER AUTHORS' NAMES
AND MANY GROUPED FOR CONVENIENCE
UNDER THE FOLLOWING HEADINGS

	PAGE
ALLENSON'S HANDY THEOLOGICAL LIBRARY	35
ALLENSON'S INDIA PAPER SERIES	36
ALLENSON'S SIXPENNY SERIES	34
STUDIES IN THEOLOGY AND ETHICS	38
THE HEART AND LIFE BOOKLETS	35
THE TRACTS FOR THE TIMES	36
BOOKS FOR BIBLE STUDENTS	38
BOOKS FOR JUVENILES	39
BOOKS OF ILLUSTRATION FOR SERMONS	37
,, ADDRESSES TO CHILDREN	37
,, OUTLINE ADDRESSES AND SERMONS	37
,, ADDRESSES TO YOUNG MEN AND WOMEN	38
,, MISSIONARY INTEREST	38
,, DEVOTION	39
,, MYSTICISM	39
,, SERMONS	40
,, FICTION	39
,, BIOGRAPHY	39
HISTORICAL LONDON CHURCHES (PICTORIAL POST CARDS)	2
OLD AND VANISHING LONDON (,, ,,)	2

LONDON
1 & 2 IVY LANE, PATERNOSTER ROW, E.C.

PICTURE POST CARDS.

OLD AND VANISHING LONDON. Reproductions of
Six Original Pen and Ink Drawings by E. M. Roughton.

SIX PICTORIAL POST CARDS SIXPENCE.

1. CLOTH FAIR.
2. THE DICK WHITTINGTON, Cloth Fair, (the oldest public-house in London).
3. A CORNER AT THE BACK OF CLOTH FAIR.
4. THE OLD BELL, Holborn.
5. ST BARTHOLOMEW - THE - GREAT, Smithfield.
6. OLD HOUSES, St Giles, Cripplegate.

"Among the prettiest and most interesting of picture post cards."—*T. P.'s Weekly.*
"One of the most interesting and attractive series of picture post cards at present on the market."—*British Weekly.*

FAITHFUL PICTURES OF HISTORIC LONDON CHURCHES.
These Pictures are beautifully reproduced from Collotype Photographs specially taken for this Series, and will prove of real use to Architects and all others interested in Archæological subjects as well as being a choice addition to any collection or album.

24 PICTORIAL POST CARDS.

WREN'S CITY CHURCHES.

FIRST SERIES.   SIX CARDS SIXPENCE.

ST MARY ALDERMARY, Queen Victoria Street.
ST LAWRENCE JEWRY, Gresham Street.
ST MARY THE VIRGIN, Aldermanbury.
ST DUNSTAN IN THE EAST, St Dunstan's Hill.
ST MARGARET PATTENS, Rood Lane.
ST MAGNUS THE MARTYR, Thames Street.

SECOND SERIES.   SIX CARDS SIXPENCE.

ST NICHOLAS COLE ABBEY, Queen Victoria Street.
ST ANDREW BY THE WARDROBE, Queen Victoria Street.
ST BRIDE, Fleet Street.
ST STEPHEN, Wallbrook.
CHRIST CHURCH, Newgate Street.
ST ANDREW, Holborn.

OLD LONDON CHURCHES.

FIRST SERIES.   SIX CARDS SIXPENCE.

ST MARY WOOLNOTH, Lombard Street.
ST OLAVE, Hart Street.
ST KATHERINE CREE, Leadenhall Street.
ST ETHELBURGA, Bishopsgate Street.
ST ANDREW UNDERSHAFT, Leadenhall Street.
ALL HALLOWS BARKING, Tower Street.

SECOND SERIES.   SIX CARDS SIXPENCE.

ST CLEMENT DANES, Strand.
ST MARY LE STRAND.
ST DUNSTAN IN THE WEST, Fleet Street.
ST SEPULCHRE, Holborn.
ST AUGUSTINE, Austin Friars.
ST BOTOLPH, Aldgate.

"Picture post cards are not always a blessing but some few are so, among which may be noted an admirable series of Wren's city churches and old London churches. The photographs are excellent and the printing very good. Lovers of old London will do well to buy them."—*Academy.*

Catalogue
OF PUBLICATIONS
AND
IMPORTATIONS OF
H. R. Allenson
1 & 2 IVY LANE
PATERNOSTER ROW
LONDON E.C.

Which may be had of all Booksellers, or will be sent post free to any part of the world, for the published price, except net books, where postage must be added.

Information as to other Publishers' books supplied promptly from H. R. ALLENSON'S Retail Department, 1 & 2 Ivy Lane, Paternoster Row, E.C.

ALLEN. CONTINUITY OF CHRISTIAN THOUGHT. A Study of Modern Theology in the Light of its History. By Prof. A. V. G. ALLEN, Author of "Christian Institutions." Crown 8vo, cloth, 471 pages, 3s. 6d. net. Postage 4d.

CONTENTS.

THE GREEK THEOLOGY.
THE LATIN THEOLOGY.
THEOLOGY IN THE MIDDLE AGES.
THEOLOGY IN THE AGE OF THE REFORMATION.

CONFLICT OF THE TRADITIONAL THEOLOGY WITH RATIONALISM.
RENAISSANCE OF THEOLOGY IN THE NINETEENTH CENTURY.

"To the revised edition of his fascinating and enlightening volume Prof. Allen prefixes a new preface, in which he replies briefly to criticisms made upon his treatment of St Clement of Alexandria and St Augustine, upon the doctrine of the divine immanence and the higher criticism. This inspiring work has been at once a product and a cause of the spread of the conviction 'that the spirit of Christianity possesses a living commentary, not only in the New Testament, but in the life and thought of the Church from Age to Age.'"—*New World.*

ATKIN. BRIGHT AND BRIEF TALKS TO MEN. A series of twenty-one P.S.A. Addresses. By F. W. ATKIN. Crown 8vo, cloth, 1s. 6d.

SOME OF THE CONTENTS.

A MAN'S INFLUENCE.
GOD'S PRISONERS.
WHY NOT A SINLESS WORLD?
SATAN IN KID GLOVES.

GOD'S TRIANGLE.
THE RULE OF THE ROAD.
MORTGAGING THE FUTURE, ETC.

This little volume just fits the question the publisher has often received for something manly for men.

"Twenty-one vigorous addresses."—*Scotsman.*

"Short, pithy, pointed, and logical."—*Aberdeen Free Press.*

"A book which fulfils its title."—*Local Preachers' Magazine.*

"Helpful addresses, full of helpful hints, and each capable of expansion by other workers."—*The Signal.*

BALLARD. WHICH BIBLE TO READ—REVISED OR AUTHORISED? By Rev. F. BALLARD, M.A., Author of "Miracles of Unbelief." Second Edition, revised and enlarged, 2s. 6d. net. Postage 3d.

CONTENTS.

MERITS AND PEDIGREE OF THE AUTHORISED VERSION.
THE NEED OF REVISION.
MATTERS RELATING TO THE ORIGINAL TEXT.
MEANINGS OF WORDS.
ARCHAISMS. GRAMMAR.

MISREPRESENTATIONS—OLD TEST.
MISREPRESENTATIONS—NEW TEST.
AMBIGUITIES, OBSCURITIES, AND DELICATE TOUCHES.
NAMES, TITLES, LITERARY FORM, ETC.
OBJECTIONS.
PROSPECTS OF THE REVISED VERSION.

"Seems likely to be very useful. It is a very great advantage that you deal with the Old Testament."—*Bishop Westcott.*

"His plea is vigorous and convincing,

and will guide many to the right use of the new Version."—*Glasgow Herald.*
"We strongly recommend it, especially to Local Preachers and Sunday School Teachers."—*Methodist Times.*

BROCK. A YOUNG CONGO MISSIONARY. Memorials of Sidney Roberts Webb, M.D. By Rev. WILLIAM BROCK. Crown 8vo, cloth, 1s. 6d. [Second Edition.

WORKS BY BISHOP PHILLIPS BROOKS.

LECTURES ON PREACHING. The Yale Lectures. By PHILLIPS BROOKS. Uniform with his Works, issued by Macmillan. Crown 8vo, cloth, 2s. 6d. net. Postage 4d. extra.
For small pocket edition see "Allenson's Handy Theological Library." Limp lambskin, 3s. net. Cloth semi-limp, 2s. net. Postage 3d. extra.

CONTENTS.

THE TWO ELEMENTS IN PREACHING.
THE PREACHER HIMSELF.
THE PREACHER IN HIS WORK.
THE IDEA OF THE SERMON.

THE MAKING OF THE SERMON.
THE CONGREGATION.
THE MINISTRY FOR OUR AGE.
THE VALUE OF THE HUMAN SOUL.

"A book of permanent value."—*Expository Times.*
"Well worth reading and re-reading by young clergy. They can hardly study the great preacher's methods without learning much, very much, to help and strengthen them."—*Church Times.*
"We have more than once commended

this delightful book. There is no preacher of the Gospel, there is hardly any public speaker on any subject, who can read any one of these lectures without learning something profitable. We only wish all our preachers could own, and make their own, the sterling truth of this delightful and valuable book."—*Methodist Times.*

THE INFLUENCE OF JESUS. The Bohlen Lectures. By Bishop PHILLIPS BROOKS. Uniform with "Lectures on Preaching." Crown 8vo, cloth, 2s. 6d. net. Post free, 2s. 10d.

CONTENTS.

THE INFLUENCE OF JESUS ON THE MORAL LIFE OF MAN.
THE INFLUENCE OF JESUS ON THE SOCIAL LIFE OF MAN.

THE INFLUENCE OF JESUS ON THE EMOTIONAL LIFE OF MAN.
THE INFLUENCE OF JESUS ON THE INTELLECTUAL LIFE OF MAN.

"'The Influence of Jesus' is theologically the most characteristic of all Bishop Brooks' works. Mr Allenson has given us a new and attractive edition." — *Expository Times.*

"The purpose of the book is established with an irresistible force of logic and a wealth of choice illustration. The reissue of the book is altogether timely."—*Baptist Magazine.*

H. R. ALLENSON'S CATALOGUE 5

LETTERS OF TRAVEL (1865-1890). By Right Rev.
PHILLIPS BROOKS. Large crown 8vo, 368 pages, 2s. 6d. net. Postage 4d. extra.

These letters of travel cover periods of Phillips Brooks' life that were always of the greatest delight to him. They convey not only an interesting story of travel, but also evidence of that personal charm, ready wit, and genial appreciation which those nearest to him loved so well.

"Those who have not had the good fortune to hear Phillips Brooks will be surprised with this glimpse of what must have been a delightful character."—*Academy.*

THE PURPOSE AND USE OF COMFORT. A Sermon by PHILLIPS BROOKS. Fcap. 8vo, artistic wrapper, 6d. net; also cloth, 1s. net; leather, 2s. net. Postage 1d. [Heart and Life Booklets.

AN EASTER SERMON (Rev. i. 17 and 18 v.). By PHILLIPS BROOKS. Fcap. 8vo, artistic wrapper, 6d. net; also cloth, 1s. net; leather, 2s. net. Postage 1d. [Heart and Life Booklets.

"Two of his greatest discourses."
"The purpose is thoroughly devotional. The former appeals to many hearts afflicted by sorrow, and the latter contains a hopeful message based on the Resurrection of Christ."—*Northern Whig.*

THE LIFE WITH GOD. A Sermon by PHILLIPS BROOKS. Fcap. 8vo, artistic wrapper, 6d. net; also cloth, 1s. net; leather, 2s. net. Fourth Edition. Postage 1d. [Heart and Life Booklets.

"It is almost overwhelming in its power, eloquence, and tender pleading. It is also essentially human, as is the religion which it sets forth. The preacher's great point is that the religious is the only natural and complete life."—*Christian World.*

BROWN, A. R. WHAT IS WORTH WHILE. By A. R. BROWN, Ph.D. Artistic paper wrapper, 1s.

"Not since Drummond's 'Greatest Thing in the World' has there been published anything in the same vein so beautiful and inspiring as Dr Brown's crystal clear exposition of things worth while in life."—*Dundee Advertiser.*

BROWN, CHARLES. TALKS TO CHILDREN ON BUNYAN'S HOLY WAR. By the Rev. CHAS. BROWN, Ferme Park (Hornsey). Crown 8vo, 2s. 6d.; also cheap edition, cloth, 1s. 6d. net. Postage 3d.

The Pilgrim's Progress has often been used by preachers as a subject for children's addresses; the Holy War much less often, and the publisher questions if it ever has been so successfully treated as in this instance by Mr Brown.

"Vivid addresses sound and manly."—*Examiner.*
"Best thanks for Mr Brown's beautiful book. I shall place it on my Bunyan shelf, and shall not forget it when I am consulted about the best Bunyan literature."—*Dr Alexr. Whyte.*

"Many parents will be glad to have them to read to their children, and we can imagine that many ministers will be glad to take a hint from the book and speak on the same lines to the young people of their congregation,"—*Christian World.*

THE MESSAGE OF THE GOSPEL. By Rev. CHARLES BROWN. An Address delivered at the opening of a Mission. Crown 8vo, One Penny. Post free, 1½d. [Tracts for the Times.

B

BROWN, R. M. FORTY BIBLE LESSONS AND FORTY ILLUSTRATIVE STORIES; OR, THE BIBLE IN LESSON AND STORY. By R. M. BROWN. Crown 8vo, cloth, 3s. 6d. Second Edition.

Forty chapters upon Bible truths and Bible characters, each chapter written in a manner that will immediately interest the children. Accompanying each lesson is a delightful illustrative story, together with a "Memory Gem" and an "Occupation," in which the children are given something to do that will help impress the truths that have been taught. There is a wealth of information and suggestion about this book that will delight all who have anything to do with the training of children.

This book is strikingly new. Ministers and other speakers will find the numerous good stories (forty) eminently useful for illustrative purposes.

"The suggestions for object lessons to impress the stories and lessons upon the mind are wise."—*The Outlook.*

BROWNING, MRS. AURORA LEIGH. By E. B. BROWNING. Beautifully printed on India Paper. The choicest and smallest edition of this famous work ever printed. 489 pages Imperial 32mo, limp leather, 2s. 6d. net; also in cloth, 1s. 6d. net. Postage 2d.

The most perfect pocket edition, the measurement is only 5¼ × 3¾ inches and under half an inch in thickness, weight under 4 oz.

[Allenson's India Paper Series.

—— **AURORA LEIGH.** 126 pages, clear good type, demy 8vo, 6d. [Allenson's Sixpenny Series.

"It is wonderful. Mr Allenson's experiment in issuing a sixpenny edition of Mrs Browning's masterpiece should be watched with interest."—*To-Day.*

BROWNING, ROBERT. EASTER DAY. Fcap. 8vo, 6d. net. Also cloth, 1s. net; limp leather, 2s. net. Postage 1d. extra.

[Heart and Life Booklets.

"All lovers of Browning will enjoy having this beautiful poem in handy pocket size. The print and paper are beyond praise."—*Saint Andrew.*

—— **CHRISTMAS EVE.** Fcap. 8vo, 6d. net. Also cloth, 1s. net; limp leather, 2s. net. Postage 1d. extra.

[Heart and Life Booklets.

CAIRD. RELIGION IN COMMON LIFE. By Principal JOHN CAIRD, D.D., LL.D. With Introduction by JONATHAN NIELD. 64 pages, fcap. 8vo, 6d. net. Also neat cloth limp boards, 1s. net; limp leather, 2s. net. Postage 1d. extra. [Heart and Life Booklets.

A sermon preached before Queen Victoria and Prince Consort at Crathie Church, Balmoral, and published by command of the Queen. Dean Stanley spoke of it as "the greatest single sermon in the language."

CARLYLE. HEROES AND HERO WORSHIP. Beautifully printed on India paper in a clear type the size of next line.

wonder for which there is now no limit

516 pages, Imp. 32mo, limp leather, 2s. 6d. net; also cloth, 1s. 6d. net. Postage 2d.

The most perfect pocket edition extant. The measurement of this little classic is only 5¼ × 3¾ by under ½ inch thickness. Weight only 4 oz.

[Allenson's India Paper Series.

CARLYLE. HEROES AND HERO WORSHIP. 134 pages, demy 8vo, 6d. [Allenson's Sixpenny Series.

"This wonderful series of lectures, it will be remembered, deals in Carlyle's inimitable vigorous style with such men as Dante, Shakespeare, Luther, Knox, Johnson, Rousseau, Burns, Cromwell, and Napoleon. These are classics, everyone of them powerful deliverances, and much quoted. To possess them all at the cost of a humble sixpence is indeed a surprise."—*Hastings and St Leonards Times.*

"The publication of such standard works in a cheap form is highly to be commended."—*Aberdeen Daily Journal.*

———— **SARTOR RESARTUS.** With Introduction by JONATHAN NIELD, Author of "Guide to Historical Novels." 117 pages, demy 8vo, 6d. [Allenson's Sixpenny Series.

"The perusal of it will be worth a dozen novels to an intelligent young man."
"A wonderfully cheap edition of this famous classic."—*To-Day.*
"The first demy octavo sixpenny edition, in a clear and quite readable form."—*Daily News.*

WORKS BY BISHOP BOYD-CARPENTER, D.D.

THOUGHTS ON PRAYER. By W. BOYD-CARPENTER, D.D., Bishop of Ripon. New Edition. 16mo, cloth, 1s. net; also limp leather, gilt edges, 2s. net. Postage 2d.

CONTENTS.

NECESSITY OF PRAYER.
TIMES ADVERSE TO PRAYER.
HEARTWORK IN PRAYER.
REALITY OF ANSWERS TO PRAYER.
EFFICACY OF PRAYER.
UNANSWERED PRAYER.
BARRENNESS IN PRAYER.

REGULARITY IN PRAYER.
MEDITATIONS AND PRAYERS FOR ONE WEEK.
SUGGESTIVE OUTLINES ON CONFESSION, SUPPLICATION, INTERCESSION, AND THANKSGIVING.

"Bishop Boyd-Carpenter's much-appreciated little book of 'Thoughts on Prayer,' including meditations and prayers for one week, and suggestive outlines on confession, supplication, intercession, and thanksgiving."—*Aberdeen Free Press.*

FOOTPRINTS OF THE SAVIOUR. New Edition, with Thirteen Illustrations, printed on art paper. Cr. 8vo, cloth, 2s. 6d.

Twelve devotional chapters on places visited by our Lord: Bethlehem—Cana—Sychar—Nazareth—Capernaum—Gennesaret—Decapolis—Bethany—Gethsemane—Calvary—Emmaus—Olivet.

"Great Lessons from the Life of Christ grouped round the cities in which He did His mighty works are told here simply for simple folks. It is a new edition of a foremost favourite of the sick-room or prayer-meetings."—*Expository Times.*

CAWS. THE UNRECOGNISED STRANGER. And other Sermons. By L. W. CAWS. Cheaper issue. Crown 8vo, 2s. 6d. net; post free, 2s. 10d.

"Throughout fresh and suggestive."—*Christian World.*
"Strong and spiritual sermons that stir and still."—*Evangelical Magazine.*

CHILD. ROOT PRINCIPLES IN RATIONAL AND SPIRITUAL THINGS. By THOMAS CHILD. 164 pages, demy 8vo, 6d. [Allenson's Sixpenny Series.

"Mr Child knows more of science, is a better philosopher than most 'orthodox' apologists, and makes many good points against the dogmatic evolutionists and the monists."—*Westminster Review.*
"A detailed point to point refutation of Haeckel's famous work, full of acute reasoning, and fresh and vital in every page."—*Christian Leader.*

CLARKE. HUXLEY AND PHILLIPS BROOKS. By Prof. W. NEWTON CLARKE, D.D., Author of "Outlines of Christian Doctrine." Fcap. 8vo, 6d. net; also neat cloth, 1s. net.
[Heart and Life Booklets.

"Dr Newton Clarke's appreciation of these two so widely different men is one of the finest pieces of analysis and of suggestively constructive criticism with which we are acquainted."—*Baptist Magazine.*

"It shows how the spiritual world which the Agnostic knew nothing of was the sphere in which the great preacher had his being. It is a little book that will give new hope and strength to every Christian worker. It is beautifully written and full of suggestive matter."—*London Quarterly Review.*

DAILY MESSAGE FROM MANY MINDS, A. Thoughts for the quiet hour from Fenelon, Jeremy Taylor, Wordsworth, Robertson, Phillips Brooks, Hawthorne, etc.
This choice devotional book is provided in two sizes.
Pocket Edition, on India paper, 32mo, limp leather, 2s. 6d. net, by post, 2s. 8d. (uniform with India Paper Edition of "Great Souls at Prayer").
And in demy 16mo, handsome bevelled boards, red edges, silk marker, 2s. 6d. net, by post, 2s. 10d. (uniform with large edition of "Great Souls at Prayer").
Also in white cloth, suitable for Wedding Gift, 2s. 6d. net.

"A dainty little book which will be treasured by many. The thoughts are excellently classified and indexed."—*Great Thoughts.*
"A particularly well chosen day-book of beautiful verses and prose passages. The selection is unusually varied and unhackneyed, and ranges from cheery practical encouragement to high ideals."—*Bookman.*

DARLINGTON. EFFECTIVE SPEAKING AND WRITING. By Rev. JOHN DARLINGTON, D.D. Crown 8vo, cloth, 1s. 6d.

"The careful study of such a manual as the present one will help the writer or speaker to avoid those faults against which the best natural but uncultivated parts give no security, and will at the same time suggest to him the sources whence the necessary aids of topics, arguments, illustrations, and motives may best be drawn."—*Glasgow Herald.*
"Mr Darlington's book is packed with matter, the earnest student will be amply rewarded."—*New Age.*

WORKS BY CHARLES F. DOLE, D.D.

THE THEOLOGY OF CIVILIZATION. By CHARLES F. DOLE. Second Edition. Crown 8vo, 3s. 6d.

CONTENTS.

THE REALM OF DOUBT.
THE MORAL STRUCTURE OF THE UNIVERSE.
THE WORLD OF OPPOSITES.
THOROUGH-GOING THEISM.
THE GOOD GOD.
GREAT QUESTIONS.

RATIONAL OPTIMISM.
BEGINNINGS OF PERSONALITY.
WHAT PERSONALITY IS.
THE COST OF PERSONALITY.
THE RELIGION OF THE CHILD AND THE RELIGION OF THE MAN.
THE PROCESS OF CIVILIZATION.

"We have found the volume a thoughtful and stimulating contribution to an important study of the true inward relation of the religious inquiries of our time with the fuller outlook of the modern, as distinct from the mediæval outlook in the realm of life and thought."—*Literary World.*
"We cannot do without theology even to-day. But we are civilised now, and our theology must fit our civilisation. So it is a new book, full of new thoughts. It is even prophetic. And though we may not live to see its prophecies fulfilled, it stirs new hopes within us."—*Expository Times.*

THE COMING PEOPLE.
A Study of Life in its Social and Religious Aspects. By C. F. DOLE, D.D. Fifth Edition. Crown 8vo, cloth, 3s. 6d.

CONTENTS.

THE PROPHECY.
CERTAIN CLEAR FACTS.
HEROISM, OR THE IRON IN THE BLOOD.
THE DIVINE UNIVERSE.
THE POINT OF VIEW.
SHORT CUTS TO SUCCESS.

THE LAW OF COST.
THE PROBLEM OF THE PROSPEROUS.
THE IDEAL DEMOCRACY.
POSSIBLE REVOLUTION.
THE MOTTO OF VICTORY.
THE HAPPY LIFE.

"It is distinctly refreshing to read this book, written in a style quite admirable, and under the impulse of a generous and reverent spirit. This book ought to be widely read, and we are sure that he who begins the work will finish it. Mr Dole has the insight that discerns principles, and a keen eye for facts."—*Methodist Recorder*.

"This is a healthy and virile essay which the reader, especially if he should be in that stage when his mind is 'on the make,' will be thankful to Mr Dole for having given him. There are in the book the outlines of ideas of which we shall probably hear a good deal in the future, as the attempt to interpret the Christian world and the Christian spirit in terms of the modern doctrine of evolution becomes more developed."—*The Spectator* (leading article).

THE RELIGION OF A GENTLEMAN.
By the Rev. CHARLES F. DOLE, D.D., Author of "The Coming People," "Theology of Civilization." Second Edition. Crown 8vo, cloth, 3s. 6d.

CONTENTS.

WHO IS THE GENTLEMAN?
A CIVILISED RELIGION.
A BIT OF ARGUMENT.
SPIRIT—WHAT IT IS.
WHAT IT IS TO LOVE GOD.
PRAYER AND REASON.
WHAT FREEDOM IS.

WHAT IT IS TO BE GOOD.
THE GREAT RENUNCIATION.
THE SOLDIERLY LIFE.
A PRACTICAL QUESTION.
WHAT IS THE USE?
MEMENTO MORI.
OUR RULE OF LIFE.

"The religion of Mr Dole is attractive and commands respect. It is the expression of a clear mind and a noble heart. No one will read without comfort the chapter entitled *Memento Mori*, whatever his views may be in respect to the future."—*The International Journal of Ethics*.

"The book has merits of sagacity and good sense that are not too common in works of pious exposition, and should find favour with many readers."—*The Scotsman*.

"This book is certainly one which young men will do well to read. The things that are pure and lovely, and of good report, are held up with earnest impressiveness and vigour of speech. . . . Will serve as a moral tonic to those who read."—*Week's Survey*.

"There is a freshness and originality about this book which marks it as the work of a man who has thoughts of his own. . . . He writes with the evident desire of interesting the young, and especially of that class of youth—generous, intelligent, and energetic—who are destined to be the leaders of their generation. . . . This remarkably suggestive book."—*Public Opinion*.

EAMES. SERMONS TO BOYS AND GIRLS.
By JOHN EAMES, B.A. With complete index. Second Edition. Crown 8vo, 1s. 6d. net. Postage 3d.

"Examples of what children's addresses ought to be—simple in language, but pointed in teaching."—*Methodist Times*.

"The illustrations made use of are excellent and instructive, and always help to fix the point they illustrate on the memory."—*Liverpool Post*.

EDWARDS. TIN TACKS FOR TINY FOLKS, and other Outline Addresses for Teachers, Preachers and Christian Workers amongst the Young. By Rev. C. EDWARDS. Crown 8vo, 2s. 6d.

"A mine of thought and illustration."—*Methodist Times.*
"We could wish this handbook were placed in the hands of every preacher. Even those who shape their own outlines will find abundant helpful ideas, and just the kind to kindle thought."—*Local Preachers' Magazine.*

——— **A BOX OF NAILS FOR BUSY CHRISTIAN** WORKERS. Ninth Thousand. Crown 8vo, 1s. 6d.

"Here are 'Nails of many sorts.' The pages abound in material for evangelists and other workers, sound in substance and direct in aim."—*The Christian.*
"Living and suggestive. There is an unfailing point, a keen edge about these outlines, as well as a genuine and earnest spirituality."—*The Sunday School Chronicle.*

ELIAS. THOUGHTS ON PRESBYTERIAN UNION IN ENGLAND AND WALES. By E. A. ELIAS. With Prefatory Notes by Rev. A. H. DRYSDALE, M.A., and Rev. GRIFFITH ELLIS, M.A. Demy 8vo, 6d.

WORKS EDITED BY JOHN ELLIS.

OUTLINES AND ILLUSTRATIONS. For Teachers, Preachers, and Christian Workers. Comprising 600 Outlines of Addresses, Bible Readings, and Sunday School Talks, together with over 250 Illustrations and Incidents. Compiled by J. ELLIS. Being "Tool Basket," "Seed Basket," "Illustrations and Incidents," bound in one volume. Fcap. 8vo, 2s. 6d.

"Here is the scaffolding on which to build hundreds of addresses."—*The Christian.*
"We have so frequently referred to these books in our columns that we need not do more now than wish the little volume the success it deserves. It is daintily bound, of a size convenient for the pocket."—*The Methodist Times.*

"A very treasury of helpful, well-arranged matter. Excellent in spirit and suggestiveness."—*Local Preachers' Magazine.*
"Hundreds of hints, outlines, and illustrations are here supplied in compact and attractive form. A valuable storehouse of good things."—*Out and Out.*

THE PREACHER'S AND TEACHER'S VADE-MECUM. A Second Series of "Outlines and Illustrations." Being "Evangelist's Wallet," "Outline Sermonettes," and "By Way of Illustration," bound in one volume. Fcap. 8vo, cloth, 2s. 6d.

"Right honest and good work, to be despised by nobody."—*Expository Times.*
"It might be called 'Preaching made easy.'"—*Daily News.*

TOOLS FOR THE MASTER'S WORK. 250 Sermon Outlines and Children's Addresses. Collected by J. ELLIS. Crown 8vo, 1s. 6d. [Third Edition.

"Mr Ellis seems to have excelled himself in this volume. The best of these Outlines is that they are not mere skeletons, but suggestive thoughts, leaving plenty of room for the individuality of the speaker."—*The Local Preachers' Magazine.*
"Another valuable volume. Just the suggestions and hints we so often want."—*The Methodist Times.*

TOOL BASKET FOR PREACHERS. 300 Outline Addresses for Preachers, Sunday School Teachers, and Open Air Workers. Compiled by J. ELLIS. Fortieth Thousand. Fcap. 8vo, 1s.

"Admirable; invaluable to busy workers."—*Rev. Mark Guy Pearse.*
"Clever, suggestive, valuable, and thoroughly practical."—*Methodist Times.*
"The quality is very good and the number very great."—*Expository Times.*

SEED BASKET FOR MINISTERS. Being a Collection of 300 Outlines, Seed Corn, Sunday School Addresses, and Band of Hope Talks. By J. ELLIS, Editor of "The Tool Basket." Thirtieth Thousand. Fcap. 8vo, 1s.

"Deserves its name."—*Rev. F. B. Meyer.*
"The work is well done."—*New Age.*
"A wealth of suggestion."—*Christian Commonwealth.*

"Three hundred excellent outlines."—*Primitive Methodist.*
"Contains at least a year's sermons or addresses, easily made and sufficiently worth making your own."—*Expository Times.*

ILLUSTRATIONS AND INCIDENTS. For Preachers, Teachers, and Christian Workers. Being a Collection of 250 Anecdotes and Facts, with Index of Subjects. Twenty-fifth Thousand. Fcap. 8vo, 1s.

"A choice and well-arranged collection of anecdotes marked by much freshness, and likely to be of service to many busy workers in providing 'windows' for their lessons and discourses."—*Methodist Recorder.*
"Quite a number of the illustrations are new to us."—*Sunday School Chronicle.*

EVANGELIST'S WALLET FOR PREACHERS, TEACHERS, AND CHRISTIAN WORKERS. An entirely new Series of Outlines of Addresses by J. ELLIS, Compiler of "The Tool Basket," etc. etc. Tenth Thousand. Fcap. 8vo, 1s.

"The compiler of 'The Tool Basket' has thrown us all under another debt of gratitude by the issue of 'The Evangelist's Wallet.'"—*Expository Times.*
"In small compass, there is here a great fund of information, methodically arranged, for the use of those whose time or whose libraries are limited."—*Methodist Recorder.*
"Brimful of excellent suggestive outline addresses and sermonettes."—*Local Preacher.*

BY WAY OF ILLUSTRATION. A Handbook for Preachers, Teachers, and Christian Workers. Tenth Thousand. Fcap. 8vo, cloth, 1s. An entirely new Collection of Illustrations for Public Speakers.

"Wonderfully fresh, one of the very best compilations of the kind that we have seen."—*Local Preachers' Magazine.*
"Will prove a boon."—*Methodist Sunday School Record.*

EVANS. A PRIMER OF FREE CHURCH HISTORY. By A. JOHNSON EVANS, M.A. Cheap Edition. Crown 8vo, cloth, 1s. 6d. net; postage 3d.

"Mr Johnson Evans has laid the Free Churches under a great obligation for his true story of the origin and early developments of the Free Churches of England and the United States. The book should be read by our young Free Church people throughout the land."—*Dr Clifford.*
"I am delighted with it."—*Rev. Charles Brown.*

"An excellent handbook, clear and cogent."—*Sword and Trowel.*
"The book is a useful, interesting, and opportune compendium. It can do nothing but good."—*Free Church Chronicle.*
"It is well done."—*Expository Times.*
"A very excellent history of Nonconformity. Short and well written."—*The Glasgow Herald.*

FABER. SELECTION FROM F. W. FABER'S HYMNS.
Fcap. 8vo, 6d. net; also cloth, 1s. net; paste grain leather, 2s. net; postage 1d. [Heart and Life Booklets.
Twelve of Faber's beautiful spiritual hymns, printed in large clear type, making a most acceptable gift, particularly for the invalid or aged who have little in the way of literature provided for them.
Each hymn is given complete, the book contains "The Will of God," "Come to Jesus," "The Right must win," "The Greatness of God," "Our Heavenly Father," "The Thought of God," "Peevishness," "Perfection," "Harsh Judgments," "Sweetness in Prayer," "The Starry Skies," and "After a Death."
" Have taken a permanent place in our religious literature."—*St Andrew*

FAULKNER. JOSEPH SIDNEY HILL (First Bishop in Western Equatorial Africa). By R. E. FAULKNER. Three Portraits. Second Edition. Crown 8vo, 1s 6d. net; postage 4d.
"To a young man it should be an inspiration."—*C. M. Intelligencer*.
"It is just the book to give away to young men and boys."—*C. M. Gleaner*.

FORSYTH. THE HAPPY WARRIOR. By Rev. Dr P. T. FORSYTH, M.A. A Sermon Preached as a Memorial Sermon upon the late Mr W. E. Gladstone. 32 pages, 3d.; post free, 3½d.
A fine inspiring address to young people. [Tracts for the Times.
"The sermon is suggestive, bold, and warmly appreciative."—*British Weekly*.
"A masterly memorial sermon."—*Methodist Times*.

FOSTER. WORKS by the Rev. J. EDGAR FOSTER, M.A., Cantab., can now be obtained of Mr Allenson. A list of these useful books on Elocution and Composition will be sent post free on application.

GANT. FROM OUR DEAD SELVES TO HIGHER THINGS. By F. T. GANT, F.R.C.S. Crown 8vo, 2s. 6d.
A capital book for young men and women.
"The author uses his technical knowledge and experience of human nature to a very good purpose. ... In a series of very powerful descriptions no reader can fail to be impressed by a sense of the misery and bondage of sin, or fail to be helped by the hopeful possibilities of the soul's awakening."—*The Guardian*.

GASKIN. A TALE OF SIX LITTLE TRAVELLERS. Written and pictured in colours by Mrs ARTHUR GASKIN. Square 16mo, paper boards, 1s. net; cloth gilt, gilt edges, 1s. 6d. net; postage 1½d.
The colour-printing is by Edmund Evans. Parents will recall Kate Greenaway's delightful illustrations as rendered by this firm, and the work in this volume fully maintains the old standard of excellence.

GIBBON. THE FOUR LAST THINGS. Four Sermons on Death, Judgment, Hell, Heaven. By Rev. J. M. GIBBON. Fcap. 8vo, 1s. net; by post, 1s. 2d.
"Lucid, fresh, and thoughtful sermons."—*Methodist Times*.
"In 'Four Last Things' subjects of sublime and great import are discussed, not always in terms which we approve, nor to conclusions which we endorse, but uniformly, with reverence, and often helpfully."—*Christian*.

——— **TWELVE SERMONS.** By Rev. J. M. GIBBON, selected from the monthly issues of the Stamford Hill Pulpit, containing 12 Sermons and 12 Children's Addresses. 1s. 6d. net; post free, 1s. 9d.

GORDON. THE CINDERELLA OWL-BOOK. The old fairy tale re-told and pictured in colours by MARY LINDSAY GORDON. Square 16mo, paper boards, 1s. net; cloth gilt, gilt edges, 1s. 6d. net; postage 1½d.

This book is printed by the well-known firm of Edmund Evans. It depicts in delightful fashion the old narrative with charmingly drawn owls as characters in the nursery drama.

GREGORY. AN INTRODUCTION TO CHRISTIAN MYSTICISM. A Lecture by ELEANOR C. GREGORY, of the Deanery, St Paul's Cathedral, London, editor of "A Little Book of Heavenly Wisdom." With Prefatory Letter by Dr ALEXANDER WHYTE, Edinburgh. Fcap. 8vo, cloth, 1s. net; by post, 1s. 2d.

Of late years many books have been devoted to Christian Mysticism, but these works have either been upon one exponent only, or else have been large and expensive general treatises. The comprehensiveness of Miss Gregory's "Introduction" may be readily seen by a glance at the following :—

CONTENTS.

PLATO. PHILO. ORIGEN.	MODERN MYSTICISM. MAETERLINCK.
PLOTINUS. EPICTETUS. DIONYSIUS.	SELF-SURRENDER. CHRIST'S LIFE IN US.
ERIGENA. VICTORINES, ETC.	THE THREE STAGES. SYMBOLISM.
ECKHART. PARACELSUS.	REALITY OF THE IDEAL. VISIONS.
JACOB BÖHME. TAULER.	DISPARAGEMENT OF FORMS.
LAW AND ENGLISH MYSTICS.	UNDUE EXALTATION.
THEOLOGIA GERMANICA. À KEMPIS.	INDIVIDUALISM; AND ITS TWO SAFE-
RUYSBROEK. SUSO.	GUARDS—
ST JOHN OF THE CROSS, ST THERESA.	I. PRAYER AND THOUGHT.
MOLINOS. MME. GUYON, FÉNELON.	II. PURIFICATION FOR SERVICE.

"I rejoice in the publication of anything that helps to turn the public mind to the study of the great spiritual writers: and this lecture will form an admirable introduction to the greatest and best of all studies."—*Dr Whyte.*

"The comprehensiveness and wide appreciativeness of the writer are quite beyond the ordinary run, and the booklet is a delightful guide to the subject of which it treats."—*The Rock.*

"A decidedly lucid and interesting account of the great mystics."—*Daily News.*

"We cordially endorse Dr Alexander Whyte's opinion."—*School Guardian.*

"A welcome little volume."—*The Christian.*

GUYON. Life of Madame. New Edition. 6s. See *Upham.*

HALSEY. THE BEAUTY OF THE LORD. Twenty Sermons. By Rev. JOSEPH HALSEY. Crown 8vo, cloth, 5s.

HAMILTON. THE MOUNTAIN PATH: Forty-four Talks to Children. By Rev. JOHN A. HAMILTON, Author of "The MS. in a Red Box." Crown 8vo, cloth, 2s. 6d.

"One of the most delightful children's books we have met with for a long time. Each talk is based on some fable or story, or on some fact of nature with which an ordinary walk through garden or field may make one familiar. These addresses, spoken or read, must capture the children, we are sure."—*Examiner.*

"Full of metaphor, parable, incident and illustration, freshly put and original in the best sense."—*Methodist S. S. Record.*

HANDLEY. WHAT ENGLAND OWES TO THE PURITANS. By Rev. S. B. HANDLEY. 6d. net; post free, 7d.

"The Free Church Federation would do real service by scattering his little work broadcast over the land. The Nonconformist memory, like its conscience, needs stirring up; this little historical and descriptive work is admirably adapted for this purpose."—*Sword and Trowel.*

C

HANDY THEOLOGICAL LIBRARY. See p. 35.
HEART AND LIFE BOOKLETS. See p. 35.

HERRON. SOCIAL MEANINGS OF RELIGIOUS EXPERIENCES. By G. D. HERRON. Crown 8vo, cloth, 3s. 6d.

"Dr Herron is a fearless preacher of righteousness. The note struck is sufficiently evident from the title of the book."—*New Age* (*full page review*).

"Mazzini does not lack disciples, but Professor Herron perhaps has grasped more thoroughly than any one else the inner meaning of his message. 'Social Meanings' is a book well worth reading."—*Review of Reviews* (*full page review*).

—— **THE CHRISTIAN SOCIETY.** By G. D. HERRON. Introduction by Dr CHARLES A. BERRY. Crown 8vo, cloth, 3s. 6d.

"Never in our day have we had the moral foundations and spiritual law of a Christian Society preached with such prophetic fervour and power as in this volume."—*Christian World.*

WORKS BY C. SILVESTER HORNE, M.A.

THE RELATIONSHIPS OF LIFE. New Sermons to Young Men and Women. By the Rev. C. SILVESTER HORNE, M.A. Crown 8vo, 3s. 6d.

"Mr Horne's book is worth reading, its style is simple and direct, its observations are often fresh, and are always wise and true."—*Examiner.*

"A book of sermons by one of the most brilliant preachers of the present day. It abounds in proof of good sense, sound feeling, and genuine Christianity."—*British Weekly.*

THE LIFE THAT IS EASY. Ten Sermons on the Christian Life. By Rev. C. SILVESTER HORNE, M.A. Crown 8vo, 2s.

"It is impossible to avoid the impression that this young preacher has a message for the human conscience and heart. His manner of treatment is strenuous and intense. Is certain to be read and pondered by thoughtful young men and women."—*Literary World.*

"This suggestive volume of sermons."—*British Weekly.*

THE PRIMER OF CHURCH FELLOWSHIP. By Rev. W. PIERCE and Rev. C. S. HORNE, M.A. Fourth Edition. Cloth, 1s.; Paper Wrapper, 6d.

"I have read it with much interest, and think it extremely well adapted for the purpose intended. I shall recommend it in my own congregation and elsewhere as opportunity serves. I am sure that many pastors will join me in thanking you for a very necessary and well-done piece of work."—*Rev. Alexander Maclaren, D.D.,* Manchester.

"Full of wisdom and of good feeling. I know no book which speaks a more needed word."—*Rev. Principal Fairbairn, D.D.,* Oxford.

"Admirable from first to last. Precisely the kind of book that Congregational ministers must desire to put into the hands of Church members, and of candidates for Church membership. It is a triumph of simplicity, clearness and earnestness."—*The late Dr R. W. Dale,* of Birmingham.

"I think the 'Primer' will be of the greatest use, not so much as a rigid text-book for pastors and teachers to employ in classes, but as a model or pattern of the ground which has to be covered, and filled, according to the individual conviction, in instructing the young."—*Dr R. F. Horton,* Hampstead.

THE SPIRIT OF DIVES. A Sermon on Indifference. By C. S. HORNE. Crown 8vo, One Penny. [Tracts for the Times.

THE SOBRIETY OF HOPE. By C. S. HORNE. Crown 8vo, One Penny. [Tracts for the Times.

H. R. ALLENSON'S CATALOGUE 15

HORWILL. WANTED—AN ENGLISH BIBLE. By Rev. H. W. HORWILL, M.A. 2d.; post free, 2½d. An Essay reprinted from *The Contemporary Review* by special permission of the Editor.
[Tracts for the Times.

—— **FOUNDATIONS. A Sermon** by Rev. H. W. HORWILL, M.A. 1d.; post free, 1½d. [Tracts for the Times.
A fine and inspiring appeal to young people to build on Christ.

HUMBERSTONE. THE CURE OF CARE. By Rev. W. J. HUMBERSTONE. Fcap. 8vo, cloth, 1s. 6d. net; by post, 1s. 9d.

CONTENTS.

THE UNCHANGING CHRIST.	THE WHISPERS OF FAITH TO DOUBT.
THE CURE OF CARE.	REMEMBERED GOODNESS.
HIDDEN MANNA.	AN EASTER PROMISE.
GLADNESS IN THE HEART.	A WHITSUNTIDE BLESSING.
THE GOSPEL OF PURITY.	MAN'S ANXIETY AND GOD'S CARE.
CHRIST IDENTIFYING HIMSELF WITH MAN.	

"Eleven chapters of a comforting, cheering and stimulating character. The thoughts are clothed in chaste and appropriate language."—*Aberdeen Free Press.*
"This little volume of short sermons is full of wise and tender feeling."—*Christian Leader.*

INDIA PAPER SERIES. See p. 36.

JAMES. TALKS TO YOUNG FOLK. Seventeen Addresses to Children. By Rev. G. H. JAMES. With Index of Subjects and Anecdotes. Second Edition. Crown 8vo, 2s. 6d.
"A volume of simple sermons for children."—*The British Weekly.*
"These talks are full of sound teaching, in simple homely language, enforced by telling illustration."—*Christian Commonwealth.*

WORKS BY J. H. JOWETT, M.A.

BROOKS BY THE TRAVELLER'S WAY. Twenty-six Week-night Addresses. By the Rev. J. H. JOWETT, M.A., Carr's Lane, Birmingham. Crown 8vo, 3s. 6d. Third Edition (Sixth Thousand).

"Mr Jowett's religious addresses need no recommendation. We know what to expect and we are not disappointed. As of Dr Maclaren, so of Mr Jowett, it may be said that whenever he treats any religious theme, he invariably sheds fresh light on some passage of Scripture. In a sentence is the sure seed of a sermon."—*British Weekly.*
"Full of life all through, they serve to explain the speaker's rapidly acquired reputation, and to justify the wisdom of the congregation which chose him to occupy the pulpit of the late Dr Dale."—*Glasgow Herald.*
"Many of the addresses might profitably be extended into long sermons."—*Baptist Times.*
"The very titles are worth the cost of the volume."—*Methodist S.S. Record.*

THIRSTING FOR THE SPRINGS. By the Rev. J. H. JOWETT. Being a further selection of Twenty-six Addresses delivered at Carr's Lane. Crown 8vo, 3s. 6d. Fifth Thousand.

"To read this volume is to understand why the week-night meeting at Carr's Lane is one of the most successful in England. Mr Jowett gives his people of his best—his best in thought, observation, and reading."—*Independent (New York).*

THE DUTY OF BEING YOUNG. An Address to Young People. By the Rev. J. H. JOWETT, M.A. 1d.; post free, 1½d.
[Tracts for the Times.

KEEP. OLD TESTAMENT LESSONS. Delivered to a Bible Class. By Miss M. I. KEEP. With Portrait. Crown 8vo, cloth, 3s. 6d.

" Will be found most helpful by leaders of Young Women's Bible Classes, to whom we heartily commend it."—*Life of Faith.*

" A large amount of independent practical thought has gone hand in hand with painstaking research into Eastern manners."

LAW. A SERIOUS CALL TO A DEVOUT AND HOLY LIFE. By WILLIAM LAW. With introductory letter by Dr Alexander Whyte. 188 pages, large clear type, demy 8vo, 6d.

[Allenson's Sixpenny Series.

Dr Whyte says in his letter to the publisher:—" It was a red-letter day in my life when I first opened William Law, and I feel his hand on my heart, and on my mind, and on my conscience, and on my whole inner man literally every day I live. How could I then but wish you God-speed in putting a cheap edition of Law's masterpiece before the English-reading world ! "

LAWSON. HEROIC ENDEAVOUR. A Word of Hope. By Rev. W. ELSWORTH LAWSON. Two Addresses to Young Men, one a New Year's Address. Neat enamel wrapper, 6d.

" Of this book we may confidently say that it is one of great merit. It is able, strong, and full of suggestion."—*Young Man.*

" An earnest sermon thoughtfully put together."—*Christian World.*

LAWSON, Mrs. THE WARFARE OF GIRLHOOD. A Series of Bright Papers for Girls. By Mrs ROBERTSON LAWSON. Crown 8vo, art linen, 1s. 6d.

" The tone throughout is inspiring and practical."—*Christian World.*

LEARMOUNT. FIFTY-TWO SUNDAYS WITH THE CHILDREN. A New Volume of Sunday Morning Talks to Children. By Rev. JAMES LEARMOUNT. Crown 8vo, cloth, 3s. 6d.

" Has the rare and happy art of saying things brightly and in a way likely to haunt the juvenile memory."—*Dundee Advertiser.* " Brightened with many telling illustrations, well adapted to their purpose."—*British Weekly.*	" A real children's Christian year. Mr Learmount has a fascinating way of simplifying classic legends and old traditions. His pages glitter with anecdotes and illustrations appositely introduced."—*Our Young Men.*

—— **FIFTY-TWO ADDRESSES TO YOUNG FOLK.** By Rev. JAMES LEARMOUNT. Third Edition. Crown 8vo, 3s. 6d.

" The addresses are all rich in fresh and apt illustrations from science and legend, from literature and human life, and among all these there is not one 'chestnut '! Ministers and others who have to speak to	young folk should look into this volume."—*The Examiner.* " Abundance of short and telling anecdotes, the value of which teachers will not be slow to recognise."—*The Pilot.*

LEAVES WORTH TURNING. A Fragrant Thought for Every Day. Collected by J. E. Limp leather, gilt edges, round corners, 2s. 6d. net; cloth, 1s. net; limp leather, 2s. net; postage 2d.

A Charming Gift Book Handsomely Produced.

"The selection has been excellently made. The volume is a gem of its kind."—*Weekly Leader*

" A dainty little volume."

" A treasury of wisdom and literature."

LEE, CHARLES. PAUL CARAH; CORNISHMAN. 305 pages. Crown 8vo, cloth, 6s.

LEWIS. SOME VIEWS OF MODERN THEOLOGY.
Sixteen Sermons on Vital Questions. By the Rev. E. W. LEWIS, M.A. Crown 8vo, cloth, 3s. 6d.

CONTENTS.

CHRIST THE SON OF GOD.
PERSONALITY OF GOD AND HUMAN AFFAIRS.
PRAYER AND ITS ANSWER.
CHRIST'S MIRACLES.
THE RESURRECTION OF THE BODY.
HELL AS A PLACE AND AS A STATE OF MIND.
THE TRINITY.
THE IMMACULATE CONCEPTION.
THE DEVIL.
THE BIBLE.
EVOLUTION AND CREATION.
THE FALL OF MAN.
SOLIDARITY OF HUMANITY.
SIN AND PUNISHMENT.
"ESCAPING HELL" AND "BEING GOOD."
CHRIST AS SAVIOUR.

"We have nothing but praise for this excellent volume. The clearness and candour of his arguments are remarkable. We believe in the main he represents the trend of thought in all denominations. Needless to say he parts company with the traditionalist and the literalist. The writer's work is constructive, and can only seem to strengthen and build up the faith."—*The Friend.*

"We invite our younger clergy (all who are not too old to learn) to note the difference between the thin milk-and-water stuff they often offer their famished hearers, and the solid thought, based on patristic study, which the Dissenter provides for congregations evidently willing to listen to and capable of understanding. Mr Lewis does not preach down to their supposed level, but invites them into the higher regions and leads the way. This is a good book, one that will help many to clearer thought."—*Church Times.*

"Mr Lewis is a theological 'progressive,' and he has the courage of his convictions. Practically, the whole foundation of Christianity is involved in the issues raised by these sermons; and, in bringing faith into harmony with modern feeling and knowledge, Mr Lewis is adopting the one effective way of meeting rationalistic criticism."—*Christian World.*

LEE. THE HUMAN BODY, AND HOW TO TAKE CARE OF IT.
A Tract for the People. An Address delivered to the Fulham Y.M.C.A. By WM. E. LEE, M.R.C.S.E. Crown 8vo, 22 pages, 2d.; post free, 2½d.

"An admirable tract."—*Christian.*

MACFADYEN. CONSTRUCTIVE CONGREGATIONAL IDEALS.
Edited by the Rev. D. MACFADYEN, M.A., Editor of "Madame Guyon's Method of Prayer."
Addresses and Essays by JAMES MIALL, J. A. MACFADYEN, R. W. DALE, A. MACKENNAL, A. M. FAIRBAIRN, W. HEWGILL, etc., and the EDITOR. Cheap Edition. 2s. 6d. net. Postage 4d.

The Editor has found himself repeatedly challenged to explain the meaning of "Organized Congregationalism," and asked by friends to recommend some literature on the subject. The second half of the book is an endeavour to reply to that challenge by gathering together some of the ideas, hopes, aims, and plans which have proved an inspiration to himself in denominational spade-work.

"The *pros* and *cons* of the various 'planks' in the programme of the Congregational reformers are frankly discussed by Mr Macfadyen, who, in this volume, reveals the possession of a statesmanlike grasp alike of principle and detail. He is persuasive as advocate and damaging as critic, but he seems ever possessed by an earnest and sincere desire to see organised Congregationalism adapted to meet its new needs and fresh responsibilities."—*Christian World.*

MARSH. TOM OSSINGTON'S GHOST. By RICHARD MARSH.
Crown 8vo, 3s. 6d.

"The book is certainly entrancing, but people with weak nerves had better not read it at night. I did though, I couldn't help it."—*To-Day.*

H. R. ALLENSON'S CATALOGUE

MARTIN. GREAT MOTTOES WITH GREAT LESSONS. Talks to Children on Mottoes of Great Families, etc. By the Rev. G. CURRIE MARTIN, M.A. 3s. 6d.

"In this volume we have a good idea well executed. Discourses, suited to young hearers, have been constructed, with the sentiment of some motto, of a family or a public body, for their central purpose."—*Spectator.*

"Mr Currie Martin has seized on a capital idea and worked it with consummate skill."—*Methodist Times.*

"The result is that of the numerous volumes of children's sermons published in recent years, his own is among the best."—*Christian World.*

—— **OUTLINE SERMONETTES ON GOLDEN TEXTS.** Edited by Rev. G. CURRIE MARTIN, M.A. Fcap. 8vo, 1s. [Third Edition.

Forty-seven topics by—
Rev. Prof. W. F. ADENEY, M.A.
Rev. W. J. ALLAN, M.A, B.D.
Rev. W. ARMSTRONG.
Rev. W. W. D. CAMPBELL, M.A.
Rev. JOHN EAMES, B.A.
Rev. HUGH ELDER, M.A.
Rev. R. C. FORD, M.A.
Rev. A. R. HENDERSON, M.A.
Rev. G. CURRIE MARTIN, M.A., B.D.
Rev. SYDNEY MILLEDGE, M.A.,
  and
Rev. E. PEARCE POWELL, M.A.

"They are rich in thought and exceedingly suggestive. Many a minister on the look-out for 'sermon seed' might go farther and fare worse."—*Sunday School Chronicle.*

—— **A CATECHISM ON THE TEACHING OF JESUS.** By Rev. G. CURRIE MARTIN, M.A., B.D. For use in Schools and Bible Classes. 16 pages, stout wrapper, clear type, 1d.; cloth, 2d. Post free, 2½d. [Second Edition.

"This Catechism is one of the best I have seen. The questions are most skilfully arranged, and the answers are apt and effective. A better catechetical guide for the young in acquiring a knowledge of the teaching of Jesus I cannot imagine."—*Rev. Dr Clifford.*

McWILLIAM. SPEAKERS FOR GOD. Plain Lectures on the Minor Prophets. By Rev. THOMAS McWILLIAM, M.A., Minister of New Byth, Aberdeenshire. Crown 8vo, 3s. 6d.

"I have not for a long time read a course of Lectures on scriptural characters so well fitted to be of great use to the general religious public. . . . An admirable book, which I hope will be highly and widely appreciated."—*Prof. Flint, D.D., LL.D.*

". . . has accomplished the task of making a confessedly obscure and difficult breadth of Scripture instinct with life and meaning . . . many fresh and suggestive view-points."—*Prof. A. R. S. Kennedy, D.D.*

". . . We know the grip Mr McWilliam takes of his subject, and his skill in presenting it lucidly. . . . We need all the aids at hand. Mr McWilliam is one of the best and readiest. His book may be read with ease from beginning to end, and very likely will be read for pure enjoyment by those who light upon it."—*Expository Times.*

MERCER. BREAD FOR THE BAIRNS. Outline Addresses to Children. By the Rev. HENRY F. MERCER. Cloth, 2s. net; paper, 1s. net; postage 2d. Both interleaved for Notes.

"From the letters I receive there is an undoubted need for works of this sort, and I would counsel Christian workers to add this book to their stores. The addresses are brief outlines built up about a blackboard plan. The teaching is direct, strong, and true."—*Sunday School Chronicle.*

"Simple and ingeniously devised religious lessons for children. It should prove helpful to ministers and Sunday School teachers."—*Scotsman.*

H. R. ALLENSON'S CATALOGUE 19

MILLARD. THE QUEST OF THE INFINITE; or, THE PLACE OF REASON AND MYSTERY IN RELIGIOUS EXPERIENCE. By BENJAMIN A. MILLARD. Handsome cloth, crown 8vo, 3s. 6d.

CONTENTS.

THE PLACE OF MYSTERY IN RELIGION.
THE PLACE OF REASON IN A RELIGION OF MYSTERY.
THE LIMITATIONS OF REASON IN THE SPHERE OF RELIGION.
RELIGION AND EXPERIENCE.
THE NEW APOLOGETIC AND THE WORK OF JESUS.

THE WITNESS OF HISTORY TO THE NEW APOLOGETIC.
SOME OBJECTIONS TO THE NEW APOLOGETIC.
THE ESSENTIAL AND THE ACCIDENTAL IN THE CHRISTIAN FAITH.
THE INCREASE OF KNOWLEDGE AND THE GROWTH OF FAITH.
THE CHRISTIAN LIFE.

"This eloquent and suggestive little book, Mr Millard's presentation, impresses and even enthralls us. He forces upon us the conviction that there is a future for what may truly be called Christianity, so glorious and so potent that we who live in an age of decaying dogma can scarcely imagine it."—*Academy.*

"This is a thoroughly sound and helpful discussion in a popular form of some of the chief difficulties which prevent the average man from accepting the Christian faith. The plea that religion is so full of mystery, and therefore incredible, is shown to be utterly futile. This is a book which should make for a clear, strong faith in all who carefully read it."—*Baptist Times.*

MOMERIE. IMMORTALITY AND OTHER SERMONS. By Prof. ALFRED W. MOMERIE, M.A., D.Sc., LL.D., Author of "Personality," "Agnosticism," etc. Handsome New Edition. Crown 8vo, cloth, 3s. 6d. [Fourth Edition.

CONTENTS.

IMPORTANCE OF THE BELIEF IN IMMORTALITY.
MYSTERY OF DEATH.
THE BENIGNITY OF DEATH.
THE DESIRE FOR IMMORTALITY.
THE INJUSTICE OF LIFE.
THE INCOMPLETENESS OF LIFE.
THE NATURE OF THE SOUL.
THE GREATNESS OF MAN.
MAN'S RIGHT TO IMMORTALITY.
IMMORTALITY IN THE LIGHT OF EVOLUTION.
THE RESURRECTION.
SUBSTITUTES FOR IMMORTALITY.
THE LONGING FOR REST.
OLD TESTAMENT IDEA OF THE FUTURE LIFE.

THE GREEK IDEA OF THE FUTURE LIFE.
PRIMITIVE IDEAS OF THE FUTURE LIFE.
THE SPIRITUAL BODY.
PERSONAL IDENTITY.
REUNION.
RECOGNITION.
THE READJUSTMENT OF RELATIONSHIPS.
THE CONTINUITY OF LIFE.
THE PROGRESSIVENESS OF LIFE.
RETRIBUTION.
SECOND ADVENT.
THE END OF THE WORLD.
THE DAY OF JUDGMENT.
HEAVEN.
HELL. I. WHAT IT IS NOT. II. WHAT IT IS.
FINAL RESTORATION.

Beside the thirty-five chapters on Immortality this volume contains the three fine sermons on "Common Failings," viz.: Cowardice, Indolence, Intolerance, and also Animals and Broad Churchism.

This new edition (the fourth) of Dr Momerie's most interesting and able book is now reissued by arrangement with Messrs Blackwood.

"There is so much food for thought in the sermons that we do not wonder at such a large circulation."—*London Quarterly Review.*

"The extent of his influence on his contemporaries it is impossible to gauge. He sought to supply men with a rational faith and it may well be that there are those who looked askance at his theology, who have yet been helped by him towards a nobler and clearer conception of religion."—*New Age.*

"The book is greatly enriched by the poetical quotations which conclude most of the sermons. Many of these are unfamiliar, and most of them are very beautiful and full of spiritual suggestion."—*Examiner.*

"A serious and strong contribution to a subject which will never lose its interest while the world lasts.'—*Expository Times.*

MOMERIE. IMMORTALITY. Thirty-five Chapters. By Prof. A. W. MOMERIE, M.A., LL.D., Author of "Belief in God," etc. Popular Edition, Thirtieth Thousand. 6d. [Allenson's Sixpenny Series.
"Few sixpenny reprints deserve to be more widely read than this. Dr Momerie was one of the keenest thinkers and most concisely effective preachers that have stood in the modern pulpit."—*Literary World.*

—— **BELIEF IN GOD.** By Prof. A. W. MOMERIE, M.A., LL.D., Author of "Immortality," "Personality," etc. Second Edition. 6d. [Allenson's Sixpenny Series.

CONTENTS.

THE DESIRE FOR GOD.	SUPERNATURAL PURPOSE.
MATERIALISM.	THE INFINITE PERSONALITY.
AGNOSTICISM.	

"Professor Momerie's acute criticism of sceptical philosophies of religion is sure of a wide circulation in this popular form.—*Scotsman.*
"One of the most effective indications of theistic and Christian belief with which we are acquainted."—*Baptist Times.*

MONOD. HE SUFFERED; or, HUMAN SUFFERING INTERPRETED BY JESUS CHRIST. Six Meditations for Holy Week. By WILFRED MONOD. 2s.

THE NONCONFORMIST MINISTER'S ORDINAL, Preacher's Services for Baptismal, Dedication, Marriage, and Funeral Services. Large Type. Fcap. 8vo, cloth, 1s. net; black buckram, gilt lettered, very strong, 1s. 6d. net; limp leather, gilt edges and gilt lettered, 2s. 6d. net; postage 2d. each extra.
This book will go comfortably into a breast pocket.

"A work many Nonconformist ministers will be glad to know of. A handy and tastefully presented book; as convenient in size, type, and binding as could well be."—*Literary World.*
"Will no doubt prove most valuable to the young minister, who on leaving college needs some such guide."—*Evangelical Magazine.*
"We predict it will be largely used."—*Primitive Methodist.*

NORTON. OLD PATHS. Fifty-two Sermons. By Rev. J. N. NORTON, D.D. Numerous useful and telling anecdotes. 3s. 6d. net; postage 4d.

PALMER. THE GOSPEL PROBLEMS AND THEIR SOLUTION. By JOSEPH PALMER. Crown 8vo, cloth, 6s.
"It is an elaborate piece of work, from which, whether he accepts its theory or no, the student can scarcely fail to learn much."—*Spectator.*
"A work of real value. We are glad to call attention to his book as one that well deserves study."—*Guardian.*

PARKER. JOB'S COMFORTERS; or, SCIENTIFIC SYMPATHY. By Rev. JOSEPH PARKER, D.D. 6d.
Said by very many to be Dr Parker's finest piece of work.

—— **GAMBLING.** By JOSEPH PARKER, D.D. 3d.; post free, 3½d. Fifth Edition.
"Trenchant and telling. It should be widely circulated."—*Christian.*
"We hope this mighty address will stir the heart of England and awaken the conscience of the nation."—*Methodist Times.*
"Deserves to be in the hands of every young man."—*Baptist.*

H. R. ALLENSON'S CATALOGUE 21

PARRY. PARISH DISTRICT VISITING BOOK, AND SICK AND COMMUNICANTS' LIST. By Rev. JOHN PARRY, M.A. Second Edition. Strongly bound in buckram cloth, round corners, for the pocket, 2s. net; post free, 2s. 3d.

PEARSON. AM I FIT TO TAKE THE LORD'S SUPPER? By Rev. SAMUEL PEARSON, M.A. Seventeenth Thousand. 16 pages, crown 8vo, 1d.; post free, 1½d. 6s. per 100.
[Tracts for the Times.

WORKS BY CHARLES H. PERREN, D.D.

SEED CORN FOR THE SOWER. A Book of Thoughts, Themes, and Illustrations. Arranged in alphabetical order. Original and Compiled by Rev. C. H. PERREN, D.D. Complete Indexes to Subjects Texts, and Authors. 5s.

"An admirable collection of thoughts and illustrations. One of the charms of this book is the absence of stock illustrations. Rightly used, the book will be a boon to preachers and teachers."—*The Methodist Times.*

REVIVAL SERMONS IN OUTLINE. With Thoughts Themes, and Plans, by eminent Pastors and Evangelists. Edited by Rev. C. H. PERREN, D.D. In Two Parts. Part 1, Methods; Part 2, Outlines of Sermons and Addresses. Complete in One Volume. Crown 8vo, 344 pages, cloth, 3s. 6d.
Literally the Evangelist's Handbook.

PART I. 80 Pages on Methods.

SOME MODERN REVIVALS. By Rev. John R. Davies.
DIVINE AND HUMAN AGENCY IN REVIVALS. By Rev. John Gordon, D.D.
THE PASTOR'S VALUE. By W. H. Geistweit.
THE EVANGELIST IN REVIVALS. By Rev. E. A. Whittier.
THE PEOPLE'S PART IN REVIVAL WORK.
HOW TO PROMOTE REVIVALS. By D. L. Moody.
WORK PREPARATORY TO REVIVALS. By Rev. Herrick Johnson, D.D.
REVIVALS—HOW TO PROMOTE THEM. From a Lecture by Charles G. Finney, D.D.

HOW TO SECURE A REVIVAL. By E. P. Brown.
SOME HINTS ABOUT REVIVALS.
HOW TO AWAKEN FRESH INTEREST IN OUR CHURCHES. By D. L. Moody.
HOW TO SAVE SOULS. By Rev. F. O. Dickey.
PERSONAL WORK IN REVIVALS. By Rev. B. Fay Mills.
EXPECTING CONVERSIONS. By Ira D. Sankey.
DEFECTIVE REVIVAL WORK.
THE SUNDAY EVENING SERVICE. By Rev. Addison P. Foster, D.D.
THE INQUIRY MEETING. By D. L. MOODY.
HELPFUL PASSAGES FOR DIFFERENT CLASSES OF SEEKERS.

PART II. 244 Pages of Outlines and Sketches of Revival Sermons. Forty-four Old Testament, seventy-one New Testament. In all one hundred and fifteen Outlines from approved Evangelists, such as J. W. CONLEY, R. A. TORREY, A. B. EARLE, J. L. CAMPBELL, JOHN MCNEILL, J. WILBUR CHAPMAN, D. L. MOODY, E. W. BLISS, D. H. COOLEY, A. J. GORDON, J. H. ELLIOT, G. C. FINNEY, D. W. WHITTLE, A. F. BARFIELD, A. T. PIERSON, THE EDITOR, and others.

"A large number of Sermon Outlines gleaned from those whom God has used and owned in the blessed work."—*Sunday School Chronicle.*
"Famous sermons all passed through a capable condenser."—*Expository Times.*
"To young men desirous of engaging in evangelistic work, we can highly recommend this volume."—*Methodist Times.*

PHILLIPS. CHRISTIAN CHIVALRY. A Missionary Address to Young Men. By Rev. THOMAS PHILLIPS, B.A. Enamel paper wrapper, 6d.

"An address on Phil. iv. 13, specially addressed to young men. Workers among young men should bear this little work in mind."—*Life of Faith*.
"Friends of missions might do well to distribute copies among young men "—*Christian*.

PICTORIAL POST CARDS. See page 2.

PIERCE. THE DOMINION OF CHRIST. Sermons on Missionary Work. By Rev. W. PIERCE. Cloth, 1s. 6d net. Special Cheap Edition, stout paper, 1s. net; postage 3d.

CONTENTS.

THE DOMINION OF CHRIST.	THE BECKONING VISION.
PATRIOTISM AND MISSIONS.	THE RELATION OF THE CHURCHES TO
THE SAVIOUR OF THE WORLD.	THE WORK OF FOREIGN MISSIONS.
THE VOCATION OF THE MISSIONARY.	FOREIGN MISSIONS AND CHRISTIAN LIFE
WOMEN AS MISSIONARIES.	AND THOUGHT.
THE PLACE OF EDUCATION AS A MISSIONARY AGENCY.	THE BELOVED PHYSICIAN (MEDICAL MISSIONS).

Mr Pierce's work would well form the basis of a short series of addresses for week-night services.
"Earnest in spirit, enthusiastic and hopeful in tone, and thoroughly practical in aim."—*L.M.S. Chronicle.*
"Clear, manly, and thoroughly Protestant."—*Methodist Times.*
"Cannot fail to increase intelligent interest."—*British Weekly.*
"A good and stimulating book."—*C. M. Intelligencer.*

—— **AND HORNE. PRIMER OF CHURCH FELLOWSHIP.** 6d. and 1s. See under Horne.

PRIESTLEY. MEMOIRS OF DOCTOR PRIESTLEY. Written by Himself and continued by his Son. Centenary Edition. With Sixteen choice Illustrations and Portraits. Art linen, gilt lettered, gilt top, 3s. net; postage 3d.

"Scientists, theologians and all thinkers have united in recognising the energy and genius of this Yorkshire cloth-dresser's son."—*T. P.'s Weekly.*

"This is a Centenary Edition, with a fine set of portraits. It is an autobiography that every student of the eighteenth century has to read, and there is much to learn from this record of a strenuous life devoted to theology and science."—*London Quarterly Review.*

RANDS. LAZY LESSONS AND ESSAYS ON CONDUCT. By W. B. RANDS. Fcap. 8vo, buckram, 3s. 6d.

REICHEL. WHAT SHALL I TELL THE CHILDREN? By Rev. GEO. V. REICHEL, M.A. Thirty-seven Object Sermons with many Illustrative Anecdotes. Second edition. Crown, 8vo, 3s. 6d.

"It is rather a nice book, and will be very useful to teachers and those who preach to children. The merit of the volume is that it has freshness."—*British Weekly.*

"It is thoroughly modern and alert. There is nothing hackneyed and stereotyped in its pages. Its author is full of information and of anecdote."—*S. S. Chronicle.*

"Contains such a wealth of illustration that the Christian worker will have no difficulty in selecting material which will be helpful in securing the attention of his young hearers and leading up to and enforcing the great rock truths of Holy Scripture."—*Christian Commonwealth.*

H. R. ALLENSON'S CATALOGUE

REYD. MUTTERS AND MURMURS OF A MISAN-THROPE. By PENLEY REYD. Crown 8vo, cloth, 1s. 6d.
"The mutters are tempered with wit and good humour, well calculated to while away a gloomy mood, a morose tendency."—*Liverpool Mercury.*
"An amusing little book."—*Scotsman.*

WORKS BY LAURA E. RICHARDS.

THE GOLDEN WINDOWS. A Book of Fables for Young and Old. By L. E. RICHARDS, Author of "Captain January." Handsome cloth, crown 8vo, gilt top, 2s. 6d. net.; and presentation binding, green lambskin, solid gold edges, 5s. net; postage 3d.

A collection of forty-four delightfully told Fables or Stories, each with a moral distinctly but not obtrusively expressed. The "Wheatfield" is only one of several gems likely to be used by many public speakers who make the acquaintance of Mrs Richards' book.

CONTENTS.

THE GOLDEN WINDOWS.	THE HILL.	THE SCAR.
THE WHEATFIELD.	THE DAY.	THE PROMINENT MAN.
TO-MORROW.	THE BABY.	FOR REMEMBRANCE.
THE COMING OF THE KING.	THE SHADOW.	THE SAILOR MAN.
THE TREE IN THE CITY.	GOOD ADVICE.	THE BLIND MOTHER.
THE HOUSE OF LOVE.	THE ROAD.	"GO" AND "COME."
THE GREAT FEAST.	HOME.	CHILD'S PLAY.
THE WALLED GARDEN.	A FORTUNE.	THE WINDOWS.
THE PIG BROTHER.	THE STARS.	A MISUNDERSTANDING.
ABOUT ANGELS.	THE COOKY.	FROM A FAR COUNTRY.
THE POINT OF VIEW.	ANYBODY.	THE STRONG CHILD.
THE OPEN DOOR.	THE GIFTIE.	A MATTER OF IMPORTANCE.
THE APRON-STRING.	THE STAFF.	THE STRANGER.
TWO WAYS.	THE DOOR.	THE WEDDING GUESTS.
THE DESERT.	THEOLOGY.	

"We think there has been nothing so good as this volume since Mrs Gatty wrote her 'Parables from Nature.'"—*Bookman.*
"Those familiar with that delightful little story 'Captain January' will find all the writer's charm of style and delicacy of touch in these 'Fables for Young and Old.' Of their kind they are perfect little gems of sunlit fancy playing with unerring deftness on the recurring questions of life and duty. To young and old alike they should prove thought quickening as well as heart stirring."—*Examiner.*
"Rare grace of suggestive imagination."—*Scotsman.*

"Of all the exquisite things in late literature, 'The Golden Windows' must, perhaps, take leading place. It is a collection of brief allegorical tales, each stamped with the impress of uplifting, beautiful thought, presented in an original and striking manner, and with all the charm of style that characterises Mrs Richards."—*Lilian Whiting in Chicago Inter-Ocean.*
"I regard 'Golden Windows' as the most charming book that has come into my hands for many years. Every little casket of a story holds a gem of a truth. How in the world is it so slow in getting known?"
—*Rev. Bernard J. Snell.*

CAPTAIN JANUARY. By LAURA E. RICHARDS. Crown 8vo, cloth gilt, gilt top, Twenty Illustrations, 1s. 6d. net; postage 3d.
This is a perfect story-idyll, dealing with a picturesque old lighthouse keeper, Captain January, and a baby-girl, Starbright, whom he rescued from drowning, and brought up in his island home with, as he quaintly expressed it, "the Lord's help, common sense, and a cow." The affection of these two for one another is beautifully expressed. Certainly one of the books that once begun will not be laid down till finished.
Over one hundred and thirty thousand of this charming story have been sold.
"The volume is a delightful one, and as pretty as it is delightful."—*Glasgow Herald.*
"A charming little romance."—*Liverpool Daily Post.*

WORKS BY F. W. ROBERTSON (OF BRIGHTON).

THE LONELINESS OF CHRIST. By F. W. ROBERTSON.
Fcap. 8vo, 6d. net; cloth, 1s. net; postage 1d.
[Heart and Life Booklets.
"One of F. W. Robertson's great sermons."—*New Age.*

TEN SERMONS. By F. W. ROBERTSON. A First Selection. Second Edition. 6d. [Allenson's Sixpenny Series.

ELEVEN SERMONS. By F. W. ROBERTSON. A Second Selection, completing First Series. Demy 8vo, 6d.
[Allenson's Sixpenny Series.

"Mr Allenson is rendering a great service to the religious world by his cheap reprint of Robertson's sermons."—*Daily News.*
"Robertson's sermons are among the classics of the pulpit. The famous sermon on The Message of the Church to Men of Wealth is included in this series."—*Preacher's Magazine.*
"Many people know Robertson's unique preaching only by hearsay and quotation; to these especially will Mr Allenson's reprint appeal."—*Southport Guardian.*

"Few modern preachers have exercised so great an influence on the current of religious thought as Robertson, and few indeed are so inspiring. In this accessible form they ought to lay hold of the new generation."—*Aberdeen Free Press.*
"His sermons are among the few that have kept their vitality in a religious world in which 'the old order changeth' with such startling rapidity. Their inclusion in a series of cheap, well-printed reprints will no doubt be welcomed."—*Oxford Chronicle.*

ROGERS. THE JOY OF THE RELIGIOUS. By the Rev. EDGAR ROGERS, Vicar of St Sepulchre, Holborn. 16mo, cloth, 1s. net; limp leather, gilt edges, 2s. net; postage 1d.
"Full of devout and holy thoughts, tinged with the mysticism of the middle ages."
—*Examiner.*

ROTHERHAM. THE EMPHASISED BIBLE. Great Reduction in Price. THE OLD TESTAMENT PORTION, in three equal vols., cloth, 6s. each net (hitherto 10s. 6d. each); or in one vol., cloth, 15s. net. The COMPLETE BIBLE (Old and New Testaments), in one vol., cloth, 20s. net; French morocco, 25s. net; Persian morocco, 27s. 6d. net. Being a New Translation designed to set forth the exact meaning, the proper terminology, and the graphic style of the sacred originals; with Expository Introduction, Select Reference, and Appendices of Notes. By JOSEPH BRYANT ROTHERHAM, Translator of "The New Testament Critically Emphasised."

"The whole desire is to enable us to read the English and produce the very same effect as reading the Hebrew does. . . . It puts the English scholar on a level, as nearly as possible, with the Hebrew."—*The Expository Times.*
"The analysis of the text has been carefully done, and the precision of the work is nowhere better shown than in the many footnotes on various readings and renderings. Here the fewest words are used, but sometimes they are of great value. . . . In some cases the notes convey information that has not appeared in any previous translation in our language. . . ."—*The Christian.*

"It is a wonderful testimony to the scholarship, industry, and discernment involved in the production of it. If only people would pay due attention to what it indicates, the Bible would be lit up with fresh meaning and interest, and many a pitfall of misapprehension would be avoided."—*Rev. W. F. Adeney, M.A., D.D.*
"It is a pleasure to read a Translation of the Old Testament in which synonyms and characteristic expressions of the original are, so far as idiom permits, properly distinguished. I have read many parts of it with much satisfaction and approval."—*Rev. S. R. Driver, D.D.*

ROTHERHAM. THE EMPHASISED NEW TESTAMENT. Fourth Edition. Cloth, 5s. net; French morocco, 10s. net; Persian morocco, 12s. 6d. net.

"The various signs used are extremely simple, and after reading a few lines one almost instinctively appreciates the precise value of each emphasis."—*The Daily News*.

"This is a painstaking work which deserves recognition. No page will be read without having a clearer light shed upon some passage or verse. . . . The book is well worth study."—*The British Weekly*.

NOTE.—It has been a matter of regret to the Translator and Publisher of the Emphasised Bible that the necessarily somewhat high price of the Book has hitherto placed it beyond the reach of some Bible Students desiring to possess it. Owing, however, to the remarkable reception given to the work in many lands, the cost of production has been materially lessened, and it is now possible to offer the present and subsequent editions at the much reduced prices mentioned above and on previous page.

If readers who value this work will kindly interest themselves in making it known, by lending a Volume for inspection or by obtaining Prospectuses for distribution, they will be rendering good service.

Full (Eight-page) Prospectus on application.

——— **OUR SACRED BOOKS.** Being Plain Chapters on the Inspiration, Transmission, and Translation of the Bible. By J. B. ROTHERHAM, Translator of "The Emphasised Bible." Crown 8vo, paper covers, 6d.

"We can call to mind no small book which contains so much solid reasoning as this one. It is at once a learned and a comprehensive survey of the field. The exceedingly clever manner in which a mass of fact is summarised for the general reader speaks of the author's intimacy with his material, knowing exactly how to give the maximum of argument and proof in the minimum of space. It should be a very messenger of light to many a reader of the Bible."—*Bible Class Journal*.

"He hits the golden mean between the two extremes on inspiration. . . . The work is well argued. Its perusal will foster a livelier and more intelligent gratitude that such a book as the Bible, even in its translation, has come down to us."—*The Weekly Leader* (Glasgow).

SCOTT, C. A. THE MAKING OF A CHRISTIAN. A Guide to Personal Religion for Young People. By the Rev. C. ANDERSON SCOTT, M.A., Author of "Evangelical Doctrine—Bible Truth." Crown 8vo, 1s. 6d. Also cloth gilt, gilt edges, 2s. 6d.

CONTENTS.

WHAT IS RELIGION? A BOND.
WHAT IS SIN? THE BOND BROKEN.
THE HISTORY OF A SIN.
THE CRAVING FOR SALVATION.
SALVATION: WHAT IT IS, AND HOW IT COMES.
HOW THE BOND COMES TO BE RESTORED.

THE NEW CREATURE:
HIS BIRTH.
HIS NAME.
HIS SPEECH.
HIS FOOD.
HIS GYMNASTICS.
HIS RELATIONS, HOME, AND COUNTRY.
HIS GROWTH AND DESTINY.

"He writes for young people, and succeeds in imparting to them a complete system of Christian doctrine, apparently with the greatest ease on his part, and we are sure with the greatest delight on theirs."—*Expository Times*.

"This is just the very book to put into the hands of our young people when they come to the parting of the ways, the deciding time, when they must definitely choose Christ or refuse Him. In the plainest language, but with great skill and freshness, it explains what Christianity is, and what the Christian life involves. We think it the best book of its kind we have seen, and it has the further advantage, that while addressed to the young, it is full of suggestive teaching for the mature Christian."—*Local Preachers' Magazine*.

H. R. ALLENSON'S CATALOGUE

RUSHER, E. A. SUNSHINE AND SHADOW IN THE SOUTH-WEST. A Record of a Visit to Y.M.C.A.'s and Missions in Spain and Morocco. With Map and Illustrations. Demy 8vo. Canvas, 1s. net; postage, 1d.

SCOTT, J. MAN IN THE NET. A striking Allegory and Answer on the Question, "What is God?" Artistic Booklet by JOHN SCOTT. Long fcap. 8vo, 6d. post free.

SERMON OR MANUSCRIPT PAPER. THE PATERNOSTER SERIES.

The user of this paper enjoys the following special advantages: It is easily arranged by means of holes punched in the left hand margin, so allowing that a sheet of paper can be immediately inserted or abstracted at desire, and that without disturbance to any other sheet.

Small 4to Good Writing Paper, ruled faint lines and margin line, 1s. 6d. for 10 quires. Postage, 4d. extra.

Octavo Good Writing Paper, ruled faint lines and margin line, 1s. for 10 quires. Postage, 4d. extra.

SIME. WHAT THE CHURCH MIGHT BE. A Sermon by Rev. A. H. MONCUR SIME. 16 pages, crown 8vo, 1d.; post free, 1½d. [Tracts for the Times.

CHARLES M. SHELDON'S PRACTICAL STORIES.

May each be obtained in cloth bindings at 3s. 6d., 2s. 6d., 2s., 1s. 6d., 1s., *and in paper wrapper*, 6d. *each.*

IN HIS STEPS: What would Jesus do? With Preface by Rev. F. B. MEYER, B.A.

Please ask for Mr Meyer's Edition, which was the first to be on sale in England, and is the only authorised Edition in this country.

"This is a living book. It has the fascination of a story, and the inspiration of a prophet's message. The thought of our time is just now crystallizing round the example of Jesus. No question is so urgent as 'What would Jesus do in my place and with my circumstances?' WE MUST ANSWER IT, and it is a real gain to see how others of our own day have answered it. The book will be of great service."—*Dr Clifford.*

THE CRUCIFIXION OF PHILIP STRONG.

"The story is one of intense vigour and pathos."—*The Congregationalist.*

MALCOLM KIRK; or, OVERCOMING THE WORLD. A Tale of Moral Heroism.

This book tells the entrancing history of the regeneration of a lawless western town. The servant girl question is treated from a new standpoint in the character of Faith Kirk, and the liquor element receives some hard blows.

THE TWENTIETH DOOR; or, BATTLING WITH TEMPTATION.

"No one can read it without feeling that few sermons would be more interesting or helpful than this story."—*Golden Rule.*

"It is a story of school and college life as well as of manly service and helpfulness in more than one sphere."—*Congregationalist.*

HIS BROTHER'S KEEPER; or, CHRISTIAN STEWARDSHIP.
"The story is well written, intensely interesting."—*Episcopal Recorder.*

RICHARD BRUCE; or, THE LIFE THAT NOW IS. By C. M. SHELDON.
This story of a young man's conflicts in his attempt to live up to a high ideal should interest all, particularly young men.
"It is a truly powerful, practical, touching Christian narrative creditable to the writer and engrossing to the reader. . . ."—*The Congregationalist.*

ROBERT HARDY'S SEVEN DAYS; or, A DREAM AND ITS CONSEQUENCES. By C. M. SHELDON.
"The earnestness, the zeal, the solemnity, the kindliness, the Christianity of that week's living are pictured with a skill and dramatic power that cannot fail to make readers feel as never before how solemn a thing it is to live."—*Christian Work.*

SIXPENNY DEMY 8vo SERIES. See p. 34.

SMITH. MEASURING SUNSHINE, and other Addresses to Children. By Rev. FRANK SMITH, M.A., B.Sc. Crown 8vo, 1s. 6d. net; by post, 1s. 9d.
"They are just what talks to children ought to be, short, simple, earnest, practical, arresting the attention by admirable anecdotes and striking illustrations."—*Stirling Sentinel.*
"Bright, fresh, living talks."—*Free Church Chronicle.*
"Remarkably well done."—*Methodist Times.*

WORKS BY BERNARD J. SNELL, M.A.,

WORDS TO CHILDREN. Twenty-six Addresses by Rev. B. J. SNELL, M.A., B.Sc. Crown 8vo, cloth, 2s. 6d.
"They are models of what addresses to children should be—thoroughly practical, eminently sensible, and full of spiritual suggestion."—*Glasgow Weekly Leader.*
"Each a little gem of its kind."—*The Rock.*

THE GOOD FATHER. Twenty-six Addresses to Children. By the Rev. BERNARD J. SNELL, M.A., B.Sc. Second Edition. Cr. 8vo, cloth, 2s. 6d.
"Charming addresses to children, simple, homely, childlike instructions."—*Newcastle Daily Chronicle.*
"Bright and vigorous, full of stories drawn from a wide range."—*Manchester Guardian.*

THIRTEEN SELECTED SERMONS AND ADDRESSES TO CHILDREN. By Rev. B. J. SNELL. Crown 8vo, cloth, 1s. 6d. net; postage, 3d. (Pagination not consecutive.)

WHY ARE WE INDEPENDENTS? By Rev. BERNARD J. SNELL, M.A., B.Sc. Sermon preached on Free Church Sunday. Crown 8vo, 2d.; post free, 2½d. [Tracts for the Times.
"In these days of Anglo-Catholic reaction it is well to set forth the principles for which the Independents stand. The Rev. Bernard Snell has done this with effect in a powerful sermon in which he answers the question, 'Why are we Independents?'"—*Western Daily Mercury.*

CITIZENSHIP AND ITS DUTIES. A Sermon preached on Citizen Sunday. By Rev. BERNARD J. SNELL. M.A., B.Sc. Crown 8vo, 16 pages, 1d.; post free, 1½d. [Tracts for the Times.

SNIVELY. TESTIMONIES TO THE SUPER-
NATURAL. Parochial Sermons. By the Rev. W. A. SNIVELY, D.D.
Crown 8vo, cloth, 3s. 6d.

STANYON. THE ETERNAL WILL: a Study of the
Interpretation of Life. By J. E. STANYON, Translator of Herrmann's
"Communion with God." Crown 8vo, cloth, 2s. 6d. net; postage, 3d.
Originally delivered at an Adult Bible Class for Men in Leicester.

"A very able and interesting attempt to reason out religion from the facts of life. No bald analysis can give an idea of the brilliant way in which the author advances from point to point in his contention."—*The Baptist.*
"A carefully conducted argument to induce men to get back to sincerity and reality in religion."—*Glasgow Herald.*
"Clear and concise. A serious conscious effort is made in it to catch the two facts of religion, experience and history, and get them to plough together."—*Expository Times.*

STOWELL. WHAT IS A CONGREGATIONAL CHURCH? A Sermon by Rev. J. HILTON STOWELL, M.A. 16 pages, crown 8vo, 1d.; post free, 1½d. ['Tracts for the Times.

TAULER'S LIFE, HISTORY AND SERMONS. New Edition, 6s. See *Winkworth.*

THEW. BROKEN IDEALS, AND OTHER SERMONS.
By Rev. JAMES THEW. Second and cheaper edition. Crown 8vo, cloth, 2s. 6d.

CONTENTS.

BROKEN IDEALS.	RELIGION IN AN UNLIKELY PLACE.
POSTHUMOUS INFLUENCE.	SELF IGNORANCE.
THE EAGLE.	SELFISH SORROW.
AT THEIR WITS' END.	MORNING THOUGHTS.
THE SONG OF TRIUMPH.	THOMAS.
THE QUIET MIND.	EARTHLY TREASURE.
THE GOD OF OUR FATHERS— A Sermon to Young Men.	THE RICH FOOL. THROUGH THE GLASS, DARKLY.

"Here is good preaching indeed; preaching of a type we should earnestly desire to become general. The sermons are distinctly reflective; full of pathos; instinct with sympathy. One could scarcely wish a loftier level of pulpit talk."—*Methodist Times.*
"His sermons ought to be placed in the hands of all who are studying the art of pulpit discourse."—*Daily News.*
"Mr Thew's sermons are fresh and tender."—*British Weekly.*
"We welcome the pretty and tasteful little volume of sermons by the Rev. James Thew of Leicester."
"They are the trumpet calls to faith, to duty, and endurance."—*Christian.*

THOMAS, ALFRED. IN THE LAND OF THE HARP AND FEATHERS. Welsh Village Idylls. By ALFRED THOMAS. Cheap Edition, art linen, 3s. 6d.

"Rustic homeliness, sincerity, generosity, and godliness of the people are seen in every chapter of the book."—*Baptist.*
"Stories of the quaintest characteristics of the countryside, told with sympathetic appreciation, and not without a sense of humour."—*Westminster Review.*

THOMAS, H. ELWYN. MARTYRS OF HELL'S HIGHWAY. By Rev. H. ELWYN THOMAS. Preface and Appendix by Mrs JOSEPHINE BUTLER. Cheap edition, paper, 1s.; cloth, 1s. 6d.

"Written with graphic and remorseless power, vigour of style, and thorough honesty of purpose."—*The Star.*
"The contents are thoroughly in keeping with the title. . . . Written with quite a passionate earnestness."—*Glasgow Herald.*
"No one could read this unveiling of one of the blackest forms of calculating and fiendish iniquity without horror and indignation."—*The Christian.*

THOMAS, H. E. PULPIT TALKS TO YOUNG PEOPLE.
By the Rev. H. ELWYN THOMAS. 1s. 6d. net; postage 3d.

"The subjects are such as young people like to hear discussed, and others such as they are the better for hearing about.... Recommended to ministers as a specimen of the kind of preaching to which young people lend a ready ear."—*Glasgow Herald.*

THOMPSON. PROFESSOR HUXLEY AND RELIGION. By the Rev. W. HALLIDAY THOMPSON, LL.D., Professor of Divinity, Gresham College, London. Crown 8vo, cloth, 2s. 6d. net. Postage 3d.

CONTENTS.

PROFESSOR HUXLEY AND THE METHOD OF SCIENCE.
THE METHOD OF SCIENCE APPLIED TO RELIGION.
PROFESSOR HUXLEY'S OBJECTIONS TO HYPOTHESIS OF GOD.
FAITH THE COMMON BASIS OF THEOLOGY AND SCIENCE. SUPPLEMENTARY.

"Able and suggestive lectures."—*Aberdeen Free Press.*
"A thoughtful and temperate defence."—*Scotsman.*
"Dr Thompson is just, he is logical and he is lucid."—*Examiner.*
"Conspicuously fair to his great opponent."—*Christian World.*

TILESTON. GREAT SOULS AT PRAYER. Fourteen Centuries of Prayer, Praise, and Aspiration, from St Augustine to Christina Rosetti and R. L. Stevenson. Selected by M. W. TILESTON, Editor of "Daily Strength for Daily Needs." Fifth Edition. One of the choicest of Gift Books, a delightful alternative to the more ordinary Daily Reading Books.
Pocket Edition, 24mo, printed on Opaque India paper, pastegrain, gilt edges, with silk marker, 2s. 6d. net; postage 2d.
Also demy 16mo, handsome purple cloth, bevelled boards, red edges, silk marker, 2s. 6d. net; postage 3d. Choice limp, dark green lambskin, silk marker, gilt edges, 4s. net; postage 3d.

"A very pleasing book."—*Academy.*

"A charming book."—*Expository Times.*

"Few books of devotion are so catholic, in the original sense of the word; and it is small wonder to see the compilation so successful."—*Scotsman.*

"There is a prayer for every day in the year. None are long, and most are beautifully simple and reverent. For daily reading or for suggesting suitable thoughts to those who have to offer public extempore prayer we can imagine nothing more helpful than this volume."—*Methodist Times.*

TIPPLE. SUNDAY MORNINGS AT NORWOOD.
Twenty-two Sermons and Twenty-two Prayers. By Rev. S. A. TIPPLE. New Edition. Crown 8vo, 3s. 6d. net; postage 4d.
The Prayers are a wealth of suggestion to Ministers and others who have occasion to engage in public prayer.

"There are more original ideas in Mr Tipple's volume than in many which have rapidly run into nine or ten editions. Both the prayers and the sermons contained in it give evidence of a fresh, lucid, and forcible thinker. The sermons are short, very interesting, and always aim at impressing on the hearer one idea. No connoisseur in sermons can fail to appreciate the fine quality of Mr Tipple's Work."—*British Weekly.*
"The first edition has long been out of print, and many will be glad to know that they can obtain these rarely spiritual and suggestive sermons. Two sermons are new, the one a reply to Tolstoi's literalism, the other on 'The Silence of Christ.'"—*Christian World.*

"The natural demand for discourses so wise in spirit and so excellent in form could not be satisfied by the issue of a single edition. The few added discourses of more recent date will increase the satisfaction of the old readers and of new."—*Congregational Magazine.*

TYNDALL. OBJECT SERMONS IN OUTLINE.
Forty-five Topics for Children's Services and P.S.A.'s, attracting the eye as well as the ear. By Rev. C. H. TYNDALL, M.A., Ph.D. 3s. 6d.

"Those pastors who are wrestling with the problem how to attract, interest, and influence young people may obtain valuable suggestions from this book."—*American Congregationalist.*
"The lessons are well conceived and worked out with great ingenuity, and in good hands could not fail to be extremely effective. We advise pastors, Sunday School superintendents, and others who have young people's meetings in charge to examine this book."—*Independent.*

STORIES BY ANNIE ELIOT TRUMBULL.

The keenness, quickness, and acuteness of the New England mind were, perhaps, never better illustrated than in her stories. Her conversations are at times almost supernaturally bright; such talk as one hears from witty, brilliant, and cultivated American women—talk notable for insight, subtle discriminations, unexpected and surprised terms, and persuasive humour.

MISTRESS CONTENT CRADDOCK. A Novel. By A. E. TRUMBULL. 305 pages, 12mo, cloth, 2s. 6d. net; postage 3d.

"A faithful picture of life in the early days of our colonies."—*Manchester Guardian.*
"A strong Puritan atmosphere."—*Spectator.*

ROD'S SALVATION. By A. E. TRUMBULL. Illustrated by CHARLES COPELAND. 12mo, cloth, 2s. 6d. net; postage 3d.

"Miss Trumbull is blessed by a most delightful and unpretentious gift of storytelling. Her work suggests a twilight musician; she has a certain dainty humour in her touch."—*The Citizen.*
"The volume entitled 'Rod's Salvation'
contains four short stories, some of which are long enough to be fairly called novelets. . . . 'Rod's Salvation' is a good picture of longshore life, telling of the devotion of a sister to a scapegrace brother and well worthy a reading."—*Springfield Republican.*

A CAPE COD WEEK. By A. E. TRUMBULL. 12mo, cloth, 2s. 6d. net; postage 3d.

"'A Cape Cod Week' contains an account of the adventures and achievements of three young women who sought the seclusion, silence, and scenery of Cape Cod, and who enlivened that remote and restful country by flashes of talk often brilliant, almost always entertaining. Miss Trumbull's work is delightful reading; the sameness of the commonplace and the obvious is so entirely absent from it."—*The Outlook.*

A CHRISTMAS ACCIDENT, AND OTHER STORIES.
By A. E. TRUMBULL. 12mo, cloth, 2s. 6d. net; postage 3d.

UPHAM. THE LIFE OF MADAME GUYON. By T. C. UPHAM, Author of "The Interior Life." With New Introduction by Rev. W. R. INGE, M.A. 500 pages. Large crown 8vo, 6s.

This well-known book has been out-of-print for two years. The New Edition is issued uniform in size and price with "Tauler's Life and Sermons."

"Her opinions and experiences form, quite apart from their undeniable psychological interest, a very valuable volume worthy of being carefully studied by all who are interested in varying types of Christian character."
"Her letters make the heart glow."—*Methodist Recorder.*
"Perhaps the most fascinating of all
the spiritual autobiographies, this reissue is all the more valuable for being brought in by a studious and sympathetic introduction from the pen of Mr W. R. Inge."—*Scotsman.*
"One of the most mysterious records of the spiritual life."—*Pall Mall Gazette.*
"A most welcome reprint."—*Church Quarterly Review.*

WORKS BY REV. J. WARSCHAUER, D.Phil.

JESUS SAITH. Studies in some "New Sayings" of Christ. By the Rev. J. WARSCHAUER, M.A., D.Phil. (Jena). Crown 8vo, handsome cloth, 2s. 6d.

The recent discoveries among the ruins of Oxyrhynchus of two papyrus fragments, each containing a number of sentences uniformly introduced by the words *Jesus Saith*, constitute one of the most noteworthy results achieved in the annals of modern research.

In a series of eight chapters the author has attempted to draw certain spiritual lessons suggested by some of these "new" sayings.

"A set of sermons upon some of the New Sayings of Christ. They are readable and well written."—*Spectator*.

"This is a remarkable book. These studies are not critical or speculative, they are entirely devotional, and seek to bring out the spiritual lessons those sayings have for us. The work is one which will be read with interest and profit, it invests the 'New Sayings' with fresh dignity and importance."—*The Record*.

"That the treatment is masterly and the style singularly attractive goes without saying. Where the author's name is known no reader will put the book down unrefreshed."—*Methodist Recorder*.

THE COMING OF CHRIST. Two Courses of Advent Sermons. By Rev. J. WARSCHAUER, M.A., D.Phil. Cloth, fcap. 8vo, 1s. 6d. net; postage 3d.

"We can cordially recommend this little volume to lovers of good sermons. The eight discourses contained in it are thoughtful, full of fine feeling and spiritual penetration, and written in a chaste and cultured style marked by a spiritual insight and temper which are not common."—*Glasgow Herald*.

ANTI-NUNQUAM. An Examination of "God and My Neighbour." By J. WARSCHAUER, M.A., D.Phil. With Introduction by Prof. J. ESTLIN CARPENTER, M.A. A Strikingly Fair Reply to Blatchford.

Cloth, gilt lettered, 1s. 6d. net; post free, 1s 9d.

CONTENTS.

I. OF "INFIDELS" AND THE "SIN OF UNBELIEF."
II. "NUNQUAM'S" ESTIMATE OF THE BIBLE.
III. "NUNQUAM'S" AGNOSTICISM. PART I. THE INTELLECTUAL BASIS OF SCEPTICISM.
IV. "NUNQUAM'S" AGNOSTICISM. PART II. EVIL *v*. DIVINE GOODNESS.
V. "NUNQUAM'S" DENIAL OF SIN AND FREEDOM.
VI. "NUNQUAM'S" CRITICISM OF CHRIST.
VII. "NUNQUAM'S" INDICTMENT OF CHRISTIANITY.
VIII. THE REAL "PARTING OF THE WAYS."

"We have read several replies, but not one which is at once so scholarly and so plain as this."—*Yorkshire Post*.

"Among the many replies that Mr Blatchford's attack on Christianity has called forth, this must be placed in the front rank, not only for the intellectual ability it shows but also for its conspicuous fairness. No more trenchant criticism of the Agnostic position or more powerful statement of Christian belief has been given than this of Dr Warschauer."—*British Weekly*.

"Impresses me as being in every way excellent. Written in a popular style, it is bold and strong but never offensive. Evidently written by a liberal minded Christian who really *knows* the subject he is writing about. While it is primarily an answer to "Nunquam" it is a most informing and useful book to the general reader."—*J. Ernest Rattenbury* in *Methodist Times*.

H. R. ALLENSON'S CATALOGUE

WEIDNER. STUDIES IN THE BOOK. By Rev. Prof.
REVERE FRANKLIN WEIDNER, M.A. 12mo, cloth, 2s. 6d. each.

NEW TESTAMENT. 3 Vols.
    Vol. I.—Historical Books. Seven General Epistles and Revelations.
    Vol. II.—1 and 2 Thessalonians, Galatians, 1 and 2 Corinthians, and Romans.
    Vol. III.—Colossians, Ephesians, Philemon, Philippians, Hebrews, 1 and 2 Timothy, and Titus.

OLD TESTAMENT.
    Vol. I.—Genesis.

WORKS BY REV. R. E. WELSH, M.A.

GOD'S GENTLEMEN. Vigorous Sermons to Young Men.
By Rev. R. E. WELSH, M.A., Author of "Man to Man," etc. Crown 8vo, 3s. 6d. Fourth Edition.

CONTENTS.

THE LUST FOR LIFE.
A MEDICATED MEMORY.
GOD'S GENTLEMEN.
GOOD MEN OUT OF CHURCH.
INTERESTING SINNERS AND STALE SAINTS.
MALADY OF NOT WANTING.
MEN WHO GET ON.
TENDERFOOT.
OLD TOO SOON.

CYNIC AND ENTHUSIAST.
THE GLAMOUR OF LIFE—I. ANGELIC ILLUSIONS. II. THE APE OF GOD.
CHAMBERS OF IMAGERY.
DANGEROUS YEARS.
A DOUBLE LIFE.
WHERE TO DRAW THE LINE.
EXILES OF THE CHURCH.
THE ESCAPE FROM ONESELF.

"This is a frank and manly book, stamped with a strong and sympathetic vitality. Young men will read it because it never ignores the other side of the question. Any author who brings a young man face to face with life, weighs good and evil before him in the balance, has done a work which will not be forgotten."—*British Weekly.*

"A series of ethical essays of rare value strongly commended as a gift book for men, whether young, old, or middle-aged. The man who would fly a sermon could not fail to be attracted by the fine flow of language and by the noble aims and sane admonitions of the author."—*Dundee Advertiser.*

THE PEOPLE AND THE PRIEST. By Rev. R. E. WELSH, M.A. Crown 8vo, cloth, 2s. 6d. Third Edition.

CONTENTS.

THE SPELL OF CATHOLICISM.
RITUAL AND VESTMENTS.
SUCCESSORS TO THE APOSTLES.
THE SAFER WAY.
THE ONE HOLY CATHOLIC CHURCH.
THE APPEAL TO CHARACTER.

THE APPEAL TO AUTHORITY.
THE PRICE OF A CATHOLIC'S PRIVILEGE.
ST PETER AND GOD'S VICARS.
THE ROCK OF THE CHURCH.
THE POWER OF THE KEYS.
THE PRIESTS' POWER TO ABSOLVE.

"Mr Welsh puts the Protestant point of view briefly and sensibly."—*The Times.*
"I have read with great interest your admirable book. It puts the whole question with wonderful brevity and lucidity. It is the question of the day for English people."—*Samuel Smith, Esq., M.P.*

"Anyone desiring in a short compass a clear statement of the points at issue cannot do better than purchase a copy of this work. They will find it very readable, and so plainly written as to be easily understood."—*Manchester Courier.*

H. R. ALLENSON'S CATALOGUE 33

IN RELIEF OF DOUBT. By Rev. R. E. WELSH, M.A.,
With Introduction by the Right Rev. A. F. WINNINGTON-INGRAM, D.D., Bishop of London. Fifth Edition. Crown 8vo, cloth, 2s. 6d.

And in the Handy Theological Library limp leather, gilt top and silk marker, 3s. net; cloth, semi-limp, gilt top and silk marker, 2s. net. Postage 3d.

Cheap Popular Edition, 50,000 already sold. Demy 8vo, 6d.
[Allenson's Sixpenny Series.

THE SIXTEEN CHAPTERS OF THIS STRIKING BOOK ARE—

THE ART OF DOUBTING WELL.
THE MAKING OF SCEPTICS.
DOES IT MATTER WHAT A MAN BELIEVES?
GOOD SCEPTICS AND BAD CHRISTIANS.
WAS JESUS ORIGINAL?
OLD LETTERS OF A CONTEMPORARY OF CHRIST.
THE REAL JESUS.
THE FOUR PICTURES AND THE ONE ORIGINAL.

WATERMARKS IN THE DOCUMENTS.
THE PERSONAL VERIFICATION OF CHRIST.
STRANGE THINGS IN THE OLD TESTAMENT.
ARE ALL THE BOOKS EQUALLY INSPIRED?
THE DRAMAS OF "CREATION" AND "THE FALL."
WAS MAN, TOO, EVOLVED?
MAN'S DREAM OF HIS OWN GREATNESS.
THE WOES OF THE WORLD v. A GOOD GOD.

The Bishop of London says:

"I have found it, in a great many instances, of real service in relief of doubt. On one occasion I sent it to a leading physician, and on meeting him later, and asking him how he liked it, I found he had given away nine copies to his friends.... It has hit off exactly what is wanted. It deals with that vague atmosphere of doubt which is so common, and dispels it by its clear and pointed arguments, and it is written in so racy a style that none could put it down and call it dull."

"Mr Welsh has done his work admirably. As one reads on, it becomes clear that the author has faced the difficulty for himself and is earnestly and modestly trying to help others through. This would make an excellent gift book to a young man troubled with doubts. One of the best books of popular apologetics ever written."—*British Weekly.*

"This fifth edition testifies to the undoubted practical use of such a volume. No better text-book could be put into the hands of young men inclined to scepticism."—*Examiner.*

THE CHALLENGE TO CHRISTIAN MISSIONS. By
Rev. R. E. WELSH, M.A. Crown 8vo, cloth, 2s. 6d.

CONTENTS.

INTRODUCTORY: WHERE THE QUESTION PRESSES.
POLITICAL COMPLICATIONS: IS THE MISSIONARY THE TROUBLER OF THE PEACE?
MANY RACES, MANY RELIGIONS: "EAST IS EAST, AND WEST IS WEST."
"GOOD IN EVERY SYSTEM": THE COSMIC LIGHT, AND DARK.
LIBERAL THOUGHT AND HEATHEN DESTINIES.

WILL THE MISSIONARY MOTIVE SURVIVE?
CHEQUERED RESULTS: "COUNTING THE GAME."
CHEQUERED RESULTS: "THE MISSION-MADE MAN."
MEN AND METHODS.
THE MISSIONARY AIM: THE COMING KINGDOM.
THE RETURN-VALUE OF MISSIONS.

"Once again Mr Welsh hits the nail on the head and says precisely the needed word.... Difficulties which have puzzled wise men and made good Christians doubtful are here effectually disposed of, and the whole discussion is carried on in so lively a style that there is a great treat in store for every intending reader."—*The British Weekly.*

"This book is undoubtedly the most important attempt yet made to meet current objections to Missions."—*Church Missionary Intelligencer.*

"A volume which supplies an effective answer to much shallow and mischievous talk, and indicates the weak places in Mission work which a little care might strengthen."—*Church Times.*

WINKWORTH. JOHN TAULER'S HISTORY AND LIFE, AND TWENTY-FIVE SERMONS. Translated by Miss SUSANNA WINKWORTH. With Preface by CHARLES KINGSLEY, and an Introductory Letter by Dr ALEXANDER WHYTE, of Edinburgh. 426 pages. Large crown 8vo, handsome cloth, 6s.

"You are doing all lovers of first-class spiritual books a great service by putting on the market a new and properly edited issue of Tauler. His name is fragrant to all who know him. And many more will know him, I feel sure, through this fine enterprise of yours. Be sure I shall do my best to make your Tauler known here."—*Dr Whyte.*

"Will have a cordial welcome."—*Scotsman.*

"Mr Allenson has conferred a service on all lovers of the mystics, by this re-issue of an excellent work."—*Glasgow Herald.*

"Very handsome and convenient, the reprint is most welcome. Mr Allenson has done great service in publishing this book."—*British Weekly.*

"I find it very useful."—*Prof. Rendel Harris.*

"It is forty-two years since I made the acquaintance of Tauler in the old edition, and, knowing how much valuable matter there is in his sermons, I think you have done a public service in re-issuing them in a still handier form. I hope they will have a renewed and increased circulation."—*Dr Marcus Dods.*

"I am glad you have reprinted that excellent book."—*Rev. W. R. Inge.*

"If a public can be made for Tauler in England, this admirably conceived volume should go far to do it. The sermons have been chosen on a judicious principle that gives the modern reader a good opportunity of gauging Tauler's preaching. The reprinting of Charles Kingsley's characteristic preface and of Whittier's poem on Tauler adds interesting features to the book. A large part of the volume is taken up by Tauler's Life, so that everything possible is done to bring the reader into the atmosphere in which alone his preaching can be properly understood."—*Literary World.*

WOOD. THROUGH BATTLE TO PROMOTION. By WALTER WOOD. 333 pages, crown 8vo, cloth, 6s.

ALLENSON'S SIXPENNY SERIES.

Well printed in large clear type on good paper. First time issued in the popular demy 8vo form, at 6d. each.

"Every volume is excellent value."—*The Rapid Review.*
"The publication of such standard works in a cheap form is highly to be commended."—*Aberdeen Daily Journal.*

A SERIOUS CALL TO A DEVOUT AND HOLY LIFE. By WILLIAM LAW. With Introductory Letter by Dr ALEXANDER WHYTE.

IN RELIEF OF DOUBT. R. E. WELSH. New Introduction by BISHOP OF LONDON.
[*Fiftieth Thousand.*

IMMORTALITY. A. W. MOMERIE.
[*Thirtieth Thousand.*

BELIEF IN GOD. A. W. MOMERIE.
[*Twentieth Thousand.*

HEROES AND HERO WORSHIP. CARLYLE.

SARTOR RESARTUS. CARLYLE. With Introduction by JONATHAN NIELD.

ANTI-NUNQUAM. J. WARSCHAUER. An Examination of "God and my Neighbour."
[*Second Edition.*

TEN SERMONS. F. W. ROBERTSON, of Brighton. [*Second Edition.*

ELEVEN SERMONS. F. W. ROBERTSON. A second Selection.

AURORA LEIGH. E. B. BROWNING.

ROOT PRINCIPLES IN RATIONAL AND SPIRITUAL THINGS. THOMAS CHILD.

Please send for a prospectus of this fine series, sent post free.

H. R. ALLENSON'S CATALOGUE 35

ALLENSON'S HANDY THEOLOGICAL LIBRARY.

Clearly printed on thin paper, small crown 8vo, 6½ by 5 inches. Limp leather, gilt top, silk marker, 3s. net. Also in cloth, semi-limp, gilt top, silk marker, 2s. net. Postage 3d.

"Excellent evidence that there are theological as well as other masterpieces which may be bound in leather, and sold at a small price."—*Expository Times.*

IN RELIEF OF DOUBT. R. E. WELSH, M.A. With Introductory Note by the BISHOP OF LONDON. [*Fifth Edition.*
"No better book could be put into the hands of anyone perplexed with mental difficulties."—*Examiner.*
"It has hit off exactly what is wanted."—*Bishop of London.*

LECTURES ON PREACHING. PHILLIPS BROOKS, D.D.
"Preachers have learned to regard this as one of the most inspiring books on the subject, and this edition is so cheap and so convenient that it ought to have a large sale."—*London Quarterly Review.*
"Well worth reading and re-reading."—*Church Times.*

"These charmingly got up books are the first two volumes in the 'Handy Theological Library'; they are published both in leather and in cloth, and are of a size suitable for the side pocket."—*Publishers' Circular.*

THE HEART AND LIFE BOOKLETS.

Fcap. 8vo, 6d. net each. Postage 1d.

An entirely new series of artistically produced booklets. The speciality aimed at in the issue of these delightful little books has been to choose some sterling utterance or message from writers and thinkers of repute, and to produce them in large clear type on good paper with effective wrappers, each making a suitable and stimulating gift at slight cost, but much more permanent than the rather hackneyed card.

*PURPOSE AND USE OF COMFORT. By PHILLIPS BROOKS, D.D.
*AN EASTER SERMON. By PHILLIPS BROOKS, D.D.
*THE LIFE WITH GOD. By PHILLIPS BROOKS, D.D. Fourth Edition.
†HUXLEY AND PHILLIPS BROOKS. By Prof. W. NEWTON CLARKE, D.D.

†THE LONELINESS OF CHRIST. By F. W. ROBERTSON.
*EASTER DAY. By ROBERT BROWNING.
*CHRISTMAS EVE. By ROBERT BROWNING.
*FABER'S HYMNS. Twelve Selected. Each complete.
*RELIGION IN COMMON LIFE. By Principal JOHN CAIRD, D.D., LL.D.

† Also cloth, 1s. net. * Also Paste Grain Leather, 2s. net; and cloth, 1s. net.

"'The Heart and Life Booklets' are among the latest additions to the many daintily printed libraries which are finding great favour with the reading public. This series is particularly well printed on strong paper, and bound in artistic covers which do not come off when handled."—*Oxford Chronicle.*

"Attractive little reprints o. great utterances."—*The Friend.*
"To religious minded people who love literature these well-printed booklets should give unmitigated pleasure."—*New Age.*

"Attractively printed and right well chosen."—*Expository Times.*

"The print and paper of the booklets are beyond praise."—*Saint Andrew.*

H. R. ALLENSON'S CATALOGUE

ALLENSON'S INDIA PAPER SERIES.

Demy 32mo (5¼ inches height, 3⅜ breadth, and under half inch in thickness).

Beautifully printed in clear type on good India paper, bound artistically in limp leather, 2s. 6d. net. Postage 2d. The commencement of a most handy and delightful series of little books for the pocket or valise, making especially suitable books for gifts to travellers.

*HEROES AND HERO WORSHIP. T. CARLYLE. [516 pages.

*AURORA LEIGH. E. B. BROWNING. [489 pages.

GREAT SOULS AT PRAYER. Edited by Mrs TILESTON. [384 pages.

DAILY MESSAGE FROM MANY MINDS. [380 pages.

* Also in cloth at 1s. 6d. net.

TRACTS FOR THE TIMES.

"Admirable for putting into the hands of thoughtful young people."—*Scottish Endeavour.*

16 pages. Price 1d. each; post free, 1½d.

THE SPIRIT OF DIVES. By Rev. C. SILVESTER HORNE, M.A. An Indictment of Indifference.

CHRISTIANITY AND ART. By Rev. W. PIERCE. A Repudiation of "Art for Art's Sake."

CITIZENSHIP AND ITS DUTIES. By Rev. BERNARD J. SNELL, M.A. "Apathy is the Enemy."

THE DUTY OF BEING YOUNG. By Rev. J. H. JOWETT, M.A., Carr's Lane, Birmingham. Second Edition.

AM I FIT TO TAKE THE LORD'S SUPPER? By Rev. SAMUEL PEARSON, M.A. Third Edition. 17th Thousand.

THE SOBRIETY OF HOPE. By Rev. C. SILVESTER HORNE, M.A.

FOUNDATIONS. By Rev. H. W. HORWILL, M.A.

WHAT IS A CONGREGATIONAL CHURCH? By Rev. J. H. STOWELL, M.A.

WHAT THE CHURCH MIGHT BE. By Rev. A. H. MONCUR SIME.

THE DEVIL IN KHAKI. By Rev. W. PEDR WILLIAMS.

A PLEA FOR TOTAL ABSTINENCE. By the Rev. JOHN W. VEEVERS.

THE MESSAGE OF THE GOSPEL. By the Rev. CHARLES BROWN, Ferme Park, Hornsey.

Price 2d. each; post free, 2½d.

WHY ARE WE INDEPENDENTS? By Rev. BERNARD J. SNELL, M.A.

WANTED — AN ENGLISH BIBLE. By Rev. H. W. HORWILL, M.A. Reprinted from *The Contemporary Review.*

THE HUMAN BODY, AND HOW TO TAKE CARE OF IT. By W. E. LEE, M.R.C.S.E.

THE MODERN INTERPRETATION OF SALVATION BY FAITH. By Rev. T. RHONDDA WILLIAMS, Bradford.

32 pages. Price 3d.; post free, 3½d.

THE HAPPY WARRIOR. An Address to Young Men and Women. By Rev. P. T. FORSYTH, M.A., D.D.

The series of 17 post free for 2s.

INDEX OF BOOKS UNDER SUBJECTS.

Particulars and Reviews will be found in the body of the Catalogue, under the name in italics.

ADDRESSES TO CHILDREN.

FIFTY-TWO SUNDAYS WITH THE CHILDREN. *Learmount.* 3s. 6d.
FIFTY-TWO ADDRESSES TO CHILDREN. *Learmount.* 3s. 6d.
GREAT MOTTOES WITH GREAT LESSONS. *Martin.* 3s. 6d.
LAZY LESSONS. *Rand.* 3s. 6d.
FORTY BIBLE LESSONS AND FORTY ILLUSTRATIVE STORIES. *R. M. Brown.* 3s. 6d.
WHAT SHALL I TELL THE CHILDREN? *Reichel.* 3s. 6d.
THE MOUNTAIN PATH. *Hamilton.* 2s. 6d.
TALKS TO YOUNG FOLKS. *James.* 2s. 6d.
THE GOOD FATHER. *Snell.* 2s. 6d.
WORDS TO CHILDREN. *Snell.* 2s. 6d.
TIN TACKS FOR TINY FOLKS. *Edwards.* 2s. 6d.
MEASURING SUNSHINE. *Smith.* 1s. 6d. net.
TALKS TO CHILDREN ON BUNYAN'S HOLY WAR. *C. Brown.* 1s. 6d. net.
SERMONS TO BOYS AND GIRLS. *Eames.* 1s. 6d. net.
SELECTED SERMONS; 13. *Snell.* 1s. 6d. net.
SELECTED SERMONS; 12. *Gibbon.* 1s. 6d. net.
THE MAKING OF A CHRISTIAN. *Scott.* 1s. 6d.
OUTLINE SERMONETTES ON GOLDEN TEXTS. *Martin.* 1s.

BOOKS OF ILLUSTRATIONS FOR SERMONS AND ADDRESSES.

Many of the volumes in section above also contain numerous illustrations.

THE GOLDEN WINDOWS. *Richards.* 2s. 6d. net.
BY WAY OF ILLUSTRATION. *Ellis.* 1s.
WHAT SHALL I TELL THE CHILDREN? *Reichel.* 3s. 6d.
SEED CORN FOR THE SOWER. *Perren.* 5s.
ILLUSTRATIONS AND INCIDENTS. *Ellis.* 1s.

BOOKS OF OUTLINE ADDRESSES AND SERMONS.

OBJECT SERMONS IN OUTLINE. *Tyndall.* 3s. 6d.
PREACHER'S AND TEACHER'S VADE MECUM. *Ellis.* 2s. 6d.
OUTLINES AND ILLUSTRATIONS. *Ellis.* 2s. 6d.
TIN TACKS FOR TINY FOLKS. *Edwards.* 2s. 6d.
BREAD FOR THE BAIRNS. *Mercer.* 1s. net. and 2s. net.
TOOLS FOR MASTER'S WORK. *Ellis.* 1s. 6d.
BOX OF NAILS FOR CHRISTIAN WORKERS. *Edwards.* 1s. 6d.
BRIGHT AND BRIEF TALKS TO MEN. *Atkin.* 1s. 6d.
FORTY-SEVEN OUTLINE SERMONETTES ON GOLDEN TEXTS. *Martin.* 1s.
THE TOOL BASKET. *Ellis.* 1s.
THE SEED BASKET. *Ellis.* 1s.
EVANGELIST'S WALLET. *Ellis.* 1s.

H. R. ALLENSON'S CATALOGUE

ADDRESSES TO YOUNG MEN AND WOMEN.

RELIGION OF A GENTLEMAN. *Dole.* 3s. 6d.
RELATIONSHIPS OF LIFE. *Horne.* 3s. 6d.
OLD TESTAMENT LESSONS. *Keep.* 3s. 6d.
SOME VIEWS OF MODERN THEOLOGY. *Lewis.* 3s. 6d.
GOD'S GENTLEMEN. *Welsh.* 3s. 6d.
FROM OUR DEAD SELVES TO HIGHER THINGS. *Gant.* 2s. 6d.
THE LIFE THAT IS EASY. *Horne.* 2s.
PULPIT TALKS TO YOUNG PEOPLE. *Thomas.* 1s. 6d. net.
THE MAKING OF A CHRISTIAN. *Scott.* 1s. 6d.
WARFARE OF GIRLHOOD. *Holden.* 1s. 6d.
THE LIFE WITH GOD. *Brooks.* 6d. net.
HEROIC ENDEAVOUR. *Lawson.* 6d.

BOOKS FOR BIBLE STUDENTS.

STUDIES IN THE BOOK. *Weidner.* 4 vols. 2s. 6d. each.
OUR SACRED BOOKS. *Rotherham.* 6d.
EMPHASISED BIBLE. *Rotherham.* 20s. net. and in 4 vols.
SEED CORN FOR THE SOWER. *Perren.* 5s.
GOSPEL PROBLEMS AND THEIR SOLUTION. *Palmer.* 6s.
SPEAKERS FOR GOD (ON THE 12 MINOR PROPHETS). *McWilliam.* 3s. 6d.
OLD TESTAMENT LESSONS. *Keep.* 3s. 6d.
FOOTPRINTS OF THE SAVIOUR. *Bishop Boyd Carpenter.* 2s. 6d.
WHICH BIBLE TO READ. *Ballard.* 2s. 6d. net.

STUDIES IN THEOLOGY AND ETHICS.

CONTINUITY OF CHRISTIAN THOUGHT. *Allen.* 3s. 6d. net.
SOME VIEWS OF MODERN THEOLOGY. *Lewis.* 3s. 6d.
THE QUEST OF THE INFINITE. *Millard.* 3s. 6d.
RELIGION OF A GENTLEMAN. *Dole.* 3s. 6d.
THE COMING PEOPLE. *Dole.* 3s. 6d.
THEOLOGY OF CIVILIZATION. *Dole.* 3s. 6d.
SOCIAL MEANINGS OF RELIGIOUS EXPERIENCE. *Herron.* 3s. 6d.
THE CHRISTIAN SOCIETY. *Herron.* 3s. 6d.
JESUS SAITH. *Warschauer.* 2s. 6d.
PROF. HUXLEY AND RELIGION. *Thompson.* 2s. 6d. net.
THE ETERNAL WILL. *Stanyon.* 2s. 6d. net.
INFLUENCE OF JESUS. *Phillips Brooks.* 2s. 6d. net.
HUXLEY AND PHILLIPS BROOKS. *Clarke.* 6d. net.
ROOT PRINCIPLES. *Child.* 6d.

BOOKS OF MISSIONARY INTEREST.

THE DOMINION OF CHRIST. *Pierce.* 1s. net. and 1s. 6d. net.
JOSEPH SIDNEY HILL. *Faulkner.* 1s. 6d. net.
CHALLENGE TO CHRISTIAN MISSIONS. *Welsh.* 2s. 6d.
CHRISTIAN CHIVALRY. *Phillips.* 6d.
A YOUNG CONGO MISSIONARY. *Brock.* 1s. 6d.
SUNSHINE AND SHADOW IN SOUTH-WEST. *Rusher.* 1s. 6d.

H. R. ALLENSON'S CATALOGUE 39

BIOGRAPHICAL AND PERSONAL.

See also Books of Missionary Interest.

MADAME GUYON. *Upham.* 6s.
LETTERS OF TRAVEL. *Brooks.* 2s. 6d. net.
TAULER. *Winkworth.* 6s.
PRIESTLEY'S AUTOBIOGRAPHY. *Priestley.* 3s. net.

FREE CHURCH HISTORY AND PRINCIPLES.

CONSTRUCTIVE CONGREGATIONAL IDEALS. *Macfadyen.* 2s. 6d. net.
FREE CHURCH HISTORY, PRIMER OF. *Evans.* 1s. 6d. net.
CHURCH FELLOWSHIP, PRIMER OF. *Horne.* 6d. and 1s.
WHAT ENGLAND OWES TO PURITANS. *Handley.* 6d. net.
PEOPLE AND THE PRIEST. *Welsh.* 2s. 6d.
NONCONFORMIST MINISTER'S ORDINAL. 1s., 1s. 6d. and 2s. 6d. each, net.

BOOKS OF DEVOTIONAL READING.

THOUGHTS ON PRAYER. *Bishop of Ripon.* 1s. net. and 2s. net.
DAILY MESSAGE FROM MANY MINDS. 2s. 6d. net.
GREAT SOULS AT PRAYER. *Tileston.* 2s. 6d. net and 4s. net.
CURE OF CARE. *Humberstone.* 1s. 6d. net.
FOOTPRINTS OF THE SAVIOUR. *Bishop of Ripon.* 2s. 6d.
JOY OF THE RELIGIOUS. *Rogers.* 1s. net and 2s. net.
HE SUFFERED. *Monod.* 2s.
A SERIOUS CALL TO A DEVOUT AND HOLY LIFE. *Law.* 6d.

BOOKS OF MYSTICISM.

INTRODUCTION TO CHRISTIAN MYSTICISM. *Gregory.* 1s. net.
JOHN TAULER. *Winkworth.* 6s
MADAM GUYON. *Upham.* 6s.

BOOKS FOR JUVENILES.

GOLDEN WINDOWS. *Richards.* 2s. 6d. net.
CAPTAIN JANUARY. *Richards.* 1s. 6d. net.
HELEN'S BABIES. HABBERTON. 1s. net.
A TALE OF SIX LITTLE TRAVELLERS. *Gaskin.* 1s. net and 1s. 6d. net.
THE CINDERELLA OWL BOOK. *Gordon.* 1s. net and 1s. 6d. net.

BOOKS OF FICTION.

PAUL CARAH; CORNISHMAN. *Lee.* 6s.
LADY MARY OF THE DARK HOUSE. *Williamson.* 6s.
THROUGH BATTLE TO PROMOTION. *Wood.* 6s.
MISTRESS CONTENT CRADDOCK. *Trumbull.* 2s. 6d. net.
ROD'S SALVATION. *Trumbull.* 2s. 6d. net.
A CAPE COD WEEK. *Trumbull.* 2s. 6d. net.
A CHRISTMAS ACCIDENT. *Trumbull.* 2s. 6d. net.
TOM OSSINGTON'S GHOST. *Marsh.* 3s. 6d.
MARTYRS OF HELL'S HIGHWAY. *Thomas.* 1s. and 1s. 6d.
MUTTERS AND MURMURS OF A MISANTHROPE. *Penley Reyd.* 1s. 6d.
IN HIS STEPS, etc. *Sheldon.* 6d. to 3s. 6d.

SERMONS AND STUDIES.

6s.

Tauler. TWENTY-FIVE SERMONS.

5s.

Halsey. BEAUTY OF THE LORD.

3s. 6d. Net.

Norton. OLD PATHS (52 Sermons).
Tipple. SUNDAY MORNINGS AT NORWOOD.
Allen. CONTINUITY OF CHRISTIAN THOUGHT.

3s. 6d.

Dole. RELIGION OF A GENTLEMAN.
—— THE COMING PEOPLE.
—— THEOLOGY OF CIVILIZATION.
Horne. RELATIONSHIPS OF LIFE.
Jowett. BROOKS BY THE TRAVELLER'S WAY.
—— THIRSTING FOR THE SPRINGS.
Lewis. SOME VIEWS OF MODERN THEOLOGY.
MacWilliam. SPEAKERS FOR GOD.
Millard. THE QUEST OF THE INFINITE.
Momerie. IMMORTALITY, etc.
Perren, REVIVAL SERMONS.
Tyndall. OBJECT SERMONS.
Welsh. GOD'S GENTLEMEN.

2s. 6d. Net.

Brooks. LECTURES ON PREACHING.
—— INFLUENCE OF JESUS.
Caws. THE UNRECOGNISED STRANGER.
Thompson. PROF. HUXLEY AND RELIGION.

2s. 6d.

Carpenter. FOOTPRINTS OF THE SAVIOUR.
Thew. BROKEN IDEALS.
Warschauer. JESUS SAITH.
Welsh. PEOPLE AND THE PRIEST.
—— IN RELIEF OF DOUBT.
—— CHALLENGE TO CHRISTIAN MISSIONS.

2s. Net.

Brooks. LIFE WITH GOD.
—— LECTURES ON PREACHING.
Caird. RELIGION IN COMMON LIFE. Leather Bound.
Carpenter. THOUGHTS ON PRAYER. Leather Bound.
Rogers. JOY OF THE RELIGIOUS. Leather Bound.
Welsh. IN RELIEF OF DOUBT.

2s.

Horne. LIFE THAT IS EASY.

1s. 6d. Net.

Gibbon. SELECTED SERMONS.
Humberstone. CURE OF CARE.
Pierce. DOMINION OF CHRIST.
Snell. SELECTED SERMONS.
Thomas. PULPIT TALKS TO YOUNG PEOPLE.
Warschauer. COMING OF CHRIST (Advent).

1s. Net.

Brooks. LIFE WITH GOD.
—— AN EASTER SERMON.
—— PURPOSE AND USE OF COMFORT.
Caird. RELIGION IN COMMON LIFE.
Carpenter. THOUGHTS ON PRAYER.
Gibbon. THE FOUR LAST THINGS (Advent).
Rogers. JOY OF THE RELIGIOUS.

6d. Net.

Brooks. LIFE WITH GOD.
—— AN EASTER SERMON.
—— PURPOSE AND USE OF COMFORT.
Caird. RELIGION IN COMMON LIFE.
Clarke. HUXLEY AND PHILLIPS BROOKS.
Robertson. LONELINESS OF CHRIST.

6d.

Child. ROOT PRINCIPLES.
Momerie. BELIEF IN GOD.
—— IMMORTALITY.
Robertson. TEN SERMONS.
—— ELEVEN SERMONS.
Warschauer. ANTI-NUNQUAM.

See also Tracts for the Times.

www.ingramcontent.com/pod-product-compliance
Lightning Source LLC
Chambersburg PA
CBHW022148300426
44115CB00006B/397